# my greatest day in

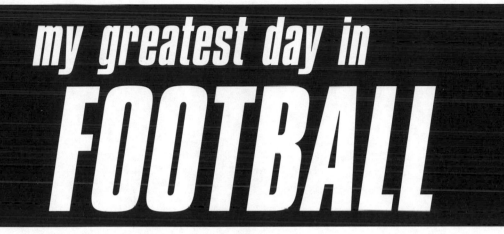

# FOOTBALL

## the legends of football
### recount their greatest moments

## as told to
# Bob McCullough

THOMAS DUNNE BOOKS / ST. MARTIN'S PRESS ≈ NEW YORK

THOMAS DUNNE BOOKS.
An imprint of St. Martin's Press.

www.stmartins.com

All photos courtesy of *The Sporting News*

ISBN 0-312-27211-1

First Edition: October 2001

10  9  8  7  6  5  4  3  2  1

*This book is dedicated to the makers of the football version of the APBA card game, who fueled a secret childhood addiction, and to the forgotten heroes of the old AFL, who made watching the game fun again by playing it the way we played in the schoolyard—wide open.*

# Contents

In the previous volumes of the "Greatest Day" series, I made a concerted effort to choose subjects whose abilities represented several different levels of excellence. I did this in part because of the sports themselves, based on the sheer variety of achievements, statistical and otherwise, that are possible in baseball, as well as a firm belief that competitive series like the PGA and NASCAR Winston Cup that produce an ongoing series of individual winners often tend to undervalue those who compete at a very high level. It was my hope that this would produce a better book, and I remain satisfied for the most part when I look back at the results.

But the football volume of the series reflects a far more singular focus: Each interview in this book was done with a Hall of Fame member. The sole exception as the book goes to press is Bill Parcells, who was interviewed several weeks before the 2001 Hall of Fame election (the bulk of the interviews were conducted just before and during the 2000 NFL season), and his omission remains a mystery to me that goes beyond the reality of the day-to-day politics that are a fact of life in professional football.

The common thread of Hall of Fame membership aside, the players, coaches, and owner in this volume were chosen to represent a cross section of eras and decades from the last half-century of football. In particular, I made an effort to include several players from the late '40s and '50s, in part to give some idea of what life in the NFL was like before the sport began its meteoric rise in popularity. Some of my favorite interviews were those with Bob St. Clair, Pete Pihos, Gino Marchetti, and other players from that era, and I hope those who read this volume will enjoy them as much as I did.

While the format of the interview itself remains largely unchanged, there are a couple of small differences between this book and the earlier volumes. Given the inextricable link between pro and college football, I asked most of the players and coaches about their greatest day in college football, an exercise that produced some pretty interesting stories. I also asked many of them to name their greatest teammate as well as their greatest opponent, an impossible pair of questions that nonetheless led to some intriguing answers.

As has been the case with each volume in the series, at the end of the day the list of great players who were bypassed because of length considerations ends up being almost as long as the table of contents listing those who were included. In the future I hope to be involved in an effort to produce a second book that would incorporate the remaining Hall of Famers, and include some of the great players from the last decade or so as time slowly validates their achievements and legacies.

Finally, the list of those who must be thanked remains the longest of all, but in the interest of brevity I'll stick to a few key contributors: Joe Horrigan of the Hall of Fame, whose steerage proved especially invaluable, and Jim Gallagher, former PR director for the Eagles, whose contributions went far above and beyond the call of duty. Frank Mara of the Giants was instrumental in setting up the many interviews with New

York's lengthy list of Hall of Famers, with able assistance from Pat Hanlon. Many thanks to all, and also to the other agents and PR folks who helped make this book possible.

Kudos also to the folks from *The Sporting News,* who came through with some great photos from their archive when the going in the artwork department got a bit sticky.

*He's been called the toughest man ever to play pro football, a throwback two-way lineman with a reputation as a vicious hitter, a savage tackler, and a tenacious blocker. Hall of Famer Chuck Bednarik played for just over a decade for the Philadelphia Eagles, and his greatest day came at the end of his career when he helped the Eagles to their most memorable championship against the team that would become football's ultimate dynasty.*

It was the 1960 championship game against the Green Bay Packers. Of course we won the game. I made sure I stopped Taylor on the 9-yard line on the last play of the game. And I played every single play in that game, offense and defense, at age thirty-five. And that was about the ninth time I did it that year. To win a game against Green Bay in the championship and to play both ways, that's got to be my greatest day.

Well, it was really a fantastic year. When the season started, of course we had a good quarterback in Norm Van Brocklin. And that's the important person. And I really didn't think that we could go all the way. I figured we'll have a good season, and I was hoping for a good season, but geez, everything went right. And it just so happened that we won our division and we were in the championship. It was a matter of a couple of key plays. Tommy McDonald came through nicely, Van Brocklin, of course, and people like that.

The competition was the Giants, with Charlie Conerly. That happens to be the year, too, when I made that play [Ed. note: the famous tackle with Bednarik standing over Frank Gifford] and I never forget it. It wasn't a dirty tackle. He was just pissed off at me and he kept yelling "cheap shot" and all. You know, that year we had a back-to-back game against New York and then back in Philadelphia and I said, You son of a bitch, I'll get you next week! And I really harassed him, and the linebackers told him I'm coming, and he fumbled the ball on a couple of occasions from the snap, and we won that game in Philadelphia, at Franklin Field.

We were going to beat Green Bay, and at that juncture I didn't care who we played. Green Bay clinched their division on the last game. And we clinched ours two weeks before that against the St. Louis Cardinals . . . was it the Chicago Cardinals? It didn't make any difference to me, but Green Bay won out on top. I can't remember who they played; it might have been the Rams.

Well, we knew they were going to be tough because they had a great quarterback in Bart Starr, a good running back in Jimmy Taylor, Max McGee was a great receiver, Paul Horning—they were loaded with top personnel, and I knew it would be a good game. My feeling about winning was about fifty-fifty. I would say the focus was on stopping Jim Taylor and also Bart Starr. Bart Starr, he had quite a good record on completions, and Jim Taylor was a bulldozing running back.

I think it was the day after Christmas, and it was a cold day. There was a little bit of snow on the sidelines, which was not on the playing field. It was an enthusiastic crowd. It was sold out, like 70,000 people at Franklin Field. It was a clear day, so for playing I would consider it perfect. The field was not frozen. The temperature was mid-forties or upper forties, which was also real good.

It was a tight game all the way. I think the clincher was when Van Brocklin hit Tommy McDonald with about a 25-yard pass in the end zone, and that put us ahead. And then the other thing I think I recall, when they scored their touchdown, Ted Dean returned the ball down to about the 12 or 13 yard line on the following kick—that I recall.

But of course I recall most the last play of the game. They called their final time-out. They were on our 16 yard line and driving. Of course I'm a little concerned, I'm a little frightened, because like I say, no more time-outs. So Bart Starr goes back to pass and of course he's on the 16 yard line, of course there's not much room to operate to throw a deep pass. So Boyd Dowler and Max McGee were pretty well covered in the end zone, the time was running, we were rushing on them, and his last resort was Jim Taylor swung out of the backfield, a swing pass.

And he caught it on about the 16 yard line and he started to take off. And I can still picture a couple of our defensive backs—they weren't very big. They come up to try to tackle him, he bounced off of them, and then he had to come and pass me on about the 9, 10 yard line, and I made sure that I wrapped my arms around him, knocked him to the ground, and I could see the clock in the upper tier of the east stands of Franklin Field, going down to 9 . . . 8 . . . 7 . . .

And when I saw it hit zero—my face was just about on top of his mask—I jumped up and I said, You can get up now. This game is over! This is what you call . . . exuberance. Not like today. This bugs my ass, people jumping around after a tackle. This was a world championship tackle and it was the end of the game, that's jubilation. Not how these jerks do it today.

So, yes, I was jumping up and down in jubilation, and so

was the rest of the football people. It was a pleasant surprise to win the championship. And lo and behold, that was 1960, we each got a winning $5,116. Can you imagine what they get today? It boggles my mind. That's why I'm not a big pro football fan anymore. I don't give a damn about it, because I read these contracts they're getting, the salaries, and I say why? Why? I can't believe it.

Unfortunately, back in 1960, television was just about coming into existence, and this is why people are making so much damn money today, because of the TV rights, and so it was not that big then. It was televised, but Philadelphia, within the radius of a hundred miles was blacked out. For $5,116 in 1960, that's forty years ago, that wasn't bad. Not like it is today, it's ridiculous.

But it wasn't so bad, to be the world champions. It was my second one. I was a rookie in 1949. I happened to be fortunate to come with a team that won in '48 and then repeated in '49. We beat the Rams out on the coast, so it took many years between then, and . . . what do you say it's been now, forty years? It was a beginning and ending for me, with twenty years playing the game. So that's a long time. Could you imagine now, they haven't won a title in forty years.

Fortunately, we had Van Brocklin. I don't think we could've won the championship without him. The great running back was Steve Van Buren. He's a Hall of Famer, and our quarterback was a guy named Tommy Thompson. He was a real good quarterback, he was a very confident quarterback. I admired the guy very much.

Let's see, Pete Pihos was one of the ends, Jack Ferrante was another one, Joe Muha was a running back along with Steve Van Buren and Bosh Pritchard, who was a little running back. On the front line, our captain was Al Wistert, who played for Michigan. One of the linebackers was Alex Wojciechowicz? Hell, he was my high school idol. The Rams had Bob Waterfield, Elroy Hirsch, Van Brocklin as a backup, Tom Fears. Yeah, they had great personnel.

We won 14–0. The field was kind of wet, in a muggy condition, it'd been raining, and the crowd, believe it or not for a world championship, could you imagine in 1949 in L.A., just under 30,000? And our big pay for winning was $1,116. That was at the Coliseum. And could you imagine another thing? Our coach, Greasy Neale, wouldn't fly, so we went out by train and back by train. So that was really something to behold.

Nevertheless, as a rookie I was on a world-championship team, and then from there on, we kind of squandered for a number of years until we came to that 1960. And again, I reiterate, I don't think we could have done it without Van Brocklin.

It was a tight game. It wasn't one of these wide-open games where you saw 40-, 50-yard touchdown passes, 30-, 40-, 50-yard running touchdowns—no. This was a hard, rock 'em, sock 'em type of football game. It was give and go slightly. The only big run we had was, like I said, that kickoff return by Dean that set up the winning touchdown. That was our longest run.

Statistically, they beat us badly. They had like twenty-something first downs, to our nine or whatever. Total yardage, they won. It was a combination of Starr and Taylor running and passing. You know they gained about 200 yards, which wasn't a hell of a lot, but our total was like 116 or 120 yards. And of course, the thing about it which I won't forget, during the week there was a convertible car sitting in a driveway there at Franklin Field and it was going to go to the most valuable player.

Nevertheless, I kiddingly went by one day and I said, I'm going to win this thing. Well, would you believe they gave it to Van Brocklin, who had a so-so day, 9 for 20-something. He led us to that championship game, but in that game, he didn't really—I'm the guy who went both ways in the game, made the game-saving tackle, and he wins the car. That kind of disappointed me, it kind of disappointed everybody, and also the people that voted for him relented later and said, Oh, I think we made a mistake.

We didn't really play the Packers many times in my career. If we played them four times, that's a lot, and I think, of the four times, that game was the only one we won. Because I remember going to Green Bay early in my career; we got beat and I don't remember, geez, playing another game against them until that championship game.

Of course the following year, 1960, we had them on the home schedule, and we got annihilated by them. Ooh, and that Taylor was giving it to me—ha-ha-ha—you know, real sarcastic. He was a tough character. He was one of these guys who never smiled, and just a hard, tough runner. He was a good football player, Hall of Famer, deservedly so.

Of course the next day, we were in the parade, and they put us in convertible cars, driving up and down the streets of Philadelphia. So that's what the city did for us. An open-car parade, which was nice. There were quite a few people. There's no question, to me, I think they're the greatest fans in the world, because I played four years at the University of Pennsylvania right there at that same field. I played fourteen years for the Eagles, so that's eighteen years.

I went to Philadelphia yesterday for some reason, and I can't believe it, 99.9 percent of the people recognized me, saying things like, Chuck, how ya doin'? We went out for lunch, and this was after I watched the Eagles play. My wife and I went to lunch, a place called Gino's Steak Sandwiches, popular for Philly cheese steaks. And everybody recognized me. They sat me down at a private table, the owner came there, gave us the steaks for nothing, the whole schmear. So it's that kind of a crowd, and you know, for eighteen years your face is pictured everywhere, so they recognize you. It's the greatest city in the world.

In college? We always had outstanding games. We won the majority of our games. I think the one game that I will never forget was against Army. They had the Blanchard and Davis teams, and so forth. It was in my junior year, I think. We had a hell of a game with them. We were seesawing back and forth and we finally went ahead 20–19. And it was like seven minutes to play in the game. We had just scored and I kicked off.

So I kicked off, and they returned the ball to about our 40 yard line. However, there was an infraction and the referee said, You kick over again, or it's first down Army. I kicked over again and put the ball in the end zone, 4 yards, and a guy named Bobby "Jet" Stewart took it and ran 104 yards for a touchdown. I made a mistake by kicking over again. I thought I made the right decision, but unfortunately, he ran all the way. We got beat 26–20.

That's one game I will always remember because we wanted to beat Army bad. When they had Blanchard and Davis, they ran all over us. And I was playing with just a bunch of young kids, because I just came out of the service. Those Army games were always spectacles, and the Navy games, the midshipmen marched in there, the cadets marched in there, and it was a great game. But that one game I certainly will always remember.

You can get 78,800 in Philly, you could get 34,000 people at West Point. Those games were always sold out. Matter of fact, the Thanksgiving game was always against Cornell. And if we beat Cornell, we got to keep our jerseys, so we beat them three times and I got to keep three of my jerseys. And would you believe that a couple of years ago, a guy from Chicago called me, one of these guys that's a collector and so forth, and asked me if I had any of my college jerseys. And I just happened to have a couple of them.

He said I'll give you $2,000 for it. I gave it to him for $2,000. But the Cornell game was a big game, and, like I say, if you beat Cornell, you got to keep your jersey. Cornell was a big traditional game. Cornell, Columbia, Princeton, we were

Ivy League schools, but at the time, we were big-time. We were always in the top ten in the country, I never played in front of less than 78,000 people. And now, unfortunately, they're drawing about 14,000 or 15,000 people because they de-emphasized it.

And I'll tell you what, if I had to go to a school again, I'd certainly go to an Ivy League school because these kids are student-athletes. They are students who have to get an SAT score of a minimum of 1,100, unlike some of these schools like Miami, Florida State, Tennessee—Christ, you can get in there with 300 SAT.

I started out at the Wharton School, which was the business school. Just coming out of the service and flying thirty missions over Germany, it got to be a little difficult, so I transferred. I went to the school of education; I wanted to be a teacher and a coach. And I got my B.S. in education. And, of course I never became a teacher or a coach. But I did get my degree from there.

We won those so-called Ivy titles three times, yes. Like I said, we were always—my freshman year to my senior year—we were always in the top ten or twelve in the country. In those days it was Army, Notre Dame, Alabama, teams like that were in the top. Princeton was up there pretty good, Cornell was up there pretty good, and they played big-time schedules.

All those schools have de-emphasized sports, and they're playing strictly amongst themselves and AA schools. We had the GI Bill. What the GI Bill didn't take care of was my food—would you believe, I was at the training table, I served one table, picked up the dishes, and I ate my meal for nothing.

My best teammate was a running back by the name of Skip Minisi. He was a good running back. He was at Penn before the war, and when war broke out he went to Annapolis, and had some good years there for two years. And then when the war was over, he transferred back to Penn. And he helped us out tremendously. There was nobody really that . . . we had a tackle that made some All-American teams by the name of George Satitsky. He made a number of All-American teams. But big-time names and all? Not really. Just a bunch of good, tough kids.

I guess I'm the only one who really went pro, believe it or not—Satitsky played one year, Minisi tried out, I don't think he made it, so I'm the only guy that probably went there who played pro ball.

The best team I played against as a pro was always the Cleveland Browns. When they came in from that streak they had with Otto Graham, Marion Motley, they had great personnel, a great team, and an outstanding coach in Paul Brown.

The best guy I ever played against was Otto Graham. I tell you the best running back I ever played against was Jimmy Brown, also of the Cleveland Browns.

I was looking at some of the Hall of Fame guys before me, those old-timers. They would play six or seven years, and that was about the average then, before the war. When pro football was just starting, you know, the guys were playing for peanuts. And that's why a lot of these things that we try to do is to help them out. And those guys would play six or seven years—and there were a number of them who got into the Hall of Fame. Now, you've got to play a good long time to be put in.

My best teammate was the running back, Steve Van Buren. No question—no ifs, ands, or buts. Quarterback, my rookie year Tommy Thompson and then Van Brocklin. Receiver, they put him into the Hall of Fame two years ago, Tommy McDonald.

Steve was faster than Taylor. And I would say Steve ran over people just like Taylor did. Unfortunately, he only played seven years, he got a bad knee—I remember that injury he had in a scrimmage. His knee was way out to the left for God sake, and he never could come back. But he's still around, goes to the races everyday.

Probably the most money he ever made was $15,000 going back then. And he lives in a one-room apartment with his cat. So, you know, things like this where you try to raise money for funding for people like that. His pension is probably about $11,000 a year. Mine is only $16,000, and the most money I ever made was $26,000. And, like I say, the pensions, if it was a baseball player that played fourteen years like I did he'd be getting $70–75,000 bucks.

And we've got this wimpy-shit thing, as a matter of fact. Last year at the Hall of Fame enshrinements, Paul Tagliabue was there, and one of the deals there was a luncheon of 2,500 people and we had five guys on the stage. I was one of them, with Art Donovan and two other guys, and they were asking questions. And one question was, if you were the commissioner of the National Football League, what one thing would you do?

And Tagliabue was in the stands and I got up and I said, This damn dancing they do after a touchdown. The people are applauding like crazy. I said, I'd cut that out. And then I said, If they could do the polka—but they don't know how to do a polka. And then the last thing I said, And, commissioner, please give us some more money in our pensions. That's what I did. Give us some more money in our pensions.

The induction, that's the highlight of all that you did, from high school to college to pro football to being inducted into the Hall of Fame. It's like I was inducted into the Hall of Fame in college. In pro ball you have to wait five years to be eligible, and I got it in my first year of eligibility. College you have to be out twenty years. So I was inducted in 1969, in 1967 in the pros.

So when you do all that hard work and you get all those honors and then you are put into the Halls of Fame of both the college and NFL, there's nothing else in life that you want.

You've reached it. You've done it all. My wife and I just got back from a shopping mall. We were in Allentown. And I can't walk through a shopping mall without every minute or two somebody stopping me saying, Hiya, Chuck, or asking me for an autograph. It's unbelievable.

If I could relive one, I think I'd have to go for the Hall of Fame. Because whatever you accomplish, this is the biggest honor I think that you can get. When you walk around the streets, people say, that's Chuck Bednarick, Hall of Famer.

# Bobby Bell

*When the AFL's Kansas City Chiefs drafted Bobby Bell out of the University of Minnesota in 1963, a new breed of linebacker entered the new league. For the next decade, the man who was quickly nicknamed "The Cat" proceeded to terrorize quarterbacks and running backs throughout the league, relentlessly pursuing the ball while outguessing the offensive strategies of the AFL's best and brightest. Bell turned his talents to taking apart NFL offenses when the Chiefs beat the Vikings in Super Bowl IV in 1970, avenging their earlier defeat against Green Bay in the inaugural Super Bowl.*

The greatest day? I guess I would pick the year we won the Super Bowl. I'm just gonna give you some background. The year we won the Super Bowl we were the wild card. We came in second behind Oakland. Oakland had won the division. And we had to play the New York Jets and come back to the Raiders and play them the third time.

So I guess one of the greatest days was that everybody counted us out, and we ended up playing the New York Jets and Joe Namath. And I guess one of the greatest plays—Joe and them was coming in to score a touchdown, they were on a drive down next to the goal line, going in for six points, and that's gonna put the icing on the cake.

And what happened was that, I always end up doing what I'm not supposed to do. So Joe, he came in, he knows that these guys are gonna be playing tight, they're gonna be trying to stop this run. Matt Snell was running the ball. And Joe Namath, instead of giving it to him, he kept the ball on a fake, and the next thing you know he faked it. I didn't go down on his deke. I'm looking right at him, and he pulls the ball right up, and he looks right at me, and he says, God durn it, Bell.

And we stopped 'em—bang. He said, any other linebacker, you'd have went in there, and it'd have been all over for you— but not you. And he was looking down my throat, and, you know, he stopped, he pulled up, he wasn't going nowhere, and me and Buck Buchanan, we just creamed him right there. Stopped him cold, that was it.

They came up and kicked, we got the ball, they kicked a field goal and came back and kicked off, and we came back and scored and beat 'em up there. That's one of the greatest days, that we beat 'em.

And on the way out to Oakland, they said there was no way we could beat Oakland, and I said, there's no way Oakland can beat us three games. They'd beat us twice, there was no way they could beat us. They were counting us out, we were an 18-point underdog.

We went out to Oakland and beat them and just kept on going. We played them and beat 'em. The Raiders, I tell you what, they knew they were gonna play either the Jets or Kansas City, and they said they had the win already in their pockets. Madden was the coach at the time. And when we got out there, we beat New York, and New York was supposedly the better team, so they were expecting New York.

So we ended up coming out, and they said, Oh, man, this

is gonna be a piece of cake. You know what they did? John Madden all of a sudden decided, all right, when we get through playing the Chiefs out here, we're just gonna leave and go straight to the airport and go right down to New Orleans. They had packed their bags.

We came out of the locker room to get on the bus after the game, and these guys, they waited for us to leave, and we were sitting there, and these guys came out of there with all these suitcases, putting them back in the car. They've gotta go home.

I don't think they were ever in the game. We had a mission. It was Coach Stram said, we're gonna beat these guys. First, we came out, and we committed to the pass, and we got the ball to Otis [Taylor], and it was just a physical control.

They were never into the game. We were just physical. And the reason we were so physical is that—I think it was the first year or the second year that Coach Stram had Alvin Roarke, he was the strength coach. I guess we were about—Dallas was the first, but Kansas City came aboard, Roarke came up from Dallas and started a weight program for us. I think Kansas City was the first one in the AFL, and then the Chargers. And in the NFL, Dallas did it for a while, but then they stopped. But Coach Stram felt like he should take every opportunity.

And when we got to Oakland for that third game, it was just awful [for them]—we were just a physical, strong team, and we just overpowered them in the third game. There was no way we were gonna let them beat us three times in a row, we were a better team. It was just an overall domination. If they beat us three times in a row, man—we felt like we just had to be really down or bad, you know?

And we felt like we had the better of anybody that year, because of the defense and the offense, you know? If you remember, that year Lenny Dawson went down for seven games, and Mike Livingston came in and played seven games until Lenny came back. And we won those seven games.

We just said, Hey, if we can score seven or nine points. We

felt defensive-wise that no one could score two touchdowns on us. We felt that our strength was defense, as long as we could put our offense in a position to win in the turnovers, takeaways, we could do it. And that time we did. The seven games that we played that year, you know, if we scored twelve points on them, the other team was like, you know, forget it. And that's the same thing that happened in the third game—you know, they already beat us, but I'll tell you what, it was going to be very difficult. It was just an overall domination of the game.

It was just a satisfaction, that, you know, they counted us out. We were wild card, we were gonna play three extra games because we were the wild card. People just said, hey, there's no way they're gonna beat the New York Jets—we proved them wrong, came out there and said, a lot of people, they just counted us out. It was the Raiders played us two games already and beat us, and said, hey, it's gonna be a piece of cake, like a walk in the garden, you know?

I guess the aftermath was that we felt that no one believed in us, and we did ourselves as a team. There was a lot of talking, guys that said, you guys lucked out, stuff like that, you know? The thing about it, back then, the AFL, the Raiders were behind us—after we beat them, they did all that talking, but they knew that we were going to represent the AFL going to the Super Bowl, so they were behind us.

It was just like the year before. Joe Namath and them won the Super Bowl, and, you know, the thrill—if you were there, all of us that went there. I mean, they thought everybody in the NFL could win the Super Bowl, all the teams. We went up to Joe and them, man, we were hugging them, congratulating them in the locker room. It was just a big celebration time.

And that's the way it was. It started in '66 when we played the first Super Bowl. And also, Coach Stram and all the players that played in the first Super Bowl, here we were we got the opportunity to play in another Super Bowl. We go to the

Jets, we beat them, and we go to the Raiders, we beat them—here's the opportunity, the door's there. All we've gotta do is open it and go in again.

So we went to the first Super Bowl and we lost, and we thought we were still in the game in the first Super Bowl. I think we just got overpowered. We played against a veteran team. Green Bay was so strong veteran-wise—Bart Starr, you make a mistake, they capitalized on three mistakes, and they scored on them. We turned the ball over three times and they scored.

Going into the second Super Bowl, that was the fourth Super Bowl, and the year before Joe Namath had won, people were saying, these guys, they might be here to stay. They were saying that the Minnesota Vikings, the Purple People Eaters, they were so strong and physical and all that, and we were saying, hey, these guys have not met us. It was an 18-point underdog, said we were going to lose . . . no way.

And also, they put some other flags out there. They put out that Lenny Dawson was gambling and all that stuff, you know? They put that out there, and everybody had flak about it, the press jumped on that, and we had people check it out, we all had a meeting, like a team meeting. We got together, the players stood up and said, Hey, Lenny, we don't believe it, and we're gonna go out there and put it behind, we're not gonna talk about it anymore, and we're behind you 120 percent, so let's just get this job done that we came down there to do.

The thing is, we knew that the Vikings were a big team, and physical, and that they overpowered people, you know. They had Joe Kapp, who was a big quarterback, one of the biggest quarterbacks. They had Bill Brown, one of the biggest running backs, a big, strong running back. Defensive-wise, they had Carl Eller, Page, and Marshall and them—they just had a great team, offense and defense. They moved the ball, they played tough defense.

We came in there saying, hey, there's no way they can beat

us today. Right before the game, we went up and told Lenny Dawson and the offense, you know, If you guys score a couple touchdowns, these guys, we are not gonna let 'em score a touchdown. If you get us twelve points, this is gonna be our day. And that's how we won. We went out there and played physical and we beat 'em down.

I talked to Joe Kapp after the game, about six months later, and he said—I'm just gonna be honest with you, Bob—he said, we have never been beat up like that. But you know, we knocked him out, we pounded him, every time he went back for a pass, we had Jerry Mays and Aaron Brown around his neck all the time. Every time they tried to run a play, we collapsed the defense with Lanier and Jim Lynch, we just collapsed and filled the holes, jammed the holes. These guys were being pounded—I think they had 26 yards the whole game. We just shut 'em down completely.

And then Lenny came out, you know. They knew that we had fast guys like Frank Pitts and Otis Taylor as outside receivers, and they were just laying back so far. And coach said, Hey, Lenny, if they want to give us the short stuff, take it. We kept getting the short stuff, and then they came up, this was the game plan. We had a game plan that was unbelievable. They came up, and when they finally came up tight, we'd go deep on 'em.

We got Carl Eller and Jim Marshall. They put so much pressure on the pass, so we said, OK, fine, they came up, we'll take that ball, they'll collapse, and we'll do the end around. Frank Pitts came around on the end around, and then Carl and Jim Marshall, they're trapped inside, they don't know where they're going. Whatever they'll give us, we'll take it.

We came out in the second half, and we felt like, hey, whatever we did in the first half, we had to continue to do it. Now we know, we realize that we cannot let up now—hey, we've got this game. If we continue to play the way we played the first half, we're gonna be in this game.

So we came out the second half, and we kicked off to them, and the turning point was we kicked off to 'em, and we came down off the kickoff team and hit the guy. He fumbled the ball, and we ended up with the ball. And we scored. Boom. That was the turning point.

And then we came back to Otis, and Mike Garrett scored on a 5-yard run, a trap play, after a 68-yard punt return. Then we came back and threw a little flare pass out there, on the corner. He came up on Otis, Otis caught the ball on a little flare-out, Otis turned around, so now it's gonna be difficult one-on-one to tackle Otis. He came up, boom, Otis gave him the limp leg and went down the sideline. The safety comes over, he gave him the limp leg.

Two touchdowns, the game's over.

Now, it's like, once we got the two touchdowns on 'em, it was down. And Joe Kapp could not move. He had to go into his passing game, and every time he cocked his arm we were knocking him down. They finally took him out of the game—every time he got rid of the ball, every time he moved with the ball he was hit, we were letting him know. We took him out of the game, we took the running attack out of the game, so they couldn't do anything now except try to put some points on the board. They tried to throw the ball, and they couldn't do it, and finally they took Joe Kapp out of the game and put another quarterback in.

It was kind of like downhill in the fourth quarter, no way they were catching up with us, we just kept pouring it right on. And our offense, Lenny just kept moving the ball—keep the ball, move the ball, run the ball. We had Wendell Hayes, we had Mike Garrett, you know, just trying to keep them off balance all the time. And that's the kind of offense that we had. They didn't know whether we were gonna come up the middle, to stop us up the middle, or outside, we'd go outside, reverse 'em, pull the short stuff on 'em. They didn't know what was going on, man.

I tell you what, after the game, I guess it took me two or three weeks to figure out, we are really world champs. You know, right after that, I think the day after that I had to fly out. The team flies back to Kansas City and has a parade—I missed that, because I had to play in the Pro Bowl. And we had to leave, all the guys in the Pro Bowl had to leave and go straight out to the Pro Bowl. We missed all the fun, the confetti, the parade, man, that's what I really missed, man. There were three of us, me, and Buck and Willie, and I thought it was Johnny Robinson, I don't think it was Johnny, it might have been Ed Budde, too.

We missed the big party, I missed the big party—I tell you, that's what I really miss. Everybody was like, Hey, I saw you in the parade, and I said, Well, you saw the rest of 'em, because everybody went back to Kansas City and I had to fly out and go to the Pro Bowl. All I got to see of the parade was what I could see on TV. I didn't get no 'fetti in my car, and I didn't get no 'fetti in my hair.

The Hall, that's just a different pyramid of your life, that's a fraternity—you've gotta understand, here's a guy that came from North Carolina. I came from North Carolina, I was a quarterback, small town, little cotton town. No one gave you the opportunity, I mean, no one could give you the credit to say that, Hey, man, it's a possibility that you'll be in the Hall of Fame. That was so far out of my mind.

All I wanted to do was go to college and get an education and stuff, get a forty-hour job, and that was it. If you did that you had made it. But here was the opportunity that started when I was in high school, somebody said, Hey, man, the way you play, you keep that up and you can get a scholarship. I said, really? I mean, my parents were poor, man, so I said, really? In North Carolina you go to Antille, which is the white school, or Florida A&M, that was it.

Then the next thing I think I heard was Notre Dame. Then I had the late Jim Taylor from North Carolina State call a friend, Jim Campbell from Minnesota, and say, Hey, there's a kid, I saw him play in the All-Star, they had an All Star game here, and he played in that, and man, he's a heck of a quarterback. He played six-man, but they played eleven-man in the All Star game, and this guy can do it, you ought to look at him.

So Minnesota had one scholarship left, and without any questions, they said, Well, we'd like to know a little bit more about it. Our school was so small, we never had any film or anything like that, and the guy called. Jim Tatum called my principal and said, Can you send some film to me so I can send it to Minnesota, I think we can get Bobby a scholarship at Minnesota. And the principal said, What kind of film are you talking about? He said, Maybe I can find snapshots—and there were two snapshots, one of me running away, and one of me laying flat on my back. He sent that to Minnesota.

And that's how it started, you know? I went up there, my father said, You're going way up there, you've never been on a plane before, boy. So I went up to Minnesota. I called my dad that night, and I said, Dad, it's like dying and going to heaven, this is the place. But you know, the fortunate thing is I went up there in the spring, and there's no snow. And the people in North Carolina would go, Hey, man, it's like cold up there, snow and ice, and I said, it was so beautiful, the sun was out, I said, there's no ice and snow.

But, you know, not being nowhere, I said, Hey, man, this is spring. So I said, I want to go, I want to go there. And my dad said, If that's what you want, if you want to go. And I signed, and went back, and never looked back. My freshman year at Minnesota, you couldn't play. I ran quarterback, and my sophomore year they switched me to offensive tackle and defensive end. And that's where it started. I made All Big Ten, and All-American during that year, and the next year, I just told the coach, Hey, Coach, I don't care where you play me, because I'm coachable.

My greatest college day? You know, I'll tell you an incident that happened. My parents had never seen me play in college, and they came up, and my dad and mom came up there. We were playing, I think it was Iowa. What happened is that I played, and in the first quarter and the second quarter, and there must have been twenty guys piled on top of me. What it did was they cracked my ribs, and I was so in pain, and finally I come off the field and into the locker room, and my dad—I'll never forget this.

And the doctor looked at me and said, uh-huh, you know, he's got a cracked rib, he's in a lot of pain, but there's no damage the way they crushed me. They pushed me out and the rib buckled back in. And he said, we can tape 'em up and you can play if you want to if you can stand the pain.

And about that time the door opened up, and boom, my dad comes down from the stands. He wants to find out what's wrong, something's going on in the locker room. He walks up to the trainer, and he says, Where's my son, Bobby Bell? And they said, He's in there on the table. And he said, Oh, well, what's wrong with him? And they said, Oh, he cracked some ribs, he's in a lot of pain, we're gonna maybe let him sit out the game. And he said, Well, what happened? And he said, Play him, tape him up.

My dad walks in and walks up to me on the table, and he said—and you gotta understand, you gotta know my dad, to me he's just the biggest giant in the world. He walks up to the table, and oh my gosh, he says, Boy, I didn't come up here to see you lay up on this table. And I go, What? Boy, I didn't come up here to see you lay here on this table. What're you gonna do? And I said, Uh, Dad, I'm gonna get dressed and I'm gonna go back out there.

I went back out there, and in the third quarter the coach had thrown in somebody else, and I'm sitting there looking up in the stands, and I said, Oh, man, I gotta play. I ran out on the field, told the coach. I ran out on the field, and he said, Where are you going? I played the rest of the game.

And then, you know, we won the Big Ten, and we went out to play in the Rose Bowl. I played in the Rose Bowl with cracked ribs, with a cast on, man. Then we came back the next year and played again in the Rose Bowl. I played in two Rose Bowls. First time a Big Ten school ever played in two Rose Bowls, because you play one year, you can't go two years in a row, that was the contract with the Big Ten.

But that year we didn't have a contract, and we were like Big Ten champs, and they invited us. The next year we were Big Ten champs and national champs, and they could have had a ruling, to sign a contract, and the coach called a lawyer and said, Hey, we didn't have no contract last year, you can't count that against us. So they said, Hey, we've gotta invite 'em then. So that's the first time a Big Ten school played, I played in two Rose Bowls back-to-back.

Washington beat us the first year, and we beat UCLA. Beating them in the Rose Bowl, that would be my college greatest day.

You played the one year, and I guess you could mention it like the Super Bowl, playing in that one Super Bowl and then coming back to win. It was UCLA. I remember Smith, the tailback. They ran a single wing, and Coach Biden, the defensive coach for Minnesota, he got us out there, and he got us so worked up, he said, Look, if you let this Smith, he's gotta run five yards to get to the line of scrimmage. If he gets five more yards, then that's a first down, that's what he's getting on you.

I mean, this was how he approached it. This guy's gonna run a single wing, he's gotta run five yards to get to the line of scrimmage, the tailback. He was killing everybody. He said, if this guy gets two or three yards, hey, man, I'm gonna be all over you. I mean, he ran eight yards to get that three yards. And we're going, wow, hey, shut it down.

They didn't have a chance. We were an underdog going in there. They said we couldn't stop the single wing. Hey, we never played a team in the Big Ten that ran the single wing, it was the first time. So we just shut that team down, pass-wise, running-wise, they didn't have a chance, we were just all over the field. We come out, won the Rose Bowl, that's got to be the top of my college career. I don't have my ring, the score's on my Rose Bowl ring. It wasn't that big in points, but we beat 'em comfortable.

Going into the Hall of Fame is the top of the pyramid. Your dream come true, man. Back when you were in high school, you never thought about this. I didn't think I was gonna play college football that much. I played college, and I was good enough to get a pro contract with the Chiefs, and the next thing you know they said, Hey, man, you might have an opportunity here. And they did call me, and guess what, this boy could be in the pro football Hall of Fame. And I tell you what, that was it.

From that point on, the whole aspect of football in my life changed. Pro football, when I went in, there was 118 in the world, man—118 players in the Pro Football Hall of Fame. That's saying that your peers think that you were one of the greatest players that ever played to put you in there. And of the thousands and thousands of football players over the years, you are one of 118.

People looked at you differently—Pro Football Hall of Fame, right here, yeah—it's hard to describe. The tears just come to your eyes, to be considered a part of the history that will always live, the bust will be there, and my family, everybody in my immediate family, my brothers, sisters, dad, everybody assured it, coaches, all the coaches, all my teammates were a part of it. And, you know, going in there, I go back just about every year, and every time I walk through there, you see your bust and jersey, and when I die, when I'm gone, they're gonna be there, for my people, my friends, people who do not know me.

Well, the ceremony is a very emotional thing. You know, you try to prepare something. You get up there, you look out there and you see all your friends, you see your teammates—I mean, playing football's easy, but getting up in front and trying to remember all the people in your life that touched you, to share some of this with the fans, to let 'em know that they were behind me, what pushed me, what motivated me. The coaches, my parents, were part of it, you know, my brothers, my sisters, my daughter, my kid, my wife. It was just—oh, man, it was just really devastating. Your heart, you know, my knees shake, you get up there and you break out in a cold sweat. Is this really me? I start pinching myself.

And the first ceremony, they keep you so busy, they try to keep you away from all of it. And when I went through the ceremony, it was like being in a tube or something until I got up on the stage. It's like you went through the motions. When you got up on that stage, and they said, here I am, and Coach Stram was the presenter, you know? And he did so much research. I mean, he called my coach, my high school coach, he talked to Vern Wallman, he talked to friends all over the country that knew me, and times that I had forgotten about.

When he first entered me and turned it over to me, I'm sitting there listening, and I'm thinking, where did you get all this?

And it brought it all back. I mean, I thought it was pretty cool going in, but when you brought all that up, what my coach said about my playing, my attitude, my friends that were not involved in football that knew me, and what they said. Coach Stram brought it all up there. And then he turns around and tells me, This is one of the greatest football players I've ever coached who played the position. He brought that up, too.

And I said, Coach—and I'm looking at him, I used to tell him, the reason I want to play for the Chiefs is that I'm gonna give you the ball, on average, at least three times a game. I'm gonna turn the ball over to you. That's my average. It might be five one game, but I'm gonna average three. I'm gonna hand you the ball on an interception or a fumble. I'm gonna turn it over to you.

And I would go ahead and negotiate my contract like that. I said to him, Coach, all you've got to do is find a couple more players to do that. Can't you win a game with nine turnovers? He used to go, Ah, come on, Bell, come on, Bell. But he gets up there and says, He comes to play, he doesn't care whether he's under contract or not under contract. And that's the way I was. If I'm negotiating a contract, I didn't talk about it, I just continued to play. I didn't deviate from my plan because I hadn't signed a contract. He brought that up, stuff like that.

So going in there has gotta be the top of the pyramid. And, you know, the relationship that I have with the Hall of Famers now, and then—you know, once you become a Hall of Famer, and also, being the first Chiefs player to go into the Hall of Fame, and being the first outside linebacker to go into the Hall of Fame. It's just the top of the pyramid, you know?

So, the friends that I have made once I was in the Hall, everybody that you played against in the Hall of Fame, we all get together and we all do things together. We all know each other's family. And, you know, I went in with Sid Gillman, Paul Warfield, Bobby Mitchell, and Jurgensen—all offensive. You know something? We are the closest, closest friends. Sid Gillman is very sick, and his wife was up there, and his daughter, and we talk. In fact, his daughter called me every week.

Bobby Mitchell, his wife, it's like part of the family. Paul Warfield, we do stuff together all the time. Sonny Jurgensen— hey, man, I don't know how to explain it. You know, the Raiders, we hated the Raiders, Willie Brown, Ted Hendricks, we're just hugging each other all the time. And the thing that gets me is that professional football, the National Football League guys notice that the American Football League, they noticed—you know we see you guys together and you grab each other and hug each other. I said, Hey, we started this league, man. We were fighting to stay alive, and Lamar Hunt started this league. It's the greatest thing that ever happened to us. He created some friction, but the AFL got better, and the NFL got better, and once we were there it was fate.

You know, when Lamar and the AFL came along, there wasn't that many blacks in the NFL. Lamar just started it, and they just started recruiting from places like Grambling, Florida, North Carolina, and they said, Where are y'all getting all these players. You're taking a lot of black players. I mean, I can go back and look at this, and at that point they started recruiting blacks—do you know in '69, I think the Washington Redskins didn't have a black player on their team except for one. Bobby Mitchell was the first black. Can you believe that?

The other thing, like Coach Stram and the multiple offense, the defense, we were playing the defense they play now, three linemen and four linebackers. Everybody ran the four-three and we turned it around, and that's how I started playing linebacker. I'd be the defensive end, and I'd get up and be the fourth linebacker. The moving pocket, you know, Lenny Dawson with the moving pocket. They said, they can't play that with the moving pocket . . . what's the game like now?

Sid Gillman went into the Hall because he had the passing attack, you know, John Hadl and Lance Alworth,—God almighty, man, Paul Lowe and Keith Lincoln, Ernie Ladd and Earl Faison. They had a big team then, but quick, spread the offense out, and boom, boom, open up the game and score a lot of points, and the NFL said, Ah, you guys'll never make it with that stuff, that spread offense. What are they doing now? They spread their offense out, score some points. Look at the Rams, they put those four guys out at receivers, those flankers, they run the same thing that we were running. It was just too bad that he was coaching before his time.

If I had to pick one, it would be the Hall of Fame, because that would sum up everything I did.

The greatest player, teammate? I'd have to pick Buck Buchanan. He was my soulmate—Big Giant, I called him, God rest his soul, man. I can't believe the guy's gone. The player I played against—I loved playing against Joe Namath. Oh, yeah. I played against great quarterbacks, but I just loved playing against Joe. It was just a challenge. He believed in what he was doing, just like I did. I see some of myself in him.

Oh, man, you never knew what he was gonna do. We'd come up and intercept his pass, two of the same passes, he ran it twice, and I intercepted the ball—and the third time, touchdown. And I'd say, Joe, we intercepted you twice, and he said, Goddammit, Bell, I knew it would work. I knew it would work. Chess game, man, I mean, stuff like that.

I loved to play against him. I told him one time, I cut across and went right at him, and I'd yell at him, Joe! He'd turn around and look and go down. I'd go by and I didn't hit him. I'd hit his shoulder pads. His heart dropped, he thought he was gone, he'd try and fake. And I'd tell him, Goddammit, you ever dodge me, I'm gonna kill you. I looked at him, and he looked at me, and I'd look at him as I went back into the huddle. And every time I had a shot at him I'd yell, Joe, and he'd go down—don't dodge me. That's the respect I had for him. Hey, you know, I want him in the game, he's got a bad leg.

This past year, I did the coin toss at the Super Bowl, and as the game went over with, I'm going down the ramp at the club level, and I heard somebody go, Bell! Hey, Bell! And I turned around, and he said, Where are you going? God almighty! Just yelling, Goddammit, there goes the best linebacker who ever played the game. He turns around, we hug each other, and we walk out the gate together with his daughter. That's a great feeling.

*Raymond Berry chose two greatest days, each one a climactic victory in which Berry felt the unique spirituality that occurs when a football team comes together to pursue a common goal. The first was the championship that came when Berry was a defensive star for Paris High School in his hometown of Paris, Texas. The second game was the championship that became known as the Greatest Game Ever Played, the 1958 title game in which the Baltimore Colts beat the New York Giants in overtime by a score of 23–17. Berry's greatest moments in that game came during the final drive in regulation, when he caught three consecutive passes from John Unitas as the Colts tied the game with a field goal.*

Two experiences. One was my senior year in high school. We ended up winning a very, very, very big game, the final game of the regular season, to win a championship that our class had been pointed toward for both years. And Yankee Stadium in New York in 1958 when the Colts beat the Giants in overtime.

During that championship in the NFL, I experienced the realization that those two experiences were so similar I could hardly put one above the other.

You know, over the years I have also had my perspective switched around. The game in New York against the Giants, I now realize was without question . . . well, I guess there's still some question in my mind. I had a big game defensively when we won this championship, the best game I ever played in high school. I was sixteen years old, I weighed 150 pounds. But I think the experience of coaching and gaining the perspective on that game in New York that I had never thought about.

Because the fact of the matter was, we played the game in New York, and then I played, roughly, another nine seasons after that. And I never really stopped to reflect on that game against the Giants, because of the movement of time. I was involved in football as a player, and during the season I never thought that much about it. I was always focused on the next game, and I never did come back to it in the off season. And when I was coaching, the demands of coaching don't leave you time for anything except what's coming up next week.

But I don't know, I've been out of coaching since the '92 season, the last year I coached, and I think it was about two years after that, somebody asked me to write my recollections of the 1958 championship game. And it just kind of happened to coincide with an experience I had. We've been living out here in Colorado since 1992, and my dad lived in east Texas. He just died a year ago. He was ninety-five when he passed.

But because of the location we made the drive to Texas a few times, and one time I was making the drive by myself, and I had something I had to listen to on the radio in the car. I went back and got a box I hadn't been into in a long time, and quite by accident I came back with two cassette tapes. I didn't even know I had 'em. Somebody sent them to me when I was living in New England when I was coaching, and I never had time to listen to 'em. Someone had sent me a copy of the radio broadcast of that '58 championship game.

So I got in the car, driving from Colorado to Texas and listening to that game, and it just started bringing back a lot of memories, you know, of a game that was so remarkable. And then about that time, somebody asked me to write an article about it. So I sat down and put my thoughts down on paper. I called Weeb Ewbank and Charlie Conerly, and I called Johnny Unitas, just to sort of help with some questions that I had.

So I really spent some time thinking about it, and I think it was at that point that I realized, that game . . . as a matter of fact people have asked me, what was the greatest play that I ever made in pro football. Steve Sabol [of NFL films] asked me that in an interview last summer. And I said, Steve, you know, I've come to realize that it wasn't one catch, it was three. In the drive that tied that ball game up I caught three passes in a row to put the ball in field goal range.

The perspective of years really brought it clear to me that that particular drive and that particular game was really the high point of my career.

I think one is the significant background of the first of those three catches. It was a play that was successfully executed because of groundwork that had been laid for four years. John and I spent a lot of time talking football together and working after practice together, and in Weeb Ewbank's system we were part of the offense in a way that we were allowed to do things that we found out on our own.

He gave Johnny Unitas the responsibility of calling the plays, and that kind of a system leads to a really interesting communication between the quarterback and his offensive people. Invariably you find out that some people are students of the game and they come up with a lot of information that leads to successful play calling.

So that was the system we were operating in, and one of

the things John and I used to do was talk about different situations to work on, and really it was just the two of us after practice. And one of 'em was the background on this first catch that I made. It was a 12-yard square-in pattern— we called it an "L" pattern.

We discussed what we would do on an "L" pattern if the defense ever put the linebacker out on me. So we came up with an adjustment, and we called it the linebacker slant. And when the ball was snapped and the linebacker came out on me, I would just fake an outside release and then slant underneath. And so we would change what we were doing.

The time would come when we would work on different things. We would do it by ourselves and come back to it and review the linebacker slant and rehearse it. That was just a list of different things that we did.

Well, as we prepared to play the Giants, we put a tremendous amount of time into studying that defense. It's my knowledge . . . I don't think we had ever seen them do this, we had never seen them walk a linebacker out like that. I'm not sure when we played 'em that we even talked about it. I don't really recall, but I suspect that we didn't, because we didn't do it before.

Huff was the middle linebacker; he didn't figure into it. Harland Svare was their outside linebacker. I always split to the left; we were going against the Giants' right defensive side. So when we got in the situation where we were behind, 14 to 17, with a little over a minute and a half, and we were almost 80 yards out. So John hit Lenny Moore for a first down from third-and-11 after a couple of incomplete passes, and then he came to the line, and I think he called a couple plays in the huddle. We didn't have any more time-outs left after that.

And so we had this "L" pattern called, and lo and behold here comes Harland Svare walking out there—you know, again, you have not really discussed a situation like this. Based on several years of understanding and confidence and trust in each other—we didn't have time to use a cell phone—the cards were on the table. The ball was snapped, I took a couple steps outside, and Svare came after me. He ran underneath me, and John hit me about five yards deep, he drilled me. We picked up about 30 yards that time.

We weren't running out of the huddle anymore, so we go to the line for the next play. We run the next play and we end up inside the 20 yard line after the third one, and the clock is still running, we had no time-outs. Weeb had rehearsed us for a situation like this. Our field goal team ran out on the field, our offensive team ran off. They came in and kicked the field goal to tie the game with seven seconds left.

So that was . . . I think there are two reasons why that three-play sequence was the peak of my career. One was the linebacker slant—the first play. That was one of the great examples of how the preparation paid off. And the second reason is that, from my coaching experience, I know that you don't ever catch three passes in a row—it never happens.

And I never really thought about it, I think, until 1994, when I sat down to put a bunch of my thoughts on paper about that game. But after I did that little writing exercise, it really set through my head that that, without question, was the highlight of my career in professional football.

The weather was perfect for the Baltimore Colts. This was a December 28th game in New York, so we could have had all kinds of weather situations that we didn't get. We got a day without any wind, and it never was above freezing. When I look back on it I realized that Weeb knew that the New York Giant defense was of such caliber that—John told me this later, that Weeb told him that we were gonna just throw and throw a lot.

So we went into the game with that thought in mind—well, that's great, but if you don't get the weather you can't do it, and we got a great break on the weather for that game, without question.

The way we felt in overtime had a lot to do with what happened in our last drive. But if you analyze this game, we jumped out on the Giants early. We did pretty well in the first . . . we got all our points in that quarter and a half or less. And after that the Giants shut us out for the second quarter and the third quarter and the fourth quarter. We really didn't do much after that at all.

So when we took the field for that drive—that was the two-minute drive—Unitas ended up driving us the length of the field for a field goal to tie it. That was our first drive that we'd had since real early in the game.

The change in our confidence was just a hundred percent turnaround, because—and this is something you don't ever plan or think about, and I'm not sure you're even aware of it. But when we took the field for overtime and got the ball, there was no doubt in our mind that we were gonna move it all the way into the end zone and win the game. And that was totally ridiculous, because the Giant defense had stopped us all day except for that one drive, and at the end here we are, going through two of these drives in a row. And it really didn't make any sense that we had such confidence.

And we got in the overtime, we weren't following the clock, and we began to be very effective with L. G. Dupre going off the right side, and he made a couple of real good gains. And he got sacked, and we ended up with third and 17 or 18. And here was another incident that presented in this game later. He hit me on this third down and real long situation, for about 20 yards. But the key thing was that Carl Karlivacz, the Giant defensive back covering me, slipped on the play.

And the reason that's significant is that before the game started I went out—playing at Yankee Stadium, I went over the whole field, you know, yard by yard, looking at the condition of that field. I had two types of shoes that I wore, and if there was any possibility of slipping on that field, I wanted a shoe that had extra and very long—a couple of very long cleats right underneath the ball of my foot.

So when I saw this spot—it was over there in front of the New York Giant bench—the other part of the field was dry. But I remember thinking to myself, here's a spot right here where if anything critical happens, I don't want to take a chance on falling down—I went with those shoes. On 99.9 percent of that field, I really didn't need those shoes. I know that this patch where Karlivacz fell down was in front of the New York Giant bench, roughly. I don't even know where the pitching mound is, because I've never been to Yankee Stadium since then. I'm not really familiar with the field that much.

But I do know that that was a critical play, and having the right shoes on at the right time made the difference.

After that third down and real long situation. I think that within a play or two there, John went to an audible, pulling Huff away from his middle linebacker position. He went to a trap up the middle. Ameche broke, and . . . I don't know, it was a 25-yard gain at least, maybe 30. That got us down in there pretty close, and then I remember—I don't remember the down and distance situation, but within another play or two, he picked me out on another slant pattern that took the ball, I think then, to about the 8 yard line.

And I remember after that that we tried to run on first and 8, and didn't make much. Eventually he called a pass to Jim Mutscheller in the right flat, and he said later that the reason he called it—because it scared everybody, not us, because we weren't into second-guessing Unitas—but obviously all the people watching, evidently it must have scared a lot of those people. But not Weeb, because all Weeb told him to do was score.

So Jim put the ball on the 1 yard line, and that's when Ameche went in after that.

I can tell you exactly what happened [after that]. All of us had had a very frightening experience in Baltimore Stadium about a month before that. We played the 49ers in a late November game there in Baltimore—we win the game. We were losing and we came back on the 49ers, from a 28–7 halftime score, and we beat 'em 35–28. It was a heck of a comeback with that 49er offense. For our defense to shut 'em down in the second half was an accomplishment. We did get 28 points in the second half to win that game, and of course everybody in the stands knew that if we won that game we were guaranteed to be in the world title game.

And the game ended, something that nobody had ever seen, and nobody had prepared for—the fans came down onto the field, and caught all the players out there on the field. And if you've never been in a situation like that, you can't really realize what the dynamic is—the dynamic is the center of the field is where they're trying to get [to], and it's a total circular situation, and everything starts compressing into the middle. And people start falling and getting trampled. I was there that day, and the thing that saved the players was that the fans lifted us, but I saw people going down and getting—it was a very scary situation.

I think we were fortunate—I'm not really sure to this day, I don't remember if anybody got seriously hurt out there. But everybody remembered it. And I'll tell you, you look at a film [of the championship game], when Ameche scored, I'll bet you that with the exception of Buzz Nutter, our center, who went to get the ball from Alan, everybody else turned and ran. We didn't know whether it might happen again. Thousands and thousands of fans, because of the geographical location between Baltimore and New York, came up from Baltimore for that game. So there were a lot of people from Baltimore that day.

Well, I went into the locker room, and I was really . . . I had a very personal experience. I really wasn't inclined this way at all, I never really gave it too much thought, I just had this very strong feeling in my mind that God had done something there that was remarkable. And I was aware of that, and that kind of dominated my whole thinking. I know I went into the locker room, fully dressed, and I went into the toilet area, and I went into one of the stalls with my full uniform on, and I just shut the door and I just sat there. I really don't know long I sat there for. It was just overpowering, what had just happened.

I guess you just call it some spiritual awareness, but it really did make a tremendous impression on me.

No, I don't think it had anything to do with the significance of the game, because—I can only speak for myself, but I think I speak for most guys on our team there—all we were thinking about was that we were in the very biggest game of our lives, and as football players we loved to play, and we had just won the world championship of professional football. And I really don't think our thoughts went any further than that.

I'll tell you what happened—and there's a link to what you're saying [re: the historical significance of the game]. Out on the sidewalk, outside Yankee Stadium by our bus, I saw Bert Bell standing there. I still have this picture of him in my mind, of him there, and he was crying, he had tears in his eyes. And I remember—see, I'm at this point in my life, I'm like twenty-five years old, twenty-six at the most—Bert Bell, which I don't realize, it just stuck in my mind, the emotion of this man.

It took years and years to understand why he was that way. This man had been nursing the NFL for years and years, and he knew the significance of this game. He understood that his baby just got born. And it took me years to understand that, and it took me many years to understand the significance of the game historically. We just didn't have the perspective to understand what we had just experienced.

You know, the league was small enough that we all knew Bert Bell. He came to training camp with every team, we met him, and he would come and talk to the team every year down in training camp. So it was a personal touch, with the commissioner in those days, so when I saw him over there, it just stuck in my mind, that picture.

[The high school championship] Well we came into this

final game against Gainesville, Texas—Paris, Texas, was where I grew up, in the upper-right-hand corner of the state. I think at that time we had only lost one ball game that year, and prior to the season we were picked to finish fourth in the league. And Gainesville was a team that returned a veteran football team from the year before, but had gone to the quarterfinals and semifinals in the state playoffs, and were actually favored to win our district. They had a lot of very good football players.

And our little team had no reputation whatsoever and we were not picked, but we ended up playing in this ball game, and we beat 'em 13–7. They were on our 5 yard line when the game ended, and we held them. And then the game ended, and it was probably the best defensive game I ever played at school.

In today's terminology, I would be an outside linebacker. But most of the time in our defense I wasn't just standing there, I was usually coming in, and against Gainesville that day our defense had me coming a whole lot. And really, when I was in high school I was primarily a defensive player. The year I got to play in college, my junior and senior year, the NCAA had gone back to one-platoon football—you had to be a defensive player in order to play. You had to play both ways, and defense was really the strongest part of my game. So that was really what I was mostly doing in those years.

In that particular game, we had pointed to this in our senior year after four years of going to school. It taught me the best lesson that I've ever learned about the power of community. I speak in places today and it's still the number one example of how potent it is to get a group of people unified and working toward a common goal. The other thing I learned was we were so fundamentally sound in the simple basics of football that we ended up winning just one close game that afternoon.

I wouldn't pick a play. I made a lot of plays that day, a lot of big plays on defense. And it was just a very long, hard-fought, very close game all the way. I really enjoyed playing defense, and one of the things that I remember so much about it was that, first of all, as a high school player, one of my greatest memories was playing defense, and the contrast of becoming an offensive player and a wide receiver, it's a total contrast, because you go from a physical, aggressive all-out effort game to a game in which you've got to be thinking all the time.

And I missed the simplicity of playing defense. Being an offensive receiver in the NFL and not being a world-class sprinter, you have to then get every inch you can and find every inch you can. And it becomes a mental game when you're compensating that way. Being a wide receiver in professional football for thirteen years was extremely—you know, it was a very difficult, hard process, because you constantly had to be thinking all the time.

Walking off the field that day is an experience that left such an impression on me that to this day, whenever anybody asks me about the greatest game, I think about what it was like that day winning that game and compare it to New York and winning that day.

And then when I coached the Patriots, we had such an unbelievable season in 1985. That entire season was just one of the greatest memories I have. There's not really one thing. It was just the experience of what that team—it was a team that came together much like the team in Paris High School did. It was just a unifying thing, it was a real team. The guys were really playing to the limit of their ability, I think, every week, and we won a whole lot of close games, and we had about as much chance of making the Super Bowl before that season as that high school team.

So to actually end up where we were, and getting to where we were was just unbelievable, the way it happened.

Well, it's interesting that you ask that [about the Hall of Fame]. I'm embarrassed to say that of all things that's probably fourth on that list. I'd have a hard time picking out of those three things I just told you. The Patriots experience wasn't just one game, it was like it was an entire season's experience. And there's so many unbelievable things that happened that year, that when I think back on all these things that I saw and experienced in that year, it was just here and there. It's not like you can pinpoint one game. It was just the experience from the year.

With those other two, I don't know, I just feel . . . I know without question, I've got some sense of mathematics, and I understand the odds of being a player on a championship team—and we didn't win the state championship, but we won all we were capable of. We won our district, and that's about all we were capable of doing. And then with the Colts winning that game that day in such a dramatic type of game, that was something. And we defied all the odds with that Patriot team to get as far as we got, and I don't know, we just . . . I haven't had many conversations like the one we're having right now, where you really reflect on it.

It's not easy to put into words.

I think you are forced to do two things [going into Hall of Fame]: One, you have to be away from the game for five years. And you know, that sounds like a simple thing and it may not be significant, but five years is a long time. So you're out of the arena, and you're away from all the game preparation and playing and doing all that. And so distance starts to become a part of your perspective. That's one that's required. The five years after I was out, I was inducted, so I didn't have to wait for the five years.

And then the other thing that happens is that when they call you up and tell you about this, you realize that you're gonna have to talk about it. So you've got to then prepare and think about what are you gonna say, and that brings you to reflecting, how in the world did I ever end up in the Pro Football Hall of Fame?

I wasn't gifted, you know. When I was in high school all I

ever wanted to do was make the high school team. And when I went to college, all I wanted to do was play in the Southwest Conference. Then when I finished at SMU I had gradually started hearing about pro football, and I saw a movie about Elroy "Crazy Legs" Hirsch, and I thought, I sure wish I could catch passes like that guy. And I started thinking about the chance to play pro football, and it never occurred to me—when I went to Baltimore, I was just trying to stay around one year.

It never entered my mind to be at the Pro Football Hall of Fame one day—it just never entered my mind.

So when you start reflecting back on how all of that happened, it makes you do alot of thinking. And you also start becoming aware of so many people who, at this turn in your life and this place in your career, here and there, you can just pinpoint the critical nature of a person being in your life, whether it was a coach that made a decision on you, or a doctor that could get you healed, and you start thinking about all the people that you need to thank that you remember this for.

I don't really remember too much about the speech, other than that I remember—I think identifying the people I needed to acknowledge that were so critical in my career. And I had Weeb Ewbank there to present me that day, and I never would have had a career in pro football if it hadn't been for him. He saw something in me, and he saw something in John Unitas, at a time when neither one of us had any reputation or track record. He was one of those special people in my life, and I remember just talking about that.

I remember, too, the five years of being out of it, and you go back there and see people you've played with and played against, and these film clips. And it's almost . . . I picked this term up watching the movies here in the last couple of years— surreal? I'm not sure what *surreal* means, but it's just the sort of experience that doesn't seem real, you know?

It's quite an emotional time there.

I think I would pick those three passes in a row from Johnny U.

Well, there's not really too much difficulty about the greatest player—Unitas, and, I've also gained perspective through the years, when you stop to—when you come into professional football with an unproven potential receiver, and you end up getting to play twelve years with Johnny Unitas, can you figure out any better scenario?

There's no way you could ever come up with a story like that. There's no question that's an open-and-shut case. In this case, it's certainly obvious.

I've never been asked that one [greatest opponent]. I don't really have an answer to that one. No name really comes to mind. I guess I've seen too many of 'em. I think especially after you go into coaching, what you end up doing is just stating a whole lot of names. After thirteen years of playing you can almost narrow it down, but after all the people you come up against, because when you get involved in coaching . . . when I was playing I'd think about a defensive player, but the way the question is, the greatest opponent, it could be an offensive guy on another team or a defensive guy.

Well, you know, one thing in watching great defensive corners over the years, and I've made this statement to Mel Blount before—I'm just so glad that he didn't come along when I was playing. About the worst thing you can encounter is the combination of size, speed, and brains—now, if a guy's got two of those and not three of those, you've got a chance. But when a guy's got size, speed, and brains, you might as well figure it's gonna be a long day at the office.

When I was coaching with the New England Patriots, that was the first time I ever saw Mel Blount. And I happened to—I joined Chuck Fairbanks's staff there in 1978, and he had put together some tremendous players—I mean, one of our receivers, Stanley Morgan, had to go one-on-one when we played the Steelers there in Foxboro one night. So I'm up in the press box, and Stanley Morgan is one of the greatest wide receivers I've ever seen play, and you wanna pick a guy you wouldn't want to have to cover, he'd be one of 'em.

And I'm watching Mel Blount up there, at 215 pounds, 6'3", and here's little Stanley, he's 5'10" and 178, but he's like greased lightning. But Mel Blount's running step-for-step with him. And it's hard for me to believe what I'm seeing. Now Blount has got the size to overpower you, and the speed to run with you and the brains to know when to do both. And I would [pick] Willie Brown when he was in his prime with the Raiders, and "Night Train" Lane, but I never had to face Night Train, because I played on the other side [of the field]. And I never had to face Willie Brown, because he came along after I did.

So when I think about people I would not want to spend an afternoon with, I would name three of 'em—Haynes would be number four. And maybe—that's not really an accurate way of putting it. You put any one of those four out there, and I'm really not interested in playing against any of 'em. Because they all combine the same thing. But I do think that Mel Blount probably has got twenty pounds on Mike Haynes, because I think Haynes was in the 190 range.

But here's Mel Blount and Willie Brown out there, weighing 215–220—good grief, I used to have to run up against Leonard Lyles in the latter part of my career in Baltimore. And this guy was a 9.4 sprinter in college, and he weighs 210 pounds, like a proverbial fire plug—God, I was glad when practices were over. I wanted to get to the game. The game was easy compared to going up against Leonard every week. And these corners that I've named right here . . . whoo, I'm curious to know what the heck I would have done against 'em. Talk about taxing my brain, I would have been smoking after that.

Those are real collisions when you come up against that kind of back. I used to have to face Abe Woodson when we played against the 49ers, who was a Big Ten sprint champion, but Abe only weighed 180, and I weighed about 185, so I wasn't losing any collisions. But when you go up against guys like Leonard Lyles that I had to face every day in practice late in my career, those are the kind of guys you can't even afford to run into 'em, you get knocked down.

But I never gave anybody just vanilla. You were gonna get a chocolate sundae with several toppings when I ran a route on you.

I coached in New England against those Steeler teams in those peak years, and I was in Cleveland when we played 'em twice a year, in '76 and '77. So I studied that Steeler defense closely, and the fact of it was you couldn't find any weakness—they didn't have one.

So I got a real introduction in contrast in the way I was having to make a living, and when I finished that last year, Tom Landry offered me a job with the Cowboys, coaching receivers. And I went there, and Bob Hayes was in his prime, and Lance Rentzel was there. And when I studied Bob and watched him and coached him and graded him, I remember thinking, good grief, how simple it is for him to get open. All he does is leave the line of scrimmage.

He comes down the field and the fear factor is such that a guy with any brains is gonna back off and give him all the room he wants. And I thought, good grief, how simple can you get? I was looking for every way I could just to get open—his vanilla, he didn't even have to put sugar in it.

*For Terry Bradshaw, his greatest day came down to his biggest game, which meant he had plenty of choices. The Pittsburgh Steelers played in four Super Bowls from 1975 to 1980, and while the Steel Curtain defense carried the day in the club's first championship, Bradshaw played a pivotal role in the pair of shoot-outs against the Dallas Cowboys that followed. For his greatest day, Bradshaw chose the second Super Bowl against Dallas, a 35–31 victory when he came as close as he ever did to playing a perfect game with everything on the line.*

My greatest day . . . my greatest game. I've never had a great game. Never. I've had a great half, but I've never had a great game. I had a great half in Super Bowl XIII, the first half.

And the reason that was a great game, number one, it was the Super Bowl, it was against the Dallas Cowboys. I'd had an MVP year; all the pressure was on me. The focus was on stopping me. And I went out in the first half, threw an interception, lost a fumble, but then responded and threw, I think, three touchdown passes in the first half.

And, it was, without question, the biggest game, because I only care about the big games. And in the biggest game of my life, I was able to respond to all the negative things that happened. And that's a source of pride that, as a player, gosh, I had all these bad things, but I was able to do some good things too.

I'd never thrown for 300 yards. That was the first time I ever threw for 300 yards, so it was that half of football. You hear players say they're "in the zone, in the zone," but that's true, you get into a mind-set. Nothing bothers you. You're totally at ease, or you're not. You really are. This is not just copy stuff. You really are at peace with yourself.

And when you get like that, the little passes that are almost knocked down are right there. A little simple hook goes 70 yards. It just all works in your favor because you're just focused, you're just there, you don't panic, you just take it at ease. When you're comfortable like that you see the coverages, you know where your protection flaws are, where you've got a blitz coming, everything is just laid out, just like you're writing it. It's just an awesome, amazing feeling, and, honestly, I never played that good ever again.

It was a simple thing. I came right back after, I think, the fumble return. I came right back on a third down, ran "70 Basic," Stallworth did a little 12-yard hook down there. The coverage rotated over, I threw it around a linebacker, he caught it, broke a couple of tackles, Swan threw a block downfield, 70-yard touchdown. You walk off the field—voilá!

Didn't do anything fancy. It wasn't a 70-yard bomb, it was a 10–12 yard hook. But I very easily could have stayed with the safety. I could've tried to squeeze the post in. I could've pulled it down, got the safety out of the middle, tried to go to the backside on the post. But when it all unfolded, right there, just boom, there was John wide open, hit him with the ball real quick, something I probably would've tried to move around and tried to get a little more yardage out of it.

So, there you have it. That's just the real secret to it, you don't panic. You just stay with your offense, you trust the players around you, you just trust that things are going to work out, and you don't worry. You don't worry, you don't have fear, and good things happen.

I never hung my head—no! Matter of fact, after the fumble return for a touchdown, I walked off the field kind of laughing, saying to myself, Ah, crap. Can't believe I did that. But I did, I threw a wounded duck on a touchdown pass to Stallworth. He was so wide open, I couldn't even get the ball out of my hand. It was just like, my God! I saw he was going to be wide open and I wanted to anticipate it, but I knew he was going to be wide open and I held it too long and when I did lay it up it just—quack, quack, quack, and he caught it, he went up in the air and he caught the darn thing.

It actually ended up being tighter coverage, simply because normally I would have set my feet, saw the coverage, anticipated, and laid it over his shoulder and let him run and get it. I actually waited too long and dang near had it picked off. So, good things start happening, and you know in life, one good thing happens, another happens, and it just keeps going on and on and on.

And then the second half it all shut out. It just shut out until a fumble recovery on a kickoff, and we ran "42 Basic." Swan has a quick slant or a quick post, and when I got ready to throw it on the slant, Lynn took it up the field a little bit. Instead of coming across flat, he saw the coverage, he just angled it up the field, I just sat on it and just laid it up where he could get it, and it was a great read by him, and it was a read by me. I just stayed with it. Or I could have come off of it initially and thrown it to the backside. But when Lynn took it up, it's like a slant and go. He read it himself. He did that himself and I just followed him. It's not that hard, is it?

We always thought against Dallas, you beat them by throwing the ball deep. You know they're going to stuff your run because the flex was very hard, the flex defense, which is a reading front based on your sets or your backs, but sometimes they do what is called contrary. In other words, they take the right tackle, have him off the guard, and the left tackle be up on the guard, and that would be against a certain set, guaranteed.

But then sometimes you'd get in that set and they'd do what's called a contrary. They'd do it the opposite, which went against the way the defense was run. Sometimes they'd set it up like that and run tackles out, sometimes they'd tackle pinches. I mean, they were a hard football team to get a read on.

But one thing you could do. They ran what's called a key coverage, which is kind of a form of a read/man coverage, where they'd either double Stallworth, and then they'd double Swan, based on the release of the tight end. Or they set the safety out, turn him out, run underneath Lynn and lay outside of Swanny, and you want to run post, hook-and-go, same thing on the backside. And that's all we did. No cut, no take-off. We always felt that to play Dallas, we had to throw the football deep. That's how we beat them.

We had the weapons. We had the rams and all of that stuff. Except we only had two of them.

I was watching on the sideline when the defense was on the field, and you know what happened. We got a big lead, and normally, what we did back then, or what our coaching staff did defensively was going to three-man zone, where you have six defensive backs. And instead of playing what had gotten us this big lead when we played aggressive, a lot of man coverages, a lot of cover fours, cover ones, all these types of man coverage, and we shut them down.

When you go to three-man zone against Roger Staubach, you're going to give up yardage. And that's what happened, boom, boom, boom, boom, boom, down the field they go, touchdown, boom, boom, boom, boom, boom, downfield, touchdown, because we're in a three-man zone. And I know the fans were screaming, Oh, my God, get out of that!

You hear people say that now on television, oh, no, not the three-man, because two minutes before the game's over you got an 80-yard drive and it's pretty mid-zone, and occasionally they don't like to blitz, you go man-to-man because if you get beat outside you're one-on-one, it's touchdown right off the bat. So you do zones, keeps everything in front of you, give them the completion, you stop them, they can't get out of bounds, hopefully.

It happened in Super Bowl X against Roger, and it happened right down to the last pass into the end zone. And this thing was the same way. And then Jackie Smith dropped a sure touchdown pass from Roger. So you have to look around, while you're watching this. You're a nervous wreck, because when you're an offensive player in a big game, speaking for myself, I become a fan. I get more nervous. I'm not nervous when I'm on the field, but when I'm off the field, in a big game watching our defense, you're sitting there, you're eating, you're just biting it, you're just grinding it with them, because there was nothing I could do.

Even as good as our defense was. Oh, yeah. As good as they were. But we played some teams that had—we played Fouts, we played Staubach, Stabler, Brian Sipe, when they ran that back then, their form of the old West Coast offense. Kenny Anderson was there. You knew that they would scheme you so well and that offense with three great receivers, there's going to be somebody open, I don't care who you're playing. Now, do they have time to do it? Against certain teams, it'd just eat at you, it'd just gnaw at you.

Super Bowl XIV, you remember, we ran a coverage we hadn't ran—I don't know when we'd run a reverse coverage. And Ferragamo is going down the field, and all of a sudden we call a reverse coverage and he throws it right to Jack Lambert. He didn't think Jack would be there, because we hadn't shown the coverage. Mike Wagner called all the coverages. Jack would call the front, Mike would check the bases. So that's football.

When Jackie dropped that ball, I don't know what the score would have been. I think we would've still been ahead, maybe by four points, I'm not sure. When you saw Roger just get chunks of yardage—I mean, honestly, you're helpless. You know what your defense is doing, you know what they're trying to get done, and you just watch them.

Staubach was a player that I always stood up and watched. I never sat. I always watched the opposing quarterback, but I especially watched him because you just held your breath until the gun went off, and then you thought, Oh, my God, you knew, just knew, that he would pull it out. You just knew he would pull it out. And just watching these passes go down the field, 10 yards, 15 yards, 10 yards, 15 yards, and, I mean, it exhausts you. It exhausts you.

That's why after all the Super Bowls, I had these huge, massive migraine headaches. Oh, massive—I just lay in bed and not move. Oh, I went to the parties, but I didn't stay long. Normally, I'd leave the stadium late and I'd go back to the hotel. Gosh, the first Super Bowl IX I went right to my hotel room, never left it. Super Bowl X, I got knocked out, and so I stayed in my hotel room again, never went to the party. Super Bowl XIII, I think I went to the party just for a minute, because I just don't feel good. And XIV, I showed up just for five minutes. I was really late leaving the stadium. I hardly ever was there more than thirty minutes for two of them.

I don't think I ever really could enjoy them, because for some reason, when it was over with, the next day you're getting on a plane, and you're heading home and you're playing the game over and over, you're reading the papers, you're seeing the headlines, and I'm pretty exhausted. I really don't enjoy it because right off the bat my thought process was, well, we've got to get ready for next year. We've got to defend the title, we've got to face all this stuff again.

I wasn't the type of player that just went around partying and having a grand old time, having people slap me on my back. It was really draining on me to be a Super Bowl champion. I've often said this. They weren't the greatest moments of my life, simply because they were so demanding. There, for a six-year period, maybe an eight-year period, when we were one of the top four every year, it's pretty exhausting. Mentally it's extremely exhausting. Honestly, I never really have enjoyed them, until, really after I finished playing.

After I finished playing, I've been able to look back and I've seen the highlights and stuff and I really enjoyed them because I don't have to worry about going in and defending the title next year. It really wore me out, it really did.

The first Super Bowl, Super Bowl IX in New Orleans, I went straight to my ranch and fished and worked cattle. I didn't do any engagements. I think that off season, I made $1,500. Isn't that amazing? Super Bowl X would have been a little bit more, but still, I stayed pretty much on my ranch. And then XIII is when I started making tons of appearances and just went gangbusters. XIII and XIV I stayed busy from the day the Super Bowl was over until right up to training camp. I'd normally take off a month before training camp, where I'd get really focused and really get myself ready to roll.

I think it was the most pressure. Super Bowl XIV was even harder than XIII on me. But XIII was just the greatest half of football. Because I never really had a great game. I never had four quarters. Never. During my entire fourteen years that I played, four solid quarters. I screwed it up. I don't know what the closest I ever came was. That would've been regular season. I only reference big games, because, really that's all I cared about. That's all that matters.

The Hall of Fame culminates your entire career. It's the last award you ever get. You never think about the Hall of Fame. It's not something that, when you start out as a child loving football, you don't play and go, one of these days I'm going to be in the Hall of Fame, one of these days I'm going to be in the Hall of Fame. You never think that.

Your process is, I want to play quarterback, I want to see what it's like, I want to throw touchdown passes, I want to start in junior high school, how cool is this, and boy, if I could start in high school . . . Then you start in high school and you keep your fingers crossed and you say, God, would it be neat if I could get a college scholarship. Then you get a college scholarship and then you say, Man, wouldn't it be neat if I could start? And then you start, and all of a sudden you wake up one morning and go, Wow, I got a chance maybe to go into pro football. How great would that be?

It's just that each step is such a joy. To see that it all unfolds was just such a joy for me. And then you get drafted and you go into pro football, and you're just blown away by that, at least I was. I went to a small school, small-town kid, and then it's the same. It starts all over. All of the junior high, high school, and college all comes together again, and you say, how cool, if I could just start up here.

And then, after you start playing you realize this isn't any good unless you're in a playoff game, you got to get into the playoff game. So then you start to say, Man, I want to get to a playoff game, I want to see what that's like. Then, when you get into a playoff game and you win the first one, and you see the reaction to it, then you go, this is just unbelievable.

And then you say, man! You don't think we could get to the Super Bowl? Nah! Impossible. And then all of a sudden you travel out to the Raiders out there and you beat them there and you go to the Super Bowl, and you're stunned. I was just stunned. I was shell-shocked.

And then you go to the Super Bowl, and my first thoughts

were, oh, God. What if we lose? What if we lose? Then you play the game, and all of a sudden you're on a drive there, with a few minutes, eight, nine, ten minutes left, and if you can sustain the drive, you're going to win this football game. And then we did that, threw that touchdown pass to Larry Brown against the Vikings and I went to the sideline, and I was absolutely, absolutely destroyed by this whole event. Just absolutely destroyed by it.

So it's like climbing the stairs, it's like learning to walk, then learning how to run. It's like learning how to throw, how to hand off, how to complete a pass, your first long one, your first touchdown. You get hit, introduction in high school and the fans screaming and you get to break the paper thing that says, "Woodlawn Knights." I mean all of these things were so important to me because I'm just such a kid.

And then when you look at your life, and you look back on it, the Hall of Fame summed it all up. It's just people thought you were special, when in fact you know you aren't. You played pretty good football, but, you know what, if they're stupid enough to vote me in?? You know what I mean. And then that's it.

And then people treat you differently, they just treat you differently. Pretty neat.

I remember the night before the induction on the top of the hotel. All my friends, and friends that I didn't even know were coming showed up, which really meant a lot to me. And we were just sitting on top of the roof of the hotel, and all my brothers, family, my friends, and they're ordering cases of beer, icing down garbage cans, stuff's being delivered to the roof of the Holiday Inn and I'm able to sit back and enjoy this. To me that was . . . they were just there celebrating the end of my dream. And I had the people that I cared about, they were there.

And then the parade's the worst part, and then the ceremony. I just sat there. If you've ever seen the tape I'm just sitting there with sunglasses on looking out at the crowd. And actually I'm trying to think about what I'm going to say, because the speech I'd written, I'd torn up and thrown away. And I was just sitting there and looking at all this. I was just thinking, you know, look at this. These people love you, they respect you, and they're all here cheering the Steelers. And all these people I went in with and I was just trying to collect my thoughts, because I didn't know what I was going to say.

The emotional part of the speech normally would be because of my family, and then it was because Mr. Rooney had passed away and he would have been my presenter. And so much had been said about my choice of presenters, and I think I had thought so much about him that when I mentioned his name, it was such an emotional time because he and I were so close. That got me, because when I started talking, I wanted to acknowledge the people, but then again I didn't want it to be like an Academy Award performance, you know, I want to thank, I want to thank . . .

And when I got to him, that nailed me, and then the next closest guy would have been Webby, and that's when I did that spontaneous—one more time. And then I just stopped. That's enough. I was going to talk about Joe Greene—that was enough. I'd done enough, you know? I sat down.

So that's who I was. I never have been articulate, I never have been someone that gives careful thought to what he's going to say. I'm pretty much off-the-cuff, and that's how I played, and it was only right, I think, I didn't have any notes or any speech. One thing that I wanted to leave everybody with was, if you leave here today from the Hall of Fame, you can rest assured of one thing: You can say to yourself that you were at least smarter than one person.

The greatest college game was against Northwestern State at the Fairgrounds in Shreveport, packed house, 25,000 people. Time running out, I think there was about ten seconds left, and we were 82 yards away, we're four points down, what was the score? 35–32, I think. And I'm not really sure about the score, but anyway, just enough time for one play.

I dropped back in the end zone and had everybody on take-offs and I saw Kendall gaining on the go past the corner, and the safety kind of froze in the middle and I just missile-launched it. He pulled that sucker in and walked into the end zone. We beat them. Biggest play of the game, 82 yards. It was cool! Archrival, Northwestern State. It's all relative, isn't it?

My greatest teammate? Wow. I was closest with Mike Webster. And everybody's always afraid to single out one person for fear you'll hurt somebody else's feelings. I was closest to Webby. The guys I hung out with were Calvin Sweeney and Jim Smith, and a guy who was like a brother to me was Joe Greene. Put it all down like that. I love Stallworth, I love Swanny, I love all these guys, but that's kind of the order.

And then the greatest opponent? Raiders. Tough. You know what, I never focused on an individual opponent, because all I can take care of is one person. I focused on teams, and the Raiders were tough. The guy I respected the most? Then I'll take Ken Stabler. Kind of like Roger. Just cool, accurate, and it was the Raiders. The Raiders were just the hardest team to beat, they were just . . . man, you play the Raiders, boy, you took a beating, and you didn't get a lot of yardage out of it. One heck of a rivalry. Easily the Raiders and Kenny Stabler.

*Like many great championship teams, the Green Bay Packers of the 1960s had to fail before they could succeed, and it was that temporary failure—a loss against the Philadelphia Eagles in the 1960 NFL Championship game—that spurred Willie Davis to become a Hall of Fame defensive end. Green Bay's loss to the Eagles was a motivational tool he used to improve his performance going into the following season, when Green Bay beat the New York Giants to take their first NFL title.*

Well, my greatest day in football probably would have to be the day that we stood as champions in Green Bay in 1961. And I think it was my greatest day, and not so much that I had what I would consider a good game if not a great game, but more specifically, was the team's success. That ultimately had always, and to this day, meant more to me than an individual achievement. It was living in the glory, in that moment—hey, of all the teams that set out in July to do this somehow, the Green Bay Packers did it well enough to be champions of the NFL. And indeed, I guess, many times we felt that gave us the right to say we were the champions of the world.

For me, the big backdrop was the Philadelphia game the year before that. We lost in the championship, and in particular one play that, to this day, I remember painfully as a play that ran away from me where I chased it. I remembered it in many instances during that season and probably more even into the future.

And on this particular case, I think that I elected to be a little more cautious and determine a route on the play, so that if it somehow turned back I would be in good position to make the play. Instead the play continued to go away from me, and at one point the runner got a great block hit, and lo and behold he turned and stumbled and I was maybe within a step of making the tackle at that time. And in my mind, that whole off season I just relived it—there was no doubt in my mind, had I chased the play the way I typically did, I would have caught the play.

The back for Philadelphia was Billy Barnes. And I believe it was actually late in the third quarter, early in the fourth quarter, the time this happened. And it was on a play that, probably if I'd made it, if nothing else, they would probably have to punt the ball or something. But as it was they made a first down and kind of retained the ball and I believe went on and ultimately scored.

That was a play that turned my whole attitude towards how I played from then on. It was almost like anytime I felt that I had the opportunity to do something, there was never a second thought. You've got to play this game with abandon. You've got to play it with the notion that every chance you have, you must make the play. And for that reason the next year was a championship opportunity that we didn't squander, and I would say, it was something that Lombardi had said after the Philadelphia game that next year. He said earlier in the year that we would never lose a championship game. And we lived up to that. We never lost a championship game.

I think that year was probably the greatest year I had in the National Football League. I'm sure that it was the precursor to the All-Pro selections and everything else, because, as I said, the next year I played with total commitment to every play and every opportunity.

I remember Jack Stroud was the Giants' right tackle, and Jack was a very strong guy. If you managed to play him head up, you had a long day. I developed the ability to play on the corners of most offensive tackles, with the notion that if it was an inside play, I would angle my charge such that I would partly close the hole if it turned out to be a run. But more specifically, if it was a pass, I could jump and usually get a good start on the corner getting around the blocker, and that's what I did that week. I focused all week on getting on Jack's corner, and making him run with me back to the quarterback.

Probably the one thing that Lombardi described about my play was my quickness and speed along with upper-body strength, and I think that I concentrated on the fact that I needed to apply them more in that game that day than ever before.

It was a cold day. I think that the whole team was focused. Nothing was going to stand in the way of our beating the New York Giants on that day—the weather, an injury, nor anything was going to stand in the way. And I think that was the preparation all week; this is our moment and there was nothing that was going to deny us of a reasonable nature, and I think we played just that way.

Our offensive line was devastating that way. That whole five of Gregg, Kramer, Ringo, Fuzzy [Thurston], and Bob Skoronski, they were just sensational. And they blocked the New York Giants probably unlike they'd ever blocked them before. And I think that we on defense kept pressure on their quarterback all day.

I think no question one of the duels that day was Sam Huff and Jimmy Taylor. And that's why I would say our guys, our offensive line, was so devastating that day, because they blocked tough and they blocked the front-four guys and the fact that Jimmy Taylor and Hornung ran like unbelievable, undenied football players. And I think all of that stands out in my mind.

If you remember, that score was 37–0, and I think, so often you would see a game that didn't reflect that kind of difference or not. I would say to you that game in particular, we clearly outplayed the Giants to the tune of the score.

I think that we were always coached almost to the point of never taking it for granted, or never allowing a team to get back up that you had down. I think by the late third quarter, I started to say, boy, we're going to handle this thing. We're not going to be denied today. And I'd think playing at Green Bay with all the fans and all, there was nothing was going to deny the Green Bay Packers.

I think that for me personally, I'm one of those emotional individuals that do indeed build up a lot of adrenaline and excitement about playing the game. And it was really interesting, because when the game was over, I felt exhausted. I felt this whole sense that it was almost like you were enjoying the moment, but it was almost like you'd given so much of yourself you felt empty. I mean I really needed to reenergize myself.

I remember I was pretty much one of the nonconsumers of the alcohol that night. I decided I needed a couple of beers, because I needed to do something to unlock what had been this focus and this dedication and this whole intensity about the game. It was kind of hard to relax, believe it or not.

In Green Bay, one of the other things that always impacted you a little bit more than other places in my mind—and particularly at Cleveland, where I'd played two years before—to me win or lose in Green Bay, the impact of it was always a little bit more intense. And I say that because that night we went out, and clearly, you ran into the other Packers because in a town like Green Bay, it's so small that the choices of places to go are not going to allow you to not bump into teammates. And it's just a good feeling for all of us to live in this victory, and of course, the fans, they made it memorable to this day, the sense of how elated they were.

Well, the next year we played the Giants in New York, and I can tell you it was good to win again, but it was almost like it didn't rise to the '61 game, and I would say that in between, probably the next game that set itself apart was the first Super Bowl.

And I think there, it was our sense of having to protect something in terms of the reputation of the NFL. It was having to go out and protect the Packer pride. There were a lot of things that was put on the line, and it was almost like the thing that was pretty clear to us is that who we were playing had a lot to gain, but very little to lose. And I think the importance of it kind of evolved from that as a game. Frankly, I would say to you that the NFL games had been better, probably, as games themselves, but that one took on importance because it was the first NFL/AFL game played kind of as competing leagues.

Well, I was surprised, maybe just slightly. One of the things Lombardi had said to us that week in Santa Barbara, he said, you know, you only have to look at this team's lineup and think about the college headlines from these athletes and you remember the names of individuals on the Chiefs that had been very outstanding college football players. And that kind of created a sense of, well, you can't take these guys too lightly.

So I think that made a situation for us of, well, there's a job we've got to go and do, and the worst thing that could happen was we create some excitement for them. And, as you remember, the first half the Packers played probably unlike they had ever played before. I think we played defensively, we played kind of protecting something rather than being all-out aggressive, the way we typically had played over the years leading into that first Super Bowl.

And I think for that reason we didn't dominate the first

half nearly as much, I believe, as we could have if we'd took in one of the things Lombardi said at halftime. To this day it rings in my mind. He said, OK, what happened, you played thirty minutes adjusting to the Kansas City Chiefs. Now what I ask you to do is to go out and play thirty minutes of Green Bay Packer football and let the Chiefs adjust to you.

There was no truer factual statement made that day for me personally, because I had a sense that I could beat my guy in some ways that I had just refused to try before because I didn't want to make that critical mistake. All at once I said, Coach, you're so right. And the first series back in the second half, up front we started to cut loose and soon we were dominating the Chiefs.

Well, that's kind of how I recall the situation, and to this day, it's satisfying and it's gratifying to the extent that it typifies Green Bay as the exception in many ways, to this day. We had some lean days after that. I still think Green Bay represents the exception in the NFL more than it does the expected or the average.

My greatest college day? Well, it's kind of interesting to me that you'd say that. Yeah, I played in what was called the Orange Blossom Classic, which is played in Miami, and we played Florida A&M. And this was back of course I went to Grambling, which at that time and to this day is primarily a school where pretty much 90 percent of the student body is African American.

And of course we were playing Florida A&M, which was pretty much the same. And I remember the headline in the paper the next day was that Paul Brown, who supposedly attended the game to scout Adolphus Frazier and Willy Galimore, went away talking about Bo Murray and Willie Davis.

And the thing that to this day my college coach Eddie Robinson makes fun of, I was credited with twenty-seven tackles that night. At one point, because we stopped en route down to Florida, and we actually ate dinner on the Florida A&M

campus, one of their football players said to one of our defensive players, or one of our players, You'd better touch me now, because you probably won't during the game. And this was the guy I knocked out of his shoes and his shoes stayed on the ground as he went backwards, and I'll always remember that because that was one of the most often told stories around Grambling when you get the old players and coaches together.

I would say to you it probably was my greatest game in college. I was possessed that night. It seemed like every time they ran certain plays that somehow, I managed to make the tackle or be in on it. I kind of carried the memory of that game, because it was a challenge that had been laid out there that made me say, uh-huh. You're not going to talk like that and then make it happen. So, that was clearly my best college game and we went undefeated that year and everything, so it really was a fitting climax to a great year.

I believe it was something like 28–21. It was a hell of a game. Florida A&M had a good football team. They always did. Jake Gaither was a hell of a coach, and I believe they may have been undefeated at the time.

I think with Robinson and Lombardi—and that's something I've even thought about a lot—each had his superiority at the level they were coaching. There's no finer college coach in my mind than Eddie Robinson, in some phases of the game, his whole ability to motivate you, identify with life and the struggle. And I think sometime if you came from a background that was kind of mired in poverty and all these other things, he could make you play to a purpose and to a calling, if you will, that I think was just unlike any coach I ever had. That, to me, was something that worked extremely well in college.

I think when you get to Lombardi, you have the same type of motivation, but Lombardi's motivation would have been built around responsibility and commitment—kind of like, hey now, you're at another level, and now you've really got to take this on. As I said, if you make twenty-seven tackles, you're probably all over the field and you probably make a hell of a lot of mistakes, as you're just running around chasing the ball. Whereas with Lombardi, you would be required to play your responsibility and then you add your support to everything else that happens on the field. But I would say the motivation, in terms of the abilities to motivate people to play, was pretty much the same.

*Today's generation of Giants fans know Frank Gifford as one of the primary voices of* Monday Night Football, *which changed both the football and the cultural landscape of America. But those fans who followed the club for a bit longer remember Gifford as a two-way terror at USC who went on to become one of the great offensive players of the 1950s after being drafted by New York. For his greatest day, Gifford chose his Hall of Fame induction in which he was presented by Giants owner Wellington Mara, for whom Gifford returned the favor when Mara had his day in the sun at Canton.*

I think probably, it kind of encompasses everything I've ever done, and that was when I went into the Hall of Fame. And Wellington Mara, the Giants owner, presented me to the Hall of Fame, and I think being there . . . it's like everyone else who's ever done that, I guess, in that it just culminates everything.

You think back on all the games you played, the championships you won and you lost, and it goes literally back to high school for me. And I had some friends there from high school and college and the professional world, and I think most importantly it's that Wellington Mara was my presenter.

And then I guess twenty years later, I presented him, and I can't think of anything in the individual game that transcended that.

It's kind of interesting—if you've never been to Canton, Ohio, it's kind of hard to explain, because it's very . . . they've kept it almost like it's been from the very beginning when the old Canton Bulldogs played there. The Hall of Fame is a wonderful place to visit, and when you walk in there and actually see your own bust there it's kind of weird—you're not even dead yet (laughs).

And this year I'm gonna—in the fall sometime—I'm gonna take my nine-year-old out and let him look at it, because he's really just discovered football, and the fact that I played.

It's very special . . . they have the parade in the morning, it's a whole weekend, an exhausting kind of a weekend. They have the parade in the morning, and you go through the induction ceremonies right before the game. Actually, even before that. Thursday night there's a big dinner, Friday morning there's a breakfast, and Friday's the big luncheon where all the other Hall of Fame members who've come back each year—the luncheon is just exclusive for the Hall of Fame members and the newest inductees.

People like Ray Nitschke and Sam Huff, one of the real characters, Doug Atkins, very unlikely people have been really caught up in this. And they come almost every year. Lou Groza, and I just saw where Marion Motley died, but he lived over there. It's a wonderful luncheon. Everybody gets up and says something about what the Hall of Fame means to them. They're kind of telling the newest inductees how important it is—which they didn't have to tell me, because I'd been going there from the very beginning of *Monday Night Football*.

That was part of our contract, and I played in the very first [Hall of Fame game]. So it was very special for me to have played in the first one, and broadcast all those games, and there I was in 1977 standing on those steps with Wellington Mara, my friend, and the guy who drafted me for the Giants, as my presenter.

And then it was 1997 that Wellington Mara was inducted, and I felt the same thing with him, riding in the convertible with him the morning of the parade, thousands of people. I think they estimate 100,000 people come into the town—only 25,000 can go to the game because of the stadium. So it was very special.

I went in with Gale Sayers, Bart Starr, Bill Willis, and the big offensive tackle from Green Bay, Forrest Gregg—there was five of us. We just spent the three days together, and we had played against each other. Bart and I had played against each other. I lost a couple of championships to him. Forrest Gregg I remember really well. Gale Sayers, I broadcast quite a few of his games, even in the fewest number of years of any player. It was only eight years. He was unbelievable before he tore his knee up.

Everywhere you went they had highlights of you playing . . . mine were in black and white, but other than that it was fun.

I remember talking about the Giants, and how fortunate I was to come there, and having followed Wellington, who introduced me. He was the one who drafted me. He drafted me because I was both an offensive and defensive player, [that] being a cut rate on personnel. And it turned out that was the case, too.

But we later became really great friends.

And I talked about the Giants being a family. So many people today, they bounce around from team to team, I played twelve years with one team, and it was like a family. Oddly enough, when I presented him, I went back to my speech. That would have been twenty years later, and it became almost the same thing. I hardly had to change the notes, I just had to reverse the roles, coming and going.

And there's the same thing . . . I think he spoke much like I did, other than he had thirty-two grandchildren there, so they couldn't very well boo him.

You know, of all of it, I have to say I do remember that. There's a gazillion games that I played, and a gazillion more that I broadcast, and people have always asked me, what's the most memorable game? There aren't any. It's all a blur. You know, it's a wonderful blur. You think of individual things that happened, but I can't think of one game where I ran for a thousand yards or something. . . . I just can't. I would never even want to, there are so many of 'em.

It was just the culmination of everything I've done.

There's been so many changes, and everybody is so critical of them. Football makes so many changes. Football isn't like a game of dimensions, like baseball is, where people say, oh, baseball never changes. We've got offensive tackles, where twenty years ago they were 200 pounds, and now they're 350. We've got people that can really hurt each other, and they need to be protected from themselves in many ways, but I think most of the changes to pro football that I'm aware of have been for safety, and to make it entertaining.

What the hell's wrong with that?

I think it's a better game in the sense that the people who play it are better players. A lot of it is the skill of the players. They're much better, they work at it, it's a year-round thing for them. It wasn't with us. We couldn't afford it to be a year-round thing. Anything you can measure, the athlete is better today.

I don't think they have as much fun, or care about . . . they care about the individual game, but I don't think they have the same feeling that I did toward the city that I played in. I loved New York, and New York loved me. It was a great, great relationship, and still is.

I moved all over the place as a kid growing up, and my dad was in the oil field, and in my hometown, people say, well, what's your hometown? It's New York, even though I live in Connecticut. I love this town, and I loved playing here and I love the fans.

I would much rather have played when I played. First of all, I like living here, and I don't know how many players, maybe Phil Simms and Lawrence Taylor. They're both retired and they're both gone now for many years, and they played their careers here. I'm trying to think of who else, in terms of veteran time with the Giants. You could look it up, but it's not very long, on either side of the ball.

That was nothing unusual for us. A lot of guys I played with had been here eight, nine, ten years—Kyle Rote, and Charlie Conerly, Harland Svare, Andy Robustelli. Andy came over from the Rams, but he spent most of his career here.

We had a fortieth renewal of our '56 championship team recently, in 1996, out at Giants Stadium. And the guys voted me the spokesperson for them, and that's what I said. There are no fans like the Giants fans. As far as I'm concerned, all the other fan bases, they're just pretenders.

The Giants, their tickets have gone down from family to family, from generation to generation. I run into kids that were named after me, and I didn't know any of 'em. It's been that kind of wonderful relationship, and again, like I said, it was all culminated at Canton, Ohio.

Bud Grant is best known as the stoic Hall of Fame head coach who guided the Minnesota Vikings to four Super Bowls during the '60s and '70s, but the versatile, talented Grant also had a two-sport career playing basketball for the Minneapolis Lakers and football for the Philadelphia Eagles before he took to the sidelines. Grant's greatest days in football took him back to the Canadian Football League, then to the near record-breaking NFL contest that also cut short his playing career. As a coach, he chose Minnesota's first NFL championship, when the Vikings beat the Eagles and then had to wait in the locker room to see if the Green Bay Packers had lost to the Bears to clinch their inaugural title.

First of all—and I don't know if the record still holds—but I made five interceptions in a game when I was playing in Winnipeg. It was a playoff game, and that was a North American record—I don't know if it still is or not. I don't know if anybody in the NFL ever got five interceptions in one game—they may have, I haven't kept track of that.

It was a playoff game, and boy, these things go back a long way, but Frank Kochock, who used to play with the Giants, he played for Canada at that time. In those years, we all went to Canada for more money. Canadian football was paying certain Americans more money than I could make with the Eagles—this was 1953, I think it was.

Well, I made the Pro Bowl when I was an Eagle. I asked for a raise and they said, Oh, we can't give you this much, so I went to Canada for a third more than I was making with the Eagles. And so, you know, I had to play both ways. Bednarik played both ways, and other people have done that. So I played both ways and went there and made good money, more money than the Eagles were prepared to pay me, and I went to the Pro Bowl. But I wasn't alone. There was a number of people, and their names don't mean anything to anybody, but they were first-, second-, third-round draft choices. They were players that were All-Pro down here that left the NFL just for money.

I was right at the height of my career. I'd only played two years with the Eagles. I was the number one draft choice. And I played pro basketball for two years before I went because the money wasn't there. I could live at home, play with the Lakers, win the championship, all that kind of thing and stay home. I didn't care to go and live in Philadelphia.

So then, finally, I decided I wasn't that good of a basketball player, and I went to the Eagles, and the first year I was there I was a receiver. I thought, although I played both ways at Minnesota for four years—I was a linebacker and whatever—so I went out there. Well, the first game, the defensive end gets hurt. So I'm on the bench, the coach says, get in there for him—I got two sacks and I played defense the whole rest of the year.

Well, the next year I said, I'm not going to play defense, I'm a better wide receiver than I am a defensive linebacker. So the next year I played out my option that I wouldn't sign a contract. I wanted to play offense. And to make a long story short, I was second in the league in receiving, went to the Pro Bowl, played every game, blah, blah, blah, and went in for a raise and they said, We can't give you what you want, we can give you a $1,000 raise. Well, that's a lot of money in those days, but I went to Canada for $4,000 more. So that was the scenario, that's why I went there. We weren't making a lot of money those days.

Well, in Canada, there was only nine teams in all of the Canadian Football League, five in the Western division and four in the East. And so that means you're in the playoffs almost automatically. But in those days when you played, the top teams had a bye. The second and third teams played a two-game series based on total points. It was a tough system, and then you played the first-place team in two out of three. So you could have a bad game and still come out and win. And the top team had home-team advantage.

So we get to the playoff in Winnipeg against Regina, and of course they're all rivals, but it's a big game. And we won big. And at that time, in that particular game, I started, I played corner. We had a couple of injuries, and I ended up playing free safety that game. So I just happened to be at the right place at the right time, I guess, and there was nothing spectacular about it—I mean you make an interception, and I ran it back for so many yards, I don't remember any of that, but you make some long runs. I didn't score any touchdowns on the interceptions, but I got five, and that's a record.

Playing in Canada was easier if you like to run, and I could run. I played corner most of the year, and wide receiver, never came off the field. Alot of times we played two games in a week because of the scheduling. They didn't play on Sunday in those days. We'd play a Saturday night, and a Monday-night game or midafternoon on Monday. So we'd go to Vancouver on Saturday and then play in Edmonton on Monday.

If you weren't in shape you got in shape. It was surprising, but you could recover in a day. The next day after a game you're all beat up and you could hardly walk sometimes, but you go out and loosen up and the adrenaline would start running and you could do it. And that's why it never bothered me when I was in the National Football League to play on a Monday or a Thursday as a player—it didn't bother the players.

The coaching was a little more difficult because you have less time to prepare, all the preparations you had to do. But from the player's standpoint I never felt that was a handicap to play on a Monday night and not to play on Sunday, or Thursday or Thanksgiving, or whenever they played. That never bothered me.

My greatest NFL game? There was kind of a tragic twist to that. I was playing with the Eagles the year before this interception record, played with the Eagles and we were playing Dallas. We were fighting for the playoff spots, and we were playing Dallas and we jumped out on them pretty good. I forget the score at halftime.

In the first half I got ten passes for 190 yards. So we go to halftime and the coach calls me over to the quarterback and he said, Bud's got ten receptions here for 190 yards. I think the record at that time was sixteen in a game. And I said, I wasn't aware of any of that. And he said, You know, the game's pretty well in hand, why don't—just between the three of us—why don't we go for the record?

So he said, If you got ten the first half, for 190 yards, why can't you get ten in the second half for better than that? In the meantime, you might have a record that would stand for all time. You got twenty passes for 400 yards, that might still be a record. So he said, Why don't we go for it? And I said, That's fine with me.

So, in the meantime, I cover all the kicks, too. Having played defense and run, I could cover kicks. The opening kickoff, I was hovering, we make the tackle, I was in at the end of the tackle, but I was coming in standing up and some guy caught me with his helmet right below the knee, tore my cruciate. So I'm on the ground and really I hadn't ever, ever missed a game or a practice. And now I'm laying on the ground and I get up and it hurts. I go to the sideline, and they're saying, how does it feel, and they tape it up. So I go back again. I caught one more pass for five yards or something, and I went to cut and I couldn't do it, just tore the anterior cruciate, so that was the end of it. It's a tragic story.

In those days also, there were no operations for that. I went in the next day and they said, Well, you tore your anterior cruciate, and I said, What do we do? And he says, Well, you've got another one. You live with one. And I said, Geez, I don't know, it's pretty sore. And he said, Well, it depends on how much swelling you get.

Anyway, we play Washington the next week to tie for the championship with Cleveland. So I get out there and played the next week. I wasn't in practice all week, but I played the whole game against Washington. Didn't do much, we lost, it was snowing, Sammy Baugh retired that day, we were in Washington, we lose by three points, but it was for the tie for the championship.

And, ironically, that game we're going for the winning score, we're four points behind, and I'm down the middle in the end zone, wide open from about the 20 yard line in. It's the last seconds of the game, wide open, quarterback throws the ball, hits the upper crossbar on the goalpost, which were on the goal line in those days. I'm wide open. I'm sure if I'd caught the ball we would've won the game and tied for the championship. And so at the end of the season, it didn't end on a good note. Although I did make the Pro Bowl. But I could've set a record, I could've caught a winning touchdown if it weren't for a crossbar and a hit. Those aren't highlights, those are lowlights.

Cleveland was a dominant team in those years, although

the Eagles had won two years before with Greasy Neale and Steve Van Buren and those guys. They'd won the championship, they'd had a taste of that. And the team was an aging team, but we always gave Cleveland a lot of trouble, and it was a highlight for me because I'd played for Paul Brown at Great Lakes and I knew Marion Motley. He was on my team when I played tackle.

But beating Cleveland was my greatest game with the Eagles—when we played Cleveland, Brown would always come over and shake hands with me. He was kind of a stoic, non-emotional guy. He doesn't seem to be close to his players from an outward standpoint. After playing with him at Great Lakes, he wouldn't shake hands with the coach, he'd come over and shake my hand after the game. Players were looking at me like, Well, is he your uncle or something?

That kind of thing, that was really quite a noticeable thing, because normally Paul Brown would just put his head down and go to the locker room. He'd come across the field. I wouldn't go to him, he'd come to me. Later, to the extent that he's shared that with anybody, I found out that when I was at Great Lakes I was only eighteen, and I guess I was one of his favorites. He said, you know—I don't want to put quotes in his mouth, and I want to give you the perspective—he once said that I was one of the most coachable players he ever had. He'd never had a kid that didn't make a mistake or something along those lines.

He's a student of the game and that kind of thing. He took a shine for those reasons, because I just listened to every word he ever said to anybody, I don't care if it was me or somebody else. Because he had insights into football that a lot of people didn't even catch. And I guess he must have caught that, seen that. I didn't know that. I was just a punk kid, trying to keep my place on the team. But later he did comment on it. He wished he'd been at Ohio State and recruited me at Ohio State instead of going to college from there. He went to the Cleveland Browns, I went to college.

We didn't win any championships in college—we came close but we didn't win. I played both ways in college for four years. I made a lot of touchdowns and tackles and made a lot of catches, as much as we threw in those days, it wasn't a lot. And I don't know that there was one game, not one that defines a career.

I think I played football, then I played basketball, then I played baseball. I was probably a small forward, And I could play guard, but I was like a swing guy, a sixth or seventh guy. And I could play the defense side, and I could play the perimeters and then ball-handle a break. As I said, it dawned on me that I could play at that level [pro], but I wasn't going to make a big living. I was just an average professional player, not a great one as opposed to professional football player. I think I was at the top of the game when I played. I was at the top echelon.

You know, I coached for so many games, and one thing you do, at least I did, if you're going to survive, you can't be dwelling . . . one thing you do is if you coach long enough, you don't live with all of those games. Some guys coach for a short career and they have a defining moment or something. I don't think I ever had that. We won a lot of championships and we won a lot of games and I don't think there's a game that's a defining moment. From reading your other book [*My Greatest Day in Baseball, 1946–1997*], a lot of the guys, they come up with great games. I mean, if you coach long enough, you lose sight of that spectrum. You lose in the last second, you win in the last second.

Well, I guess probably I think I could go back, and you asked me what year this game or that game was. A lot of people come up and say I was there when this happened and I was there when that happened, I can't remember what year that was. You may jog my memory and I'd say, Oh, yeah, we beat the Bears down there, or they beat us.

We did win our first conference championship in Philadelphia on the last day of that season. And we played at old

Franklin Field, which I think is the last game I ever played there. That's at the University of Pennsylvania—well, it was like '68. And it was a snowstorm, of course. And because it was the last game, they didn't do anything for the field. I mean they might have put down some markers on it, but as far as they were concerned the field was done and they didn't want to spend any more time on it. It was at the point where I don't think they brushed anything off.

And we were playing the game and the yard markers were obliterated, and the sidelines were obliterated, terrible field conditions in terms of it was cold and snow, and I don't know whether it was frozen or not. I think part of it was. And we had to win the game and the Bears had to lose. We ended up winning the game, a couple of long passes, and Joe Kapp threw and Gene Washington caught the ball and he was five yards out of bounds for the deciding score. And they didn't even have brooms to sweep off the sideline markers.

And we looked at it later, and I remember saying on the phone, is he in bounds? And they said, I don't think so. We looked at the film, he's five yards out. But the officials couldn't tell, they just neglected the field to that extent. So we win the game.

So it's the eastern time zone, it's an hour difference in Chicago. So we get back in the locker room and Franklin had a little cubbyhole of a locker room—by today's standard you could put a junior high team in there. Now, what's going on in Chicago? Well of course the game isn't broadcast, it's not televised, so how do we know?

Sid Harper, the sportswriter, was in the locker room, so he calls back to Minneapolis, talks to somebody at 'CCO, our radio station here, and the flagship for our games, and they're relaying, they pick up a broadcast from Wisconsin, Green Bay, or Chicago. They got that on the radio. So I say, Tell me, Sid, what's happening? And Sid is on the phone. First and ten! They stopped them! He's giving us a play-by-play, third-hand.

We're all sitting there, because if Chicago loses, we win the championship. It turns out that Chicago, at the end, is driving out on the field, they score even a field goal, I don't remember any of that. But Nitschke intercepts a pass, Chicago loses, we win the championship. First one here at Minnesota. Everybody was pretty happy.

We got ready to play Baltimore. We started in the locker room. It was a great plane ride home, but we weren't a dominant team at that point. I think we were 8–8 or 8–7 or something. It was a fourteen-game schedule. We won, but we didn't win by big margins. But that was only my second year here. First year we won three games. That happened to be one I remember because of Franklin Field, the locker room.

Yeah, the next year we won 12–4 or something like that. We went on from there. So now, not only do we make the playoffs, Baltimore beat us down there, not bad, so next year we're going back as division champions, we got another goal. The rung is a little higher now. And so we kept going up that rung. But that was the first step, and we went on from there, from that point. But that was a game I remember because of the strange circumstances.

But there's a lot of games you're involved in, if you lose or win, but you can't worry about it, you go on to the next week. I never think of that game again. I know we had our fortieth reunion here, the Vikings, this past weekend. And I was looking through the book at some of these scores, and I can't remember them.

I remember the championship games, but not one over the other. We beat Dallas in Dallas, they beat us up here, we beat the Rams in a snowstorm, went out there and beat the Rams in a rainstorm, they finally got us out there. We beat St. Louis here, we beat Washington here. Those were all games that I couldn't tell you what the score was. I don't know what happened other than we won.

In those days, all your telecasts were regional. So the Midwest saw the Vikings. Nobody on either coast saw us all year.

We were just a name and now the playoffs come. Now they see the Vikings. So the only image they have of the Vikings is, Hey, those guys play with them flamethrowers out there, and it's cold and there are no heaters and in their underwear, they take their jackets off at the national anthem, and they stand in the cold, and they scrape the scabs off their elbows or their arms before the game starts.

That was everybody's image of us. They never saw us other than the playoffs. We play 90 percent of our games in nice weather, but only the ones that were shown on television were the bad games.

The induction? It's not something you can think about, at least I didn't. It's not something you can plan on, say, Well, you know, am I going to get in, or am I not going to get in, when or how. I didn't even know how the system worked.

However, when the time came, and I'd hear, you've been nominated, but you didn't make it, then finally you make it. Then when I got in there they say, Well, you've got to be here for the ceremony. We'd played a couple of games in Canton, anyway, in the Hall of Fame game. So I'd been to the museum there and everything.

But after I was in it, I started informing myself what it was all about and looking at it a little closer. Hey, it was pretty special. Of all the awards you can win, you wouldn't trade any of them for that—being in the Hall of Fame, I think there's—since whenever they started, 1920-something or '30-something—there's only been 200 people in there. And to be one of that select few is an honor that you can't minimize.

It was much better than you could imagine if you were, not having been there before. The treatment that you received from the league, from the Hall is absolutely outstanding. They honor you. You feel honored. You can win championships and you can win games, and I always said there's nothing older than Monday's newspaper. Once Monday goes, the next week there's another game, there's another hero, there's another story. And if you win a championship, it only lasts for a year at the most. Or if you're All-Pro or you're all this or something, somebody else is going to be there next year.

Sports doesn't have many residuals. You can be on top of the world one year, and you get injured and you're out the next year and two years later they can't remember you. If you asked somebody—if you go down the street and say, well, okay, four years ago who played in the Super Bowl? Unless they're real ardent fans, they'll have a hard time remembering that and the score.

The entertainment business doesn't allow you a lot of that. You're going for entertainment, and that's what people forget is that football is entertainment, not life and death. But, if you get in the Hall of Fame, they can't ever take that away from you.

I went in with Jackie Smith, Randy White from Dallas, and [Tony] Dorsett. Well, when I start thinking about it, about what an honor it was, and when I start going back in my life when I started, I never forget about the Hall of Fame, but my whole life has been football I haven't made a dollar doing anything else. And in my speech I'm sure I mentioned that the New York Giants used to train in Superior, Wisconsin. I used to be at that ballpark every day. I used to shag balls every day, field goals or punts or anything I could do.

And they used to have a tackle by the name of Dewitt Coulter for the Giants, and they had about a 200-yard walk from the field to the their locker rooms. He used to let me carry his helmet. Yeah, it was exactly the same as that commercial with Mean Joe Greene and the kid. That's me, because he was a mountain of a man in those days, he was probably 275, he was the biggest guy in the world. And I walked beside carrying his helmet. Man, I was the envy of every kid in town because the other players didn't do that. He gave it to me.

So I watched that whole thing go through. Steve Owen [Giants coach] was there. My dad got to know him because my dad ran a concession stand at the ballpark, and Steve would always say, Well, someday you'll play for us. I know my dad would say to him, someday the kid's going to play for him. And he'd say, Sure, just keep eating, whatever, running, staying in shape, whatever he said, I don't know. But my dad kept telling him, The kid's going to play with you.

So having that background, and also having two people from Superior in the Hall of Fame, which is was a small town, Toughy Leemans and Ernie Nevers. Well, those were names my dad would tell me about. The great Toughy Leemans— I'd ask, Well, why'd they call him Toughie? Because he was the toughest guy in the National Football League.

The greatest player I ever had was a guy named Leo Lewis, who I had in Winnipeg. In fact, his son now works for the Vikings. I picked him up. He was a wide receiver and a punt returner. I picked him up when he got released, when he got out of college and he spent I don't know how many years, ten or eight or something.

Lewis was a punt-return guy, and as a receiver he caught a lot of passes. But his dad was the best I've ever seen. If you remember the guy from Baltimore, what was his name? Lenny, yeah, Lenny Moore. He'd catch the ball. He was our best running back, our best receiver, our best blocker, our most durable player, returned kickoffs, set records, he was the most complete player I'd ever been around. If he'd played in the National Football League then, which wasn't much better than the CFL at that time, he'd have been a household name. He was a more complete player than the Ellers, Larsons, yeah.

The toughest guy I ever played or coached against? Probably Walter Payton. He was Mr. Everything. He reminded me of Leo a lot, if they had put Payton back to returning kicks. You never saw Payton run out of bounds. He'd put his shoulder down and he'd take your shot, but the thing that distinguishes good players from great players is durability. If you don't have durability you never achieve greatness.

Brown didn't finish his career. He quit, he could have had more records. But I think it was a personality thing there, was what that was all about. And Motley, I played with Motley at Great Lakes. And then I had to tackle him. That was a thrill. And I knew the play they were doing, you know. They ran with their little quick pitchout there, and I was playing on the left side, and they run that way about four out of five times. They came to the right, and here comes Motley, either blocking me or carrying me on his back. I came out of those games pretty beat up. But, again, I don't think he played a long time either.

I'm just being a football observer, and that's what coaches do, observe. Leo brought more to the game than any of the rest, and Payton should be in that category. Leo ought to be in Payton's category, or Payton ought to be in Leo's.

The best opposing coach was Paul Brown. He was a big innovator. He got into football and he made a lot of changes. And I thought when I was coaching in Winnipeg, I didn't have any coaching experience. I was only twenty years old when I got the job, and I'd just come back from an All-Star game. I'd scored two touchdowns. At the peak of my career, and a job opened up. Allie Sherman got fired and I got the job. And I didn't really know a lot about coaching, though I knew a lot about people and players.

So I think that I did some things like Paul Brown did, innovated, in making us a better team by doing something a little different. I don't think you can do that today. You can prepare, but most of what you do might be copying someone else. Paul Brown didn't copy anybody. He originated a lot of the things that we use in football today, and at that time. So I watched very closely what he was doing, and when he had the Browns in Cleveland he put all of that into effect and won all of those championships.

As a coach he was, I think—I don't have idols, but he had my utmost respect as a coach. He probably lasted longer than most of them. It's a thousand percent effort every week, I don't care who you're playing against. There's no letup. There's no, I hope I beat this guy, you don't want to beat anybody anymore than anyone else, you just want to beat everybody. It's not a thing where you say, Boy, if we'd only beaten Green Bay, it'll save my job. None of that kind of stuff.

I think if you brought everything into focus, the Hall of Fame, that would be the day I'd choose to relive. That brought everything into focus. I didn't realize the enormity of all that until I got there. And I started looking around, and I started going back over what happened—the roads that I've gone down, how lucky I had been to be where I was at, the timing that takes place, that became the focal point, that was the ultimate. You can't take that away from me.

Well, you coach, if you're lucky. You've got to be lucky to play a long time, you gotta be pretty durable, which I was. I never missed a game in all my high school, college, or pro careers. I made winning baskets with the Lakers and won championships with winning baskets, and I knocked home runs in the ninth inning playing baseball and all that. But football is the thing that I carried on through my entire life.

## Bob Griese

*Bob Griese had two careers as a pro quarterback. In his early years he was a scrambling, gambling dart thrower whose heroics often allowed some mediocre Miami Dolphin teams to win games they had no business being in. But when Don Shula came on board and put together the juggernaut that would go unbeaten a few years later, Griese became a methodical precision passer who orchestrated a devastating ball-control offense. In his two greatest days, Griese recalled both of those incarnations, the first when the Dolphins won the Super Bowl against the Redskins to put an exclamation mark on their undefeated campaign, the second near the end of his career when he once again filled the air with touchdown passes during a memorable Thanksgiving game.*

Individually, or as a team? I'd have to say that teamwise, the greatest day would have to be Super Bowl XII, the 1972 season, when the Dolphins—I think it was the 1973 Super Bowl by the time they played it in January—where we beat the Washington Redskins in the L.A. Coliseum to finish the season undefeated, 17–0, after we had lost the Super Bowl the year before. I would say teamwise, that would be the greatest day.

And I think individually, it would have to be a day where I threw—it was back in 1977, it was a Thursday in St. Louis. We had been in Cincinnati the week before, and we lost that game and were supposed to win. We were supposed to beat Cincinnati. It was a time when I was, I think—I just started wearing glasses when I played, and it was raining during the game at Cincinnati, and I didn't have a very good game, and we ended up losing.

We went home with that thought in mind, and the thought that we had to turn around and go to St. Louis to play a game on Thursday, which was Thanksgiving. So we were off on Monday, Tuesday we went in and got a little work done, Wednesday we traveled to St. Louis, and Thursday was the game.

Now I normally do a lot of preparation and film watching and a lot of note taking, and I take a lot of stuff—well, for this one, obviously, I couldn't do much. I remember in my hotel room on the night before the game, watching some tape of St. Louis, and I said, Well, this is silly, I ain't getting anything done. So I just stopped, and I said I'm just gonna go by my instincts, and I'm just gonna go out and play the next day. I knew what they were doing a little bit, and I said, we're just gonna go out and play. I've been in this league for probably eleven years at that point, so I said, I'm just gonna go out and play.

So the next day we went out, Thanksgiving, and away from home, and everybody was lined up defensively where I thought they were gonna line up. You know, you hear the old cliché, the game slows down. Well, that day, it was like the game really slowed down. I mean, they were doing everything I thought they were gonna do. I checked off, everything worked properly, the guys got open, the ball was there, the protection was there.

I ended up throwing six touchdown passes in a period of just over three quarters. This was back when they were calling them the "Cardiac Cards." Their offense was lighting it up—the offense like it is right now in St. Louis. That was the [Jim] Hart years, they scored a lot of points. Gray was the wide receiver—I mean, I can remember being on the sideline and having, I think, scored two or three touchdowns in the first quarter, and we were up like 21 points. And I was thinking, boy, that's not enough points, these guys score at will, we just better keep scoring while we can.

And like I said, every time I saw something defensively, I said to myself, gee, this might not work, I better check to this. And every time I checked everybody heard it, the protection was there, I threw it, and I think we ended up beating them something like 54–13 or something. That was one of those days where you didn't have a lot of time to prepare, you weren't coming off of a good week the game before, and you just go in and you just go with your instincts, and everything clicked.

I spread it around. I threw it around. I threw it to every-body. Nat Moore was a receiver then. I don't even know who the other guys were—I don't think Warfield was there any longer, I think he had moved on. I think Jim Mandich was there. I think he may have caught a pass for a touchdown, but I don't know—you can look it up.

The thing that stands out about the Super Bowl was that we were 16–0, going to the Super Bowl against the Washington Redskins, the only team that has ever gotten that far. We were underdogs—16–0, and we were underdogs in the Super Bowl. That just told us that we'd won all these games, but we weren't getting any respect from somebody. So we went out and won the game, and that's the game that Garo went to kick the field goal and he batted it up in the air—if he would have kicked the field goal, we would have won 17–0, which would have been a fitting end to a game that ended a 17–0 season.

*On every great defense there are players who have a nose for the football, a knack for being in the right place at the right time to make the big play. Jack Ham recovered twenty-one fumbles and intercepted thirty-two passes during the eleven years he played linebacker for the Pittsburgh Steelers in the '70s and early '80s, and along with Jack Lambert and Andy Russell he was part of one of the best linebacking corps in NFL history. For his greatest day, Ham chose a pair of games from the early days of the Steeler dynasty, when the Steel Curtain carried the club to their first Super Bowl victory in 1974.*

I have two greatest days, I guess. Actually, our first championship here in Pittsburgh, Art Rooney Sr., founder and owner of the team, ended up in New Orleans with Pete Rozelle receiving the Lombardi Trophy. And I think to a man on our football team, after forty years of losing, we finally win a championship, and in typical Art Rooney fashion, all he said was, thank you. I think the players probably wanted it more for him than he wanted it for himself, which is just like him.

And that year, we played the Raiders. We played the AFC Championship game and we won on the road out in Oakland, against a great football team with Ken Stabler and all those guys, Cliff Branch and Jack Tatum and everybody else. And to win on the road was, for me, very special. Winning at home's one thing, but being able to do it on the road against a great football team was a highlight, or my greatest day.

The week before the division game, the Dolphins were the two-time defending champions. They had won the one year they were undefeated, '71, I think, or '72 in the Super Bowl, and then in '73 they won it again. And they were going for their third championship, and they played the Raiders out in Oakland, and Kenny Stabler, falling down, throws a pass to, I think, Clarence Davis, to win that game. I think John Madden, after that game, said the championship game, the Super Bowl, was played today.

In our meeting that following week, because we were going on to play the Raiders, Chuck Noll, who was a very pragmatic man and not much on the Knute Rockne speeches, was absolutely livid in our locker room. Chuck Noll said the best football team is in this room here, and we're gonna prove it. I think because he had never done that to our football team, for him to say that got our attention, and maybe got us a little more resolve in preparation for going out to Oakland to play them the following week.

The Raiders at that time had great balance in their offense. They could hammer the ball at people and run the football very well, because they had the great offensive line with Art Shell and Gene Upshaw, and they really were a left-handed-type team. They had Dave Casper, who was their tight end. So they could run the football, but they also had Biletnikoff and Branch and those kind of people, so it was a challenge for our defense—we had a very good defense—to shut every aspect down, to take the running game away from them initially so that they had to throw the football.

We did that, because I think they only had 25 yards rushing in the entire game. Our front four, Joe Greene and Ernie Holmes and L. C. Greenwood and Dwight White, just played a phenomenal football game. I'm a linebacker, and I kind of watched a lot of tackles. That was a very special day.

We had played the Raiders so many times, and every time we played the Raiders it was a big football game, because we were both successful in that era, so whether it was a division game, a championship game, or whatever, it was a big game. We just, physically—that hardly ever happens to the Raiders—but physically our front four just outmanned them that day. I never saw a front four play that great, or that dominant, in my whole career.

Initially, we had to overcome a couple of things. John Stallworth makes a touchdown catch, and they rule it incomplete, and today with instant replay that would have changed, but those were not the rules back then, so we had a touchdown taken away. It was going back and forth. Actually they took the lead on us, I think. Going into the third quarter they made a play, I think they took a touchdown lead.

And then we came back, and in the second half I had two interceptions against Stabler. One stopped a drive, and one actually gave our offense the ball down on the 10 yard line, and Lynn Swann made a catch to put us in the lead. And then they had to play catch-up football late in the fourth quarter. Now, Ken Stabler had brought teams back many, many times, and I'm sure the Raiders and their fans were very confident.

Probably the other key play was in a wide-open play, Jack Lambert makes an open-field tackle on Cliff Branch on what could have been a touchdown run on a crossing route by Branch. And Lambert makes a great tackle and then J. T. Thomas ends up making an interception on a badly thrown ball by Stabler to seal the win.

And probably at that point on, when you know—I think at that point we'd scored a touchdown. I think the final score was 34–13 or something like that. When you know you're gonna win this game, and when you know you're going to the Super Bowl for the first time, I remember Joe Greene in the huddle was just absolutely ecstatic. He left the field with about a minute to go, and he's not getting a standing ovation out at the Oakland Coliseum, but he did get one from our defense, the guys who were left in the game. I mean, just to a man, the guys on our defense knew the key to the game was our front four, there were just outstanding.

In a game like that there's so many big plays, you know. They had the lead on us and they were going in to drive again when I made my first interception. They had the ball around midfield and we had a blitz on, and Stabler threw it to my side and I picked it off. I think Lambert's touchdown-saving tackle was the big one, if I had to pick one play, because they could have either taken the lead or tied that game up with that play. Jack was a rookie middle linebacker playing for us at that time, and for him to make the plays that he made that day, especially that key play in the fourth quarter, to make that tackle, was huge, I thought.

For me, because their team was so left-handed, I'm more involved in the passing game. I kidded Andy Russell, who was the other linebacker, because he was getting the running game. It was Shell and Upshaw, you're gonna run that side of the field. On the physical side, it was not that tough a game for me, because I'm involved more in the passing game and try to help out underneath coverages when we're throwing the football and so forth.

The preparation was, we went after him a little bit more, safety blitzes. That's what caused the one interception he threw to me. We saw that we were gonna go after him a little bit more, especially when we shut the running game down. Had they been able to run the football, then you can't do those kinds of things, but the running game was not a factor in that game at all, and that again goes back to our front four. If you can't run the ball, we're not stupid, you're not gonna take a play-action fake if you've only run the ball for 24 yards going into the fourth quarter.

That's why it's a special game.

There wasn't a lot of celebration, because we were on the plane back, and you have a five-hour plane trip back. It's a great feeling knowing that you have won a game to go to the Super Bowl, your first one. Obviously it was the first one for everybody on that team. It was ecstatic on the plane trip back, it was an away ball park, our fans aren't there, we were a pretty businesslike football team, but we got pretty emotional in our own locker room and on the plane ride back.

We got in at about three or four o'clock in the morning, in Pittsburgh, and there had to be 10,000 people at the airport, we could not even get off the plane. That's how crazy our fans were. They were out at the airport—I mean, I'm sure a lot earlier they were on the belt for the baggage claim, people hanging everywhere. I know it was a big game, and the fans here are great fans, but you didn't expect that kind of crowd at three or four o'clock in the morning at the airport, which actually shut down the airport. I don't think the police or anybody felt there was gonna be that kind of a crowd. It was incredible at that point.

The two weeks you have between games was kind of good for us, because it was such a big win for us, and going for the first time. To be perfectly honest with you, we watched the tape of the Vikings, and we knew they were not as good as the Raiders—the Raiders were a much better football team. On the defensive side, the way our defensive line played against the Raiders, I'm sure they were gonna play just as dominant against the Vikings, which is not as good an offensive line.

It showed up, I think. I think they had maybe 16 yards rushing in that game. I think for our three playoff games, there was a total of 100 yards—Buffalo, the Raiders, and the

Vikings added up together, they were able to run it for a hundred yards.

So, our defensive line stepped it up again. Actually I didn't do that much in that game at all to tell you the truth. I think I made two tackles. And it was really kind of anticlimactic until the end of the game and after the game. We struggled against their defense, they got a couple of plays, and I think the final score was 16–6. They blocked a punt for a touchdown, and they didn't move the ball at all, but we had a difficult time moving the ball. We made a couple of plays here and there. Franco [Harris] ran the ball just enough. I think at the end of the game he had gotten over a hundred yards.

But probably for a fan's aspect, not a very exciting game, but it was exciting for us.

It was a very confident team for us even though it was the first time for us in the Super Bowl—the Vikings had been there two or three times already. I think we felt that we had better talent, not that they weren't talented with the Alan Pages and the Tarkentons and all those guys, but it would be very difficult to score on our defense. And we'd get enough on offense. We caused a safety at the beginning of the game. We took a 2–0 lead, we were just dominant for the most part.

I think it was towards midway in the fourth quarter when we had that lead, and I think we were a very confident football team, not overconfident, but we knew that unless something crazy happened out there, this team was gonna have a tough time moving the football against us.

I remember at the end of the game, as the game ended, Fran Tarkenton sprinting off the field, and I think that made the third Super Bowl that they had lost. And I always felt for him—there's only one winner. Unless you lose a bunch of times, nobody remembers the loser, like the Vikings.

But to me, it'd be frustrating to go all the way through training camp and so on, and go through all the work, regular-season, playoffs, championship game, and then lose that game. Fortunately in my career we didn't have to experience that, but I almost felt kind of sorry for a team that had been there that many times and came up short, because they were a quality football team, and I think the following year they lost to the Raiders.

In the locker room, I'm kind of very low-key, because I didn't play . . . I didn't do much. You want to be more of a factor in a game, and I think a lot of our players felt the same way, you want to somehow make a play. And I did in the championship game, but in the Super Bowl I think I made one or two tackles. I could have played the game in shorts and a tank top. That's how good our defense was. I think Joe Greene had an interception, and L. C. batted down two or three balls.

I'm pretty low-key about that. I think for me it was the journey. To kind of realize that we'd won a championship was kind of anticlimactic for me. Because you work to get there, and to finally be able to do that, the fun part for me was the journey.

There are times in the off season when my wife and I would have lunch with Art Rooney, and he would tell stories about back when he bought the football team for $2,100 dollars, the times he would go to different tracks around the year, the betting he'd done on the horses, and so forth, and I would have that kind of off season with him for the most part. And it was just a feeling. The man had gone through so much with this team, and actually people did feel sorry for him in the sense of not being able to ever get a championship team here. So that's the feeling I had for him. And maybe it wasn't that special for him, but I thought it was, so I'll live with that memory.

I think the Raider game put our football team over the top. You're trying to get to the top, and until you win a tough game, a tough game on the road, a playoff game on the road like that, all of a sudden you become a confident football team. We were able to win the following year as well, and with the Super Bowl, to win four of six years, so I think that's probably a benchmark of what direction our team was going. And plus that year, Lambert was a rookie that year, Lynn Swann, who made big plays in a lot of those games, was a rookie as well, and John Stallworth and Mike Webster, all four of those guys were drafted that year. I think we were a good football team prior to that draft, but that draft put us over the top.

The Hall of Fame, I take that out of the [greatest day] equation—it's a great honor, a terrific honor to be among the best of everybody who's played this game. But football to me is a team game. I'm in the Hall of Fame because of the guys I've just mentioned here. This is not like golf or tennis. You need the guys in front of you, or the guys behind you to play and make your life a little bit easier. I could not have played as long as I did as a linebacker if I had lousy defensive linemen in front of me, and Joe Greene and L. C. Greenwood kept me healthy for my twelve years. So it's a great honor, and I'm very proud to be in the Hall of Fame, but it pales by comparison to winning championships.

Joe Paterno was my presenter, and my family and friends were all there, and that was a very special whole weekend. I went in with the great class of Ditka and Alan Page, and actually the guy that I played against for a lot of years, Fred Biletnikoff, and actually over the years I got to be—I hated Fred Biletnikoff when I played against him. But now that I got to know him, especially that week when we spent that much time together, we ended up being great friends with him and his wife. So you kind of change your perspective of those hated Raiders to those guys you kind of enjoy being around.

Actually I was not as nervous as I thought I was gonna be. You're thanking a lot of people and so forth, and I remember there was a huge bunch of Steeler fans there. They crowded the whole place. It's not that long a trip up from Pittsburgh to Canton. And I thought Joe Paterno did a great job in being my presenter, and in fact I thought I would be more so, more than I was.

My greatest college day . . . God, we had those undefeated teams and the Orange Bowl championships when I was there. It was probably a game where we played Syracuse, and we were on a two-year run there, we were 22–0. And we played a Syracuse team my junior year, and again I had great players in front of me there with Mike Reid and Don Ebersole.

We won a game in which I always pride myself. We won a game up in Syracuse, and at that time we had won, we were undefeated the previous year—we were 8–0 or 9–0 that year. We went up to Syracuse and we were outplayed. I think we were losing 14–0 in the fourth quarter. And I always pride myself on, when you're not playing well, some guys make plays or whatever, make a play, turn a game around. We end up winning the game 15–14 or 17–14, I think. We ended up making a couple—we caused a fumble, we got the ball back, our offense kicked it in.

When you win a game that, the next day, the writers say, you know, they were fortunate to win and they should have lost that day, but you win it because somebody makes plays. And you never know who that's gonna be. We did that that day, and I think that also told me what a good football team we had, when you can win a game against a quality football team when you're not having your best day.

There was no question that we were laying this big egg. But we just hung in there, and made a play, caused a fumble, and Franco Harris makes a big run—your playmakers. Your playmakers who end up somehow—you have that resolve, and you hang in there and you make a play.

And my college and my pro teams kind of mirrored each other. We had people like that, who, in the fourth quarter, when the game was on the line, wanted somebody to run the play their way versus trying to hide and hoping they didn't run a play your way. So that may be kind of an obscure game, but it's kind of one that sets our football team apart when I was in college.

The greatest player I ever played against was Earl Campbell, because he could embarrass a pro football player on any given Sunday, and I've seen him do that running over people. And a class act, I mean, just a terrific, terrific football player.

We were winning a championship game here in Pittsburgh two years later. Now the Oilers were kind of our competition, and we played 'em here for two AFC Championship games. And we were winning 34–5, and this is the other reason— you win the championship game, you're going to the Super Bowl, which is our third Super Bowl—now remember, the score is 34–5 with a minute to go.

And again, you're thinking, OK, just stay healthy, and you're on your way to the Super Bowl. And out of that I formation he runs a play on the other side of the field, and I go, that's good, fine, Andy Russell or somebody will make the tackle. So then he bends it all the way back and crashed into me and shattered my face mask. Actually I could have got really hurt.

And I'm laying on the ground, and I said, Earl, it's 34–5, what are you doing out here? And he said, Jack, I'm gonna go a hundred miles an hour every play. And that's the kind of guy he was.

My best teammate? Well, the guy I admired the most was a guy by the name of Mike Wagner. Free safety, very intelligent, made a number of big plays, probably the unsung hero on our team because of the Joe Greenes, the Lamberts, Mel Blounts. Always had people in the right position back there— always.

To this day, I mean, Roger Staubach, he had a big interception in the Super Bowl against Staubach. And to this day, Staubach thinks he guessed on the play. I was telling Roger, You know, you've gotta get closure on this, it happened twenty years ago. I mean, you gave it away, you stared down the receiver. I was giving him a hard time with it.

But Mike, he'd deliberately give quarterbacks a bad preread by a lineman. He'd cause an interception somewhere else on the field. And that's why that guy will not get the recognition that other people will get, but boy, I tell you, he was a guy I just admired, a tough hitter, and just a smart football player. So it would be Mike Wagner.

*For the first half of his NFL career, Mike Haynes was a great cornerback on some outstanding New England teams that somehow always seemed to come up short in the playoffs. But when Haynes was traded to the Los Angeles Raiders in the early '80s after a contract dispute, it was the Raiders' Super Bowl opponent in 1984, the Washington Redskins, who quickly learned how much of a big-game player Haynes could be. In that game, which was Haynes's greatest day, the Hall of Fame cornerback and Lester Hayes combined to hold the Redskins prolific receiving duo of Art Monk and Charlie Brown to a total of four catches, sparking the Raiders in a game that eventually turned into a rout.*

The greatest day would have to be playing in Super Bowl XVIII against the Washington Redskins. That whole year started off being a very tough year for me. The negotiations with the Patriots and things hadn't worked out, and I was able to work a trade with the Raiders. It was a very tough situation for me, but being traded to L.A. at the time was like going home for me. And being on what ended up being the best team in football made everything seem worth it, all of the hassles I went through that year.

Leaving New England was kind of a mixed blessing. I had mixed feelings, really. I had several friends there on the team, had become quite comfortable living in the New England area, guys like Stanley Morgan, Shelby Jordan, Don Hassleback, Raymond Clayborne, Steve Grogan, Steve Nelson, John Smith. You know, I had several friends, and I was very popular with the team, I think.

And also I had a job in the off season at a place called State Street Research and Management, and I enjoyed working there and the friendships I made there. Working downtown in the financial area was fun for me. I was working in a money-management firm, handled a lot of pensions, mutual funds, and I was working as an analyst. They were basically training me to be an analyst, and my goal was to one day at some point become a money manager myself. But I was just enjoying working in the market, checking out different companies and just being in the environment. I found it very exciting.

I was negotiating the contract at the time with Pat Sullivan of the Patriots. His family had given him a lot of power to make the deal, and I thought we were going to be able to work out a deal. But at one point Patrick was honest and came clean and said that there was just no way that he could pay me what I wanted, even though it was what I thought was fair based on what other defensive players were making—it just wasn't going to be able to happen.

It's been very tough to go through, but it ended up great, going to the Super Bowl, and actually a couple of years later I got a chance just to talk to Billy Sullivan and we got a chance to talk about a lot of things, and clean things up and we built the relationship again. When I was there and I was drafted by the Patriots, I was very close to the Sullivan family, and every time my contract would come up it was just a tough situation. They'd always been able to work it out, but that year it didn't look like it was going to happen.

It was very tough going to the Raiders. I guess football has probably changed from those days, but at the time I thought I was going to be a Patriot forever, and everybody that wasn't on the Patriots was kind of like the enemy. So I had a hard time realizing that I was leaving my friends and joining another team where I was unknown. I didn't know much about the guys. They all had reputations and of course, when they're the enemy, you tend to probably blow things out of proportion so that you can dislike them that much more.

And so Al Davis—I got to tell you, during the negotiations and everything, he became a good friend, and I realized that he's a football man and he understands football, dedicated to winning. I understood that about him just from talking to him, how important his team was to him and how important winning was to him before I got a Raider uniform.

So coming out there was a lot of different guys, a different team. I really was surprised that they'd won all the games they had because the Patriots team, we had more athletes, better athletes. The Patriots were younger, stronger, faster, and all that. But the Raiders just had something the Patriots didn't have, and that was they knew how to win. The only important thing was winning. That was the important thing, not if you practice on Wednesday and Thursday, not if you threw three interceptions or not, not if the defense gave up three touchdowns. People didn't hold their head down. They expected to win, and that was probably the biggest difference you can notice right away.

With the Patriots, if we knocked off a top team, we were really celebrating in the locker room, saying yeah, we beat the Jets or the Dolphins, or whoever. And with the Raiders, it was kind of expected. They would go into the locker room and the coach would say, great game guys—get your rest, we'll see you tomorrow. But it wasn't the same kind of atmosphere, it was kind of like expected to win. Not, boy, we got lucky, or we pulled one off, you know?

And so that was kind of early on, and I kind of liked that feeling because it reminded me of college when I was at Arizona State. We won all the time and we expected to win all of the time. If we won 21–7 we might be down because we thought we should have won 40–0. Getting in that situation again was great. There were fights in practice. Where you might expect that in training camp when a guy's trying to make the team and all, but not in the middle of the season. And that's what happened, stuff like that. It was great.

They had great camaraderie, and during the week they would take a day—it was Thursday—and after Thursday's practice they would have camaraderie day and the guys would get together after practice as a group. The defensive backs would hang with the group for a little bit and then they'd break off to do something as a group, the same with each other position. We became really close-knit that way, and I didn't really feel like I was going to fit in with these guys, but it turned out that I really did. Lester Hayes and Mike Davis and James Davis, Ted Watt, and Odis McKinney. They kind of welcomed me in. It made it real easy.

And the biggest reason is because [Lester] welcomed me in. He didn't try to make it a tough situation for me. He really wanted to be on the greatest defensive team that ever played. Lester was a great student of the game and he had like a little dossier built up on every single receiver he'd ever played. And so, in the AFC West, getting ready to go into a game against Seattle, he'd say, You've got to watch out for this, that, and the other, and we started talking about these things right on Monday or Tuesday. For me it made the transition pretty easy.

One of the things in the AFC East, I played against everybody, and I kind of knew what they could do, knew their

strengths and weaknesses, knew how the quarterback threw
the ball, where he liked to throw it. But in the AFC West, it
was new learning. In some ways you felt like a rookie because
it was so much time you had to put in on your opponent.
Lester made it easy on me, because we'd sit down, just the
two of us, and just go over film and break down film and talk
about receivers and talk about the idiosyncrasies that I'd see,
talk about the idiosyncrasies that he'd see, and actually he
taught me quite a bit about field positions.

He'd say, Hey, ever noticed that whenever this guy's two
yards inside the numbers he always runs out? Stuff like that.
And I'd say, I never really realized that. So we really fed off
each other and got better. We would actually stay after practice and go work out and do some extra work together. It
was just fun. And he was very, very competitive, probably the
most competitive guy that I've ever been around. He was kind
of aloof off the field, yeah, but not on the football field and
not in practice.

Being with the Patriots, we'd got to the end of the season
and never won the first playoff game. We'd always get beat.
With the Raiders, the feeling was they knew that they were
going to get to the AFC Championship game, they knew they
were going to get to the Super Bowl. There was some concern
about Seattle—Seattle had a great season that year and there
was some concern about them. But the first team we played
was the Steelers and there was no concern about them. We
had to just get through the game.

For me, it was huge, emotionally, mentally, all during the
week. I didn't say anything to anybody, but I really felt a lot
of pressure in that game because I'd never really gotten over
that hurdle. And I didn't want to be the reason that they
didn't get over the hurdle. So we beat the Steelers. Lester had
a big interception in the game, I had a big interception in the
game, and I can't even remember, I think our next game might
have been the AFC Championship game against Seattle.

And so going in that game, we played them in the AFC Championship game and it was a huge game, and I'll never forget it. The day before the game Tom Flores—now I understand what made him such a great coach was that he was able to remove pressure from the team. And this was about to be the biggest game of my life. If we win this game we go to the Super Bowl. Tom's speech was basically, Well, guys, another big game tomorrow. See you at the hotel tonight at six.

I mean they're all big games. This one is no bigger than last week's. But everyone—I was expecting a different speech. And then I realized later that that was really quite by design, and it was good timing. So we went into the game and beat them pretty convincingly, then on to the Super Bowl.

Well, getting ready for the Super Bowl, during the week of practice, it was very much like the tension you feel in practice during the season. We had guys in fights, and coaches realized it was because . . . the coaches realized that guys were uptight. Like if a receiver runs deep and catches a ball during practice for a touchdown, the defense got really pissed off. And it wasn't like, Good catch, or, I hope you do it in the game. If it was during our period, the defensive period, we actually got pissed. So guys were liable to take the receiver's head off— your own teammates.

Well, after studying a lot of film on them, I realized a lot of teams did not play them bump-and-run. And their receivers were just used to the defensive backs playing in the off position, and I knew that they'd have a lot of trouble against the bump-and-run, especially against me and Lester. And so I liked the man-to-man situations. It was the ultimate challenge. I didn't realize they were going to pass as much as they did, but because their game plan was to throw as much as they did. It really kind of played into our favor, and we were able to have a good day that day, put a lot of pressure on Theismann and delay those guys' release off the line.

Before the game, when we went out, you could tell it was

serious business. The focus was there, the attitude was there, the mental questioning that you had, if you had it, you could see we were ready for this game. But when they came out, they seemed really happy and loose, like they really weren't taking the game as serious as we were. I think it was because they had played the Raiders earlier in the season, and they had beaten them pretty convincingly, and they just felt like they were the best team in the league and we were just another game, another team on their schedule that they had to beat to prove it.

[Theismann] was very cocky, and he knew what he had. He had two great wide receivers, a great offensive line, and great running backs. And he knew that he was gonna do his job, so of course they're gonna feel confident. And because they had played us earlier in the year, I think that's why they were really confident. But the game earlier in the year, Mark Fell didn't play in that game, Cliff Branch had pulled a muscle early in the first quarter, I think—he still scored his touchdown, but he pulled a muscle and he only played one quarter. And I wasn't even on the Raiders, so there's three players that weren't even there or healthy, and all three of us had a big impact on the game.

For the most part I was on Charlie Brown, and Lester was on Art Monk. It went just the way Lester and I had talked about it, and we realized that in bump-and-run situations, they had some automatics, like all teams do—like if they're supposed to run a hook pattern, it automatically turns into a fade. So when you go up on a guy, you already know, well, he's gonna go straight up the field. And things like that.

So, things changed, I think, around the league after that game, when people started seeing what bump-and-run could do to different teams. And so they started not coming off the route, like, if we had a hook on, they'd want you to run a hook, or run across the field instead of running up the field—you know, things like that. It was just a great feeling.

So, I felt like we were ready, more mentally prepared than they were going into that game.

We knew that it wasn't gonna be a blowout, it was gonna be a tough game. And so we had trouble moving the ball the way we had moved it against some teams—but, come on, we were playing against the best team in the NFC. So we knew it was gonna be a challenge, and it was.

Those guys, they were knocking the guys off the ball. We felt like we were winning the battle on the line. Marcus was starting to make these great runs that everybody had become accustomed to. Plunkett had plenty of time to throw the ball. And then, that first drive that we scored on, it wasn't like, yeah, we scored, it was like, OK, that's one. And the defense got on the field and stopped 'em, and they had to punt the ball—it was one of those type of games where I knew we were gonna keep the pressure on no matter what. And mainly because they had beaten us earlier in the year, and they had the ability to come back quickly.

It didn't click until the last play—for the last five minutes I was thinking, damn, we're gonna win this game. I'm gonna win the Super Bowl. I just remember looking at the offense on the field and the defense off the field, and thinking, we're gonna win this thing, we're gonna win this sucker. I looked at guys on the sideline, and a couple of guys were starting to look like that, too, like, hey, ain't no way they're gonna catch us now, you know? And it was a good feeling, knowing, with seconds to go, that we pulled it off, we were gonna pull it off.

I hadn't really thought about that whole thing with Plunkett—even after I'd left New England, he'd already won a Super Bowl, beat the Eagles in the Super Bowl, what was it, like 16–15 or something back in 1980? But for me, playing with Plunkett was—I actually grew up with him in Los Angeles, we got to watch the Pac-10 schools play all the time against UCLA and USC, and so I was a Jim Plunkett fan. I knew what Jim could do.

I remember him throwing those balls to Randy Vataha, and Randy making these great catches, and the one thing that I learned coming to the Raiders was that Jim was pretty spontaneous. He could think on his feet, and he could read a defense and realize where a guy was supposed to be. If something happened, if the guy's not there, he'd look for Todd Christiansen. So they had something that was kind of unique. I thought Todd made up a lot of his routes, and he did, but Jim was right there with him, they were right on the same page. I don't know if they spent a lot of time talking about what he might do, or if it just happened, but they came through time after time to keep the chains moving and keep the ball alive.

I felt a little bit numb, if you want to know the truth. It was like, I could not believe it, I really couldn't believe that we were world champions, you know? And so in the locker room, Al Davis, he was just magnificent, you know, with what he said to the team and how proud of us he was, and Coach Flores also, about our accomplishments.

And the guys, I realized that I had just done something that very few athletes get a chance to experience. You know, you get really lovey-dovey. I ended up giving Matt Millen some ostrich boots that I had, a $500 pair of boots. But Matt Millen said, Hey, man, I love those boots, if we go to the Super Bowl and win, can I have those boots? It was incredible.

My family was there, and so I went out and celebrated with my family, and, you know, did all kind of wild stuff with my family. Marcus Allen and I were the guests on a morning show on TV the next day—I didn't sleep at all that night. I was up all night, it was awesome.

The Hall of Fame is something that—you know, it took me a long time to get there, fourteen years of playing pro football, playing with great players, and doing my part on, the defensive part, and even on returning punts or whatever I had to do for the team. It was just the greatest accomplishment you could ever have as a player, in terms of your business that you're in.

But for one season, to go to the Super Bowl, I guess it's like being the president of a company and having the top product that puts you in the number one spot for a while. But the Hall of Fame means you've done it kind of consistently, you in terms of your own performance over the years. And your peers recognized it, and it's just the culmination of a great career, and the culmination of a great season with the Super Bowl.

It was really kind of funny, my first wife that I was married to when I was playing football would have probably really, really enjoyed it and understood it a lot more so than my second wife. She really didn't understand what was going on. There was just so many celebrations going on around being inducted into the Pro Football Hall of Fame that you can't imagine. My college honored me, my high school honored me, the city of Los Angeles honored me.

I went in with Don Shula, Mike Webster, and Wellington Mara, so it was a small class. And going up to Canton, there were just tons and tons of fans there, you know, pro football fans—I wish there were more Raider fans, but you know, that didn't work out. But it was fun, it was just a lot of running you around from place to place to be recognized by one group or another group throughout the city of Canton, and as an inductee, you really don't get a lot of time to spend with your family and friends until later in the evening.

But it was great, it was absolutely great, just reminiscing with all the Hall of Famers, and looking forward to life after the induction ceremonies.

My presenter was Howard Slusser, who was my attorney throughout my entire career. And I think he may be the only agent or attorney that's ever been a presenter, at least that's what they were saying—you'd have to check that. He was with me from the very beginning. I chose him because of his ethical standards and his moral standards, and I really believe that he was gonna be there for me, and more so than pro football, more than for the NFL, more than for the owner. I recognized that, you know, tomorrow's not guaranteed, and I didn't want to do anything that was stupid, and I didn't want to take any unnecessary risks. And I definitely wanted to get paid what I was supposed to be paid.

My first meeting with the Patriots, they were talking about what a defensive back should get, as opposed to a wide receiver or a running back or a quarterback. And I said that, Well, it says on this contract here, National Football League player, it doesn't say anything about the position. And so I wanted to be paid what other good defensive players are paid.

But the first year, my first contract with the Patriots, they said, Well, you know, you were a great college player, but that was college. You have to prove yourself in this league. So I took less than probably what I could have taken to prove myself. I was All-Pro and Rookie of the Year and Pro Bowl and all that stuff for three straight years under that contract, and then when that contract was up I had to fight 'em to get what defensive players were getting. And so it wasn't good.

But thank God Howard was with me through it all, and he definitely felt the way I felt.

I remember that I was nervous, and I really had a hard time trying to put twenty-one years of football into five minutes, and making sure I thanked the right people and everything. And I just felt very fortunate to be up there, and I knew this was a moment, only one little moment in time, and I did feel like I wanted to make the most of it, because I did put a lot of value on that speech. I felt like, I wish I had enough time to thank the people that really made this all possible for me.

Because I did my part by practicing hard and playing hurt and all this other stuff, but really, I don't think you can get into the Pro Football Hall of Fame unless you play on great teams. And to play on great teams means you've had several great players, all over the place on your team. And I was really fortunate to be able to have fourteen years where I played, really, with some of the greatest players that ever played the game.

I would relive the Super Bowl [if I could choose one]— because that's what it's all about. Every single year, when I started my training, it was to get to the Super Bowl, and I wish I could have said that I played in several Super Bowls. And that also means that when I'm in the Super Bowl, I'm still playing.

Can I give a defense and an offense [greatest player]? Best defensive player I played with would be Lester, and best offensive player I played with that I really enjoyed playing with was Stanley Morgan.

On the other side of the field, I admired watching Louis Wright play, who was with Denver at the time. Oh, gosh, this guy, he was tall like me, he could run, he was great. And then offensively, geez, that's too hard to call. Offensively, I enjoyed playing against them all. The teams that were going to put the ball in the air a lot were the ones that I enjoyed playing against the most. I can't tell you I really enjoyed going up and tackling guys like Earl Campbell—I didn't really enjoy that part of it, it was part of the game. But I really looked forward more to the battles when the ball was in the air.

*The New York Giants won two of the six championship games they played in between 1956 and 1963, but the first win in '56 was by far the most memorable for Sam Huff. Huff was the marquee player on a defense that sparked New York's championship run, and along with Bill George, Ray Nitschke and Joe Schmidt, he helped redefine the middle linebacker position in the late '50s and early '60s, paving the way for Dick Butkus. Huff closed out his career with the Washington Redskins in the late '60s, but was it his early years with the Giants that opened the door for him to enter the Hall of Fame in 1982.*

I don't know—I mean when you're basically twenty years old, and you're playing in Yankee Stadium on the field where Joe DiMaggio, Babe Ruth, Lou Gehrig, all those baseball players played, and you're in the same locker room as Mickey Mantle, Roger Maris, and Bill Skowron—it's kind of almost like make-believe and you just cannot comprehend, but there you are.

You know, it's been so long I can't really remember. My first game was in 1956. Gee whiz, that was forty-four years ago. I couldn't imagine trains running underground. I'm from West Virginia, and they still don't have a train running underground. They have coal cars, that go outside, that trains pull. Hell, I said, they've got trains underground. I mean how do you fantasize about that? I never read about it and that is something that they never write about.

You see the skyscrapers and everything else in New York and you believe that it's like Disney World. At that time there was only one Disneyland and that was in California. I had never been to California, so how in the hell did I know about Disney? I mean, when you look back it's amazing to me. So that had to be exciting times—almost unbelievable.

And to win the world championship in your first year, which we did, and I was regular middle linebacker; to be coached by Tom Landry on defense, and then Vince Lombardi on offense—I was a two-way player at West Virginia, so I started out with the Giants on offense and ended up on defense, *and* I made Rookie of the Year. Those were exciting times, but it was so long ago you can't hardly remember them.

I really didn't like offense much. I was an offensive guard, and I liked defense much better. How come? I really did not like guys hitting me. The first two guys I played against were Don Colo of the Cleveland Browns in the college all-star game, and next I played against Leo Nomellini. These guys were great football players.

They would do things to you. I'm a hot-tempered guy. I mean, they would hit you in the head and slap you along the side of the head. The head slap was legal at that time, you know, and when they slapped me, well, I slugged them back. And of course I'd have to pay in penalties, so I said, well, I think I'm a better defensive ballplayer, let me do the head slapping. Let me do the hitting. And so that's where I wanted to play.

You know the whole process, as it played out, was playing middle linebacker for me when I moved there. Tom Landry moved me there because a guy by the name of Ray Beck got hurt, and he was a veteran. When Tom Landry moved me there he said: Do I want to try it?

I said: Yeah, if that's what you want me to do. It was almost like I was born to play the position. I could see everything, I could see in the backfield, basically it was very easy to play. And I was always a good tackler because I worked on it every day when I was at West Virginia University, so at middle linebacker, that's what you do. I mean, as a linebacker that's what you do is tackle, even though I intercepted passes, too. I loved playing pass defense. So in today's world, linebackers in that type of situation, they're taken out of the game. But I did it all.

It was just natural for me. It was like handing the ball to Jerry West, he knows what to do with it, shoot it. Or, you know, basketball to a great basketball player, he knows what to do with it. I put the headgear and shoulder pads on. I knew what to do: use them and tackle people. You know, that's all I ever did at West Virginia University. And I played both ways at West Virginia—I played every down.

It wasn't the greatest day [in college], the day I played Jim Brown in Syracuse. That was *not* my greatest day. In fact, I hit him so hard I knocked myself out. But it was one of my biggest learning days, and I believe from then on—because when you're ahead of him, and like I say, Rookie of the Year in the NFL, and then my second year Jim Brown came into the League—I didn't have to have a scouting report about that. Off-tackle. He could come off-tackle like no one in the world.

I told you, I got knocked out. We were ahead at half-time, and Jim Brown did not like that. So he took charge in the second half and I woke up on a training table because I hit him so hard. I never wore a mouthpiece and the enamel popped off my teeth, and my helmet came down and cut my nose, so I knew Jim Brown from then on. Isn't that exciting, when you take a hit like that? Yeah. So I got even with him. I put him down at Yankee Stadium.

We won the game 47–7, and it was a world championship game which is what they call the Super Bowl now. We beat the Chicago Bears. It was a great game and do you know why? Because we got paid extra money for it. Our winner's share I think was less than $2,000, or $2,000 or something like that. So you get the winner's share, and the Bears got the losing share.

But in my eight years with the Giants we played six of those games. And we only won that one, but boy the rest of them were really knockdown, drag-outs. The '58 greatest game I ever played against the Colts and then '59 against the Colts and then '61, '62, '63, we were right there knocking on the door.

My individual thing? It had to be against Jim Brown. I mean we were always matched against each other. And it had to be when he had 13 carries for 8 yards in a game. That was a personal victory. I don't know the year. That's a game I think it knocked him out. He said we didn't knock him out, he said he didn't stay down, and I said: Well, you should've because I probably would've knocked you out anyway. We were actually good . . . we were cordial to each other and pretty good friends. Always had the greatest respect for each other.

You know, you knew basically what the Browns were going to run just by the way they would line up—here's Jim Brown, let's see you stop him. Well, we're the Giants, we're going to stop you. And he would carry the ball 30-35 times a game. He took a pitchout right about where, at Yankee Stadium, the pitcher's mound is. I can still remember it. So he took a pitchout to his left. Most of the time he could run left, he could run right, he could run up the middle, it didn't make any difference to him. He was a big, fast back, greatest football player of all time.

So he took that pitchout, and it was a little bit slick because right around the pitcher's mound, it always freezes there first. It's always frozen there because the sun hits there last, so he kind of slipped a little bit. Modzelewski hit him low. Modzelewski got to him first, and as he was going down I came in and hit him. It might have been a helmet-to-helmet deal, which you're not allowed to do now because they want you to play with all this kind of stuff, you know, it dinged him. He still played. They didn't take him out of the game. He was really—that was the one time he was hurt. Maybe the only time he was hurt.

I think when you're told by the phone call that you're elected to the Pro Football Hall of Fame, that is unbelievable. And I waited eleven years. I don't know why. I guess—you know, it's the system, too. You have to be out five years, and then, you know, I'm sure the guy in Green Bay never liked me that covered the Green Bay Packers, and you have to be voted in by writers. And I'm sure the guy—well he told me he didn't like me, and he never voted for me. John Steadman in Baltimore—I mean, these guys, to vote me into the Hall of Fame is like voting an enemy in there. They wanted to see their own guys in there first.

I'm sure of the guy in Green Bay—why wouldn't he vote for Ray Nitschke? The guy in Detroit, why wouldn't he vote for Gentleman Joe Schmidt? The guy in Chicago, why wouldn't he vote for Bill George? And the same thing in Philadelphia with Chuck Bednarik. So we were all linebackers of a great era in pro football when the middle linebacker was the king of defense.

So you start saying to yourself, What's wrong with me? I was in New York, and all these out-of-towners didn't like me because they didn't like New York. Is Roger Maris in the Hall of Fame yet? And yet he's the yardstick everybody measures for home runs. Why isn't Roger Maris in the Hall of Fame? Because the writers in New York did not like him, because he didn't like them. He was a good guy and died of cancer, and had more home runs than anybody else. Along comes these guys that work out in the weight room, they're big guys and all this kind of stuff, and they hit the ball a country mile. But what's wrong with Roger Maris? You ask yourself.

I ask myself, what's wrong with Roger Maris, and at that time I was asking myself why wasn't I in the Hall of Fame? These guys, I played with them. I had 30 interceptions. I had more interceptions than they had. But I wasn't in. So I don't know why. It becomes a personal thing. So you feel hurt, and you feel that you're not in, and played in six world championship games, and was Rookie of the Year and in the Pro Bowl five times. How come I'm not in? You couldn't answer that question?

You know how busy you are [when you get there]. They never let you sleep. You're up at six o'clock in the morning, you're here, you're there, you're here, you're there. There's 250,000 people—it's unbelievable. I went in with Merlin Olson, George Houston, who just died at ninety years old, of the Bears, and the guy from the Cleveland Browns and the Chicago Bears, Doug Atkins.

We were all white. That was one of the things. All of a sudden we looked around . . . no speed, right? We're all defensive ball players, and that's a thing that we looked at and we said: Hey, you've got to be kidding! In this day and age? I hate to say it, but four white guys? Why with all the great black ball players that are around? Why were we selected as four white guys? I mean, I should've gone in with Jim Brown, shouldn't I?

What I remember about the ceremony is that you had five minutes to talk about your whole life. And you were supposed to stick to it, right? And I tried to do that, and that's impossible. Then somebody always, one of the presenters will always go on and on and on and on, and you think it's never going to end, that always happens. It still happens. And they've moved it up now. You're supposed to talk eight minutes. It's just, you're pushed and you're shoved, and they're so organized. You have a driver . . . they pick you up and they treat you unbelievable.

They treat you like a king. I guess if you're president of the United States, you're used to that kind of treatment or if you're Dan Snyder of the Redskins, you get that kind of treatment. But I mean, it's a fabulous ceremony, it absolutely is, and it's a ceremony you will never forget. Never. Nobody does it the way the NFL does it. That's the one thing they really, really do right.

The high school Hall of Fame, that was after, and that was different. It took place in Washington, D.C., and the first one I went in was the College Hall of Fame in 1980. I went in that, but that was different, big dinner in New York, and you have to pay your own way, your own hotel room, your own ring—but that's college. They still call it amateur.

The ceremony, another ceremony, was in Cincinnati, Ohio, at that Hall of Fame, it was a groundbreaking, so I went to that. And now it's in South Bend, Indiana, so it was different and it was all computerized. The college is all computerized. The Pro Hall of Fame is different. Everything is right there, you can have your class that you were in, it's just different. So that makes it different.

I'd relive the Hall of Fame induction—I mean you're in that class. You're sitting there with the guys that showed up, I mean, there's less than 200 guys in the Hall of Fame in this world. Sitting there with all the guys you'd played against, and guys you'd heard of way before. And then you look around and you see some guys who are not there.

Johnny Unitas—not there. Why? Because the League office and the politics of the League office. And I understand, because I'm an old football player. When you have three different retirement programs, the old ball player gets shoved aside in pro football. The league office won't do anything to help the old football players, and neither does the union, and they take care of all of the guys who make millions of dollars now so you look around and there are guys not there all because of some politics. That's unfortunate. I guess that's in every walk of life.

But it shouldn't be, because we were all one, the NFL Players Association. But they're not, because the League office and Gene Upshaw, who heads it up, don't want it to be all one, I guess, I have no idea. I feel sorry that—John and I, we think alike. I say we only have one Hall of Fame, and our lifetime now is going to be short, so enjoy it while you can. I can overlook that, but John doesn't. And he is there, and you see the great ones go in. I saw Joe Namath go in the Hall, I saw Joe Montana. The quarterbacks are all special. They're in a world all by themselves. We didn't have any quarterbacks in our group, we wouldn't allow it. We were all defense.

# John Henry Johnson

*It took the NFL two decades after John Henry Johnson re-*
*tired to put the great fullback in the Hall of Fame, but John-*
*son's defensive foes felt his impact on the game in a far more*
*immediate and visceral fashion. Johnson was a battering ram*
*of a fullback who gained over 6,000 yards in his career during*
*the late '50s and early '60s, helping the Detroit Lions win a*
*championship in 1957 before he was traded to Pittsburgh in*
*1960. Johnson saved his best games for the Steelers in their*
*big rivalry game against Cleveland, including his greatest day*
*when he gained over 200 yards against Cleveland.*

It was a Saturday night, I don't know, 1963 or '64. I gained
240 some yards against the Browns here in Cleveland. I just
knew that it was a hard game and that we had good success
running the ball, and that's what we did. It was also a rough
game, a wild game, you know? It was always a tough game
to decide who's what. But we started off good, and we had
good running, we controlled the ball, that's what we did.
They couldn't score because we had the ball. So we handled
them and ran the ball. Boy, that made a big difference.

I think my longest run was 25, 30 yards, once. But I was getting 5, 6, 7, 10 yards like that. We were running the ball like that. Just a ball-control game, so as long as we had that ball, they can't score. I think I carried the ball twenty-something times. We shimmied the ball all the way down the field. The touchdowns, if I remember right, one was on a short run, the other two were longer.

Playing the Browns, that was always our big game. You beat the Browns, you had a good season because they were a good team. We always had, I always had good success running the ball against the Browns. It was a great rivalry then, between the Browns and the Steelers, and whenever they played, if they were in Cleveland, many Pittsburgh people came to Cleveland, and then the same thing when the Browns played in Pittsburgh and the Cleveland fans went over there. It was always a great weekend. This one was in Cleveland.

It wasn't unusual for many of the fans who made the trip to be in no condition to watch the game by the time it started. Much the same as when the Browns came to Pittsburgh for a game; it was a huge party. It was a party this night, too.

I think the crowd was kind of quiet, because we were controlling the ball, running the ball a lot, and they weren't expecting that. So they was kind of cool and quiet.

I think they had Jim Brown that year, it might have been when he was a rookie. We kind of tied him up. We had the eye on him a little bit. Some of these games, some of these days, its just hard and tough to run the ball. So we had the eye on him. We had John Baker, the end, he lined up at linebacker on one side, and Glendon Thomas, who was a defensive back, at linebacker on the other side. He was kind of bottled up.

Sometimes you'd get a big hole to run through, but for the most part we were just running them. Five yards at a time, controlling the ball. As long as we got the ball, they can't score. Yeah, it was off tackle, a lot of the running was. The score was 23–7.

I ended up gained 200 yards on 30 carries, but I didn't realize it at all. I was out there running, trying to stay healthy, trying to keep my feet together and stuff. I didn't have any idea that I was close to 200 yards. We had the game under control, and it was about the minute or so when I went out of the game, and somebody told me, You know, you got 200 yards. I said, Aw, man, you couldn't tell me that. So I didn't believe it. You know how the guys are, they'll bullshit you around a little bit, say stuff like, Man, do you know how many yards you gained this game? That sort of stuff. They always got some kind of stuff going, you know. So I didn't pay them no mind.

Some of the guys come up to me, some of the people, you know, some of the writers, and said, Do you realize you had a hell of a game? And I said, What do you mean? You gained 200-yards-plus against the Browns, and I said, I did? Oh, no wonder we had the ball all day.

I had over 100 yards a few times, but I don't recall being close to 200. Playing ten games I had over 1,000 yards a few years, I know that. We had ten games or eight games or nine games or something like that and I realized that I had over 1,000 yards in those years.

The guys up front were doing a hell of a job blocking. Tommy Bradshaw and those guys, they gave me a little running room, so I'm going to make more yardage. You know, just one guy hitting me in most cases isn't going to bring me down, jolt me down, but not bring me down, so that made a big difference. I kept going, not leading in yards, but picking up yards on every carry.

Oh, man, they had a parade and all that kind of stuff. A big little party, a few little gifts, and it was a real good weekend. It was kind of a real good night when we got back.

Dan Rooney thought we were going to get killed. But after the game, he said I dominated the game, that I almost got all the yardage by myself. Dick Haley, who was a defensive back on that team, said I kept them off the field. I remember he said something in the paper about how I loved to play against Cleveland, how I saved my best games for the Browns. Every game, he said, it seemed that he would out-run, outcatch, and outblock Jim Brown, and he said, I think John Henry wanted everyone to know that he was a pretty good fullback, too.

I think Brown had one long run on a draw play, but other than that I don't think he did much. We talked a little, but I don't think we ever talked about football. We just said "hi" and "hello," little nothing things. That's the way it was with him. He wasn't all that sociable.

We took an early lead, 3–0, and then the next time we had the ball we went long down the field, and I scored on a pretty long run. The next touchdown was on a pitchout, and the last one was on a short run, maybe five yards or so. One time we had our right guard pull one way, the left guard pull the other, and I went right through the middle, which was wide open. Buddy Parker said I was like the Indian, Jim Thorpe, because I was a great back who blocked, too.

Well, it was always a good rivalry and a good weekend, and the boys up front were doing a hell of a job blocking. It made my run easier. Well, that was always the big game, you know, a lot of expectations, so you had to fulfill their expectations. That's what I did. I always had my best games against the Browns.

You want to know about Rooney? He was a hell of a guy, that's my best thing about Rooney. Because if you had any kind of problems you go to the man with it, boy. He's going to knock it out for you. Some things he found out about and you didn't even know what's happening. One of my brothers passed away New Orleans, Louisiana, and I hadn't been in New Orleans, in I don't know how many years. The old man found out about it, the next thing I know I've got a round-trip ticket, I've got a hotel room in New Orleans, I got a car to pick me up and drive me about an hour to New Orleans.

The old man did all that without even saying, Hey, John, do you want to go?

Going into the Hall of Fame was a wonderful time. You know, it was nice to see a lot of the guys I played against, and a social evening was real nice and stuff, so that was always a nice time, an enjoyable time, you know?

It took twenty years to get in. You know, you're eligible after five years, but it took twenty years, and I was at the Pennsylvania Hall of Fame one night, at a banquet, and I told the audience that I was kind of sad that they hadn't put me in the Pro Football Hall of Fame. I said, I guess they'll do it after I'm dead, and my wife and my son will have to accept the honor for me.

I don't remember what the speech was about. I guess it was a little speech saying I was glad I lived long enough to make it. It took me so long to get in. There I was the number two rusher in football. They were putting guys in there ahead of me who had no yardage, had no kind of thing like that whatsoever, but that's the way it was.

When we decided we wanted Art Rooney to be my presenter, my wife called the Steelers office, and the secretary, Mary Reese, told me that Mr. Rooney was in the hospital, that he was very ill, and that he would not be able to do it. So we started to try and find someone else, you know, that we could ask, and we got a phone call from the Steelers and Mary said, Mr. Rooney is going to get out of that hospital bed and he is coming to Cleveland to present John Henry. And he did that. And Dan had to stay with John to represent his dad the rest of the ceremony. But Mr. Rooney is the one who presented me on the steps of the Hall. That was my buddy, boy.

I went in with Gene Upshaw, Len Dawson, Don Maynard, Jim Langer. We had a good time—99 percent of the guys were a nice bunch of guys, we got along, you know? We'd have a good time and then go out and have a few afterward, and listen to the stories. Maynard had some good stories about the guys on them teams. Bring the house down. I told him, Man, you ought to be on stage somewhere, because some of them guys were excellent, you know what I mean?

My greatest college day? I know, my greatest college day was when we beat USF, when Arlen Nash was there, we beat him in the '40s. I played two years at St. Mary's and they discontinued football, so I went to Arizona State for two years. And St. Mary's had a great rivalry against USF. They had all those All-Americans. That was our big game. We played in Kezar Stadium. It was always a tough game. They always had good linemen.

I played with Bobby Lane. He was one of my greatest teammates—just playing with Bobby Lane and going upfield, because Bobby Lane was just a type of guy, a fun-type guy, but he was a serious-type guy, too, you know? You better be doing what you said you'd be doing, otherwise he'd yell, Hey, Coach, get him out of there! You'd better be running the right plays or he'd holler to the coach, Get him out of here! If you don't know what was going on, he'd do that in a minute.

When he'd come to a game he was never gushy. Clean. We'd go out after games and have a few, go to where they played some good jazz and stuff. He was a good jazz man. Nine out of ten cases he'll pay for everything.

I'd want to relive all three [days], but if I had to pick one I'd pick the Hall of Fame day. Well, that was a big day. That was a big accomplishment, and that stood out way over winning the games. That was a bigger thing than winning ten games or twelve games. That's immortality.

*When the greatest running back in the history of football re-
tired in the mid-'60s, Cleveland fans wondered where their
team's rushing yardage would come from. After they saw
Leroy Kelly step into Jim Brown's very large shoes, Browns
fans didn't have to wonder anymore. Kelly went on to have
a stellar career that eventually led to his election into the Hall
of Fame, and in the process he became one of the leading
rushers in NFL history. His greatest day came early in his
career, when he got to take the field as a rookie and play with
the man who was perhaps the ultimate mentor for a young
running back.*

My greatest day in football came during the two years I was
playing with Jim [Brown] before he retired. It was against
Pittsburgh, and Ernie Green was hurt at the time and I started
at halfback with Jim against Pittsburgh. It was a Saturday-
night game in Cleveland Stadium and it rained the whole
game, just one of those miserable weather-type games.

And we won it in the last ten seconds with Frank Ryan and

Gary Collins, on a pass over the middle on the 5 yard line, somewhere around there. I caught two passes to get them there, I had a pretty good game. And I remember that as one of my greatest moments in professional football.

This was my second year, '65, we played Pittsburgh early in the year. It was just a rivalry, you know, Cleveland against Pittsburgh. It was the first week in October so it was early in the season. The Steelers were struggling, I would kind of say, but it was still a great rivalry because I remember Pittsburgh coming into Cleveland one year and wiping us out—I mean, John Henry [Johnson] gained over 200 yards. They wasn't supposed to field a team and they crushed us. So you know you could never tell against Pittsburgh. And their defense was no party—right.

I really don't remember the score. We won it in the last ten seconds to come from behind.

With Jim, just playing with him, I loved him quite a bit. As a matter of fact, just playing with him and practicing with him, you just watched the greatest runner in the history of professional football. You have to learn something from him. And I picked up quite a bit of things, just watching Jim. And I was given the opportunity to actually play with him, just watching him and practicing with him and watching him in the games. The things that he did, you kind of pick up certain things that help you. And when I got the opportunity to start, it helped me a lot.

One very important thing I learned was a lot of times backs have a tendency to beat their guards to the hole, beat their guards to the block. And he had a way of . . . he kind of gradually eased into the play where he let that block form first before he hit that hole. This is very important with running backs, the timing between the opposite linemen and the backs.

The fact that we had different running styles didn't matter, because thankfully with the Browns' offense back then, the fullback and halfback, you could almost run the same type of plays. The halfback could really run the fullback play and the fullback could run the halfback play. That was basically how it was. There was only a few plays that actually was designated especially for the fullback. So basically the offense back then, it was sort of where both backs could run the same play, and basically we did.

Thankfully, he was very supportive of me, because I guess Jim—most football players are a pretty good judge of talent. And after I had gone through the preseason I had a few good games returning kicks and showing different things, and I think this kind of impressed him.

I know I had a bad game in my last exhibition game. I fumbled a couple of times, and he talked to me about the fact that probably everybody fumbles. And he talked to me, which kind of helped me gain my confidence back. And he even talked to Blanton [Collier] when I pulled a hamstring earlier in training camp to kind of let me know, as a rookie, you're not supposed to stop practicing, you had to be out there and try to make the team. And he talked Blanton into letting me lay off that hamstring until it healed.

It took about two weeks before it actually healed. We actually broke camp and went out to our West Coast swing where we played L.A. and San Francisco, and we didn't have two-a-days out there, we just had one-day practices, so that helped a lot. He kind of was in my corner from the get-go, and that was very impressive to me and it helped me a lot.

My thinking during the game was just to win, man. I was just concentrating on doing whatever I had to do when my number was called on, to make sure I did my job. That's basically a prerequisite for playing the game, do your job as best as you can.

I think that whole week practicing with him and knowing that, hey, man, you're going to get a chance to start with Jim. Being just my second year I kind of was a little nervous about it. Once that whistle blew and we got that first hit, it was just another game to me.

Ernie just stayed out that one time, and he was right back

the next week. You don't want to stay out too long when you've got a young guy trying to make the team, make a name for himself. Ernie was a great back, he was a great blocking back and a running back. Him and Jim worked good together. Later I got the opportunity when Jim retired early to be a starter.

He could've played at least another four or five years, easily, but mentally you just don't know where his mind-set was. Physically, he had just gained like 1,700 yards his last year. so I feel that he probably could've played another five years, easily.

You know, I didn't know he was going to act on a filming . . . endeavoring to be an actor. I didn't even know this. I don't think too many people knew it. When it came upon us, a lot of us were very surprised he decided to option out for being an actor.

Nobody replaces Jim Brown—I mean, it was a great opportunity. I kept thinking, aw, Jim's coming back, Jim's coming back, and we were in camp when Blanton, he called me into his office, and told me that Jim had decided to retire. He said this was your opportunity and he hoped I would take advantage of it. I was very thankful that he gave me the opportunity. I think I took advantage of it.

The offense was like, well, you know, I guess it was, you gotta show me. At the first game, I kind of showed them, I think. We opened with Washington and I kind of broke one for 29 yards for a touchdown. I think it was show-and-tell.

I had a good game and I had quite a few of my friends there, because I went to school in Baltimore. My college coach was at the game. I had to get quite a few tickets. I had some great support there, and I think I gained over 100 yards. I'm not quite sure, but I scored a touchdown for like 29 yards off tackle and I had a pretty good game.

Just getting the opportunity to play with the Browns, getting drafted by the Browns, and playing professional football—those are my greatest days. Your teammates who are still your friends even after football. I see guys today. I'm friends with Paul [Warfield] and Ben Davis and a lot of guys that I played with. Erich Barnes, we still get together every year.

And then making the Hall of Fame, that's the ultimate reward for a professional athlete. It's just a fraternity that's the ultimate, and guys that you played against, now you're friends with, you golf with, you socialize with. It's just great to be able to say that, Hey, I played professional football. And I'm in the Hall of Fame.

I went in with Tony Dorsett, Jimmy Johnson, Randy White, Jackie Smith, and Bud Grant was the coach. And that was a great bunch of guys going in. That week was something else. They keep you busy as soon as you get in town. With the family there and everything, you anticipate getting up there Saturday and making that speech. Finally, making it in, being a part of the ultimate dream of every professional athlete, that's to get into the Hall of Fame.

It was very emotional, because I felt it took a long time for me to be inducted. I thought that I should've probably made it my first year of eligibility. I was the fourth leading rusher in the history of professional football. My statistics didn't change. It took a while.

Guys like Chuck Heat, who were voted in, he was in my corner and he worked diligently to get me into the Hall of Fame, and that's why I made him my presenter. And Dan Dinenger, who wrote for the *Philadelphia Daily News* and covered me in high school, he was in my corner, too. I thought that I probably should have been in a long time ago. You know how that goes, politics and everything. You know that's the way it goes.

I'm in now and I've been in for six years. It's great to be in, and I understand how those things go down, because I was a consultant for the senior inductee this past week, two weeks ago where Nick Buonoconti got in. You know, as a senior, he still has to get votes in January, but he'll probably get the votes to get in.

I'm definitely a Brown, once a Brown, always a Brown. Oh, definitely. It's great to have the team back. What Art Modell did was a disgrace to football, moving the team to Baltimore. That's all about money and we know all about that. It hurt. Now that the team is back with Lerner as the owner and [Carmen] Policy and Chris Palmer, the right coach, the San Francisco connection. Hopefully, we'll get the players and the fans. We got our new stadium, and we always have the fans. So, hopefully we'll get our team together where we can get that winning position back and go on from there.

It's just great to be a part of that tradition, with Bobby Mitchell, from Marion Motley to Jim Brown, Leroy Kelly, Greg Pruitt. Now they have to get a good back and go on from there. Carry that tradition of great running backs into the future. Yeah, I doubt if you'll ever see it again, that many great backs for that long a time.

My greatest college day? College was a grind. You go both ways in college. I did a lot of things in college, it was more of a grind. We won a couple of CIAA championships, which were great, and it was just basically, going to college was more fun than playing football in college.

We finished up with . . . we played Virginia State on Thanksgiving. Each time we won. That was our last game of the season. And both times we won, we beat them to win CIAA championships. It was fun, but playing professional football was the thing. I played defensive corner back.

Actually, I thought I would be drafted as a defensive cornerback, because when they had the mini-camps in May before the camp opened up, I was worked out as halfback and defensive cornerback. Up until then, I still thought I was going to play defensive cornerback, but then Blanton told me to go back and gain some weight because he was going to use me as a running back.

I was leaning more towards being a defensive back because I really wasn't a star running back at Morgan State. My roommate was Oliver Dobbins. He was just a track god and a speed god, and I did OK at halfback, but I thought defense was what was going to get me into professional football. You never know.

Actually, at the mini-camp I weighed 188 in May, and when I got to camp in July I was 198, so I went home and gained ten pounds. And then in camp I put on like another seven pounds, because I played at 205 most of my career. It wasn't too much of an adjustment. I handled it pretty good. You're going to get hit if you're playing professional football, you're going to get hit, either way. I made the team on a special teams, where I went down and hit somebody. So I enjoyed playing defense and hitting people. I didn't mind it when I got hit.

If I started now I'd probably be a punter. You laugh, but I punted ten times for an average of 40 yards. Gary Collins was our punter, but I punted also, and I kicked off one year for a while when he was hurt.

A lot of people don't remember that—it was fun. I remember taking off one time and making the first down, and they told me, Don't do that anymore. I did it on my own, it wasn't a planned thing. I got the first down and that's all that matters. I was the backup punter, so I had to get in a few reps. I punted in college. I was the punter in high school. It was something I really enjoyed.

*Paul Krause was the NFL's consummate thief, a superb safety with deceptive speed and quickness who used guile and a knowledge of the game to set the all-time career record for interceptions. Krause had plenty of great days for the Washington Redskins and the Minnesota Vikings in the '60s and '70s, from making All-Pro as a rookie to his various successes against such stellar quarterbacks as John Unitas, Bart Starr, and Terry Bradshaw, and receivers like Paul Warfield, Charlie Taylor, and John Mackey. His greatest day came when he was elected to the Hall of Fame, an inauguration that became truly special when his wife, who had been in a tragic auto accident, came out of a coma shortly before the induction ceremony.*

I didn't have a greatest day in football—I had some pretty good days. I honestly don't know what my greatest day in football would be. One of the best days I had in football was—I was driving to training camp, I think it was my third year, and they announced that Jim Brown retired.

I even hate to say, the first rookie ever to be named All-

Pro, leading the league in interceptions my rookie year, then going to playing more games than any defensive back in history. How do you pick one best game? You don't.

The first game that I ever played professionally was an exhibition game against the Chicago Bears. The first play in that game, I got an interception, so that's a good memory. The first league game that I played in against the then Cleveland Browns, I pick off two passes off Frank Ryan in front of Paul Warfield. So—first league game—that's a big game for me.

Going on from there to become All-Pro, I think that's something that, my goodness, you don't really dream of—you don't say, Gee, I'm gonna become an All-Pro in my rookie year. As I look back at that, what a tremendous season for a young twenty-one-year-old from Michigan that really hadn't done too much.

And then going to the Vikings and winning ten Central Division championships, you get a sense of leading a pretty charmed life. I can remember the game where I picked off Bart Starr against Dowler, and I always liked to play against the Detroit Lions, because I'm from Flint, Michigan. I picked off four balls against Detroit, so those are good memories. Another good memory was picking off Johnny Unitas—so, you pick off Johnny Unitas or you pick off Terry Bradshaw or you pick off John Brodie, you can just go down the list, you know?

I go to Detroit in 1978 and tied the record in Detroit, and it just seemed like it was a great catch. I tell you, I was just laid out right on the ground. I caught the ball in front of Gene Washington. I picked it right off the ground. And in '79 I came back and got two off the Los Angeles Rams and break and set the record. Those are some tremendous games, and so for me to pick out one game, who knows what my best game would be?

Those are some of the great memories that I have. My

goodness, I can't even remember how—they sent me a tape with like forty or fifty of my interceptions—I didn't even remember half of them. I only remembered maybe forty out of the fifty, you know?

I always prided myself on the fact that if I went up for the ball, I was gonna catch it. I prided myself on having great hands. And I'll tell you, I still think I had one of the best pair of hands in football.

I have a picture—my goodness, it must be about 1964 or '65, intercepting a ball in Cleveland Stadium, leaping high into the air in front of Jimmy Brown. He's high in the air, and I go up high in the air and pick it off, and that's a great picture. I had it blown up. I'm probably the only one that has seen that picture. I've gotten to know him fairly well over the years, and that's a tremendous memory.

Those are just some of the great moments and memories that I have, in terms of my greatest game. And like I said before, I really felt like I led a blessed life—in football, I did everything that a professional football player would want to do, especially going into the Hall of Fame.

And then last year the NFL came out with their greatest all-time team and Ronnie Lott and I were named to that, and my goodness, it's almost beyond dreaming. You don't sit around when you're in grade school and junior high and then high school and college thinking, gee, I'm gonna be an All-Pro, I'm gonna be this or that. Sure, you dream of becoming a professional athlete, a professional football player or a baseball player, or whatever.

But I mean, to become a Hall of Famer. I'm just a poor kid from Michigan from a small high school. I was the first one to come out of there with an athletic scholarship. Then a few years go by, and all of a sudden I'm in the Hall of Fame. It's just a tremendous, tremendous thing to have happen.

Just to give you a little background, my wife was in a car accident a couple of years before that. She was in a coma for six months. And before that she kept saying, you're gonna get in the Hall of Fame, you're gonna get in the Hall of Fame—then she was in the accident, and my goodness, it just completely changed my life. And I'm still not in the Hall of Fame, and then she comes out of the coma, and they name me to the Hall of Fame. And she was able to see it.

As far as I'm concerned, my going into the Hall of Fame was—it was more important for me to have her see that. And sure, it's the greatest honor a football player can have.

You look around during the Friday lunch that they have at the Hall of Fame, and it's just for the guys that are in the Hall of Fame, and you look around and you see guys like Dick Butkus and Sonny Jurgensen and Ray Nitschke, and you get some idea of what they expect from you and what it takes to get into the Hall of Fame. And they're telling stories and all, and you say to yourself, my goodness, what am I doing here? I'm in awe, you know? A lot of my idols, guys I played with, Jimmy Brown, Butkus, guys I played against, and all of a sudden, you're there. It's just a tremendous honor.

Not winning a Super Bowl, that sticks in my craw a little bit. But, you know, doggone it, a lot of other people have never played in the Super Bowl, a lot of people have never gotten to the Super Bowl, and never will. Shoot, we played in four of 'em, and we had a great football team. Even though we didn't win four, I still don't think that we got our just reward from that.

Because I think that we, the Minnesota Vikings, deserved to have more guys in the Hall of Fame. And I always hear, well, they never won the Super Bowl, they never won the Super Bowl. Well, my goodness, there are guys that are in the Hall of Fame that have never been to the Super Bowl. That does make a difference, with the voters for the Hall of Fame, that has made a difference. And it shouldn't.

You talk about a Roman Gabriel—my goodness, back then, three or four guys would jump on him before he threw the ball. And nowadays you can't touch the quarterback. Well, Roman Gabriel stood back there, you talk about a great competitor, I mean, this guy stood back there with guys hanging all over him, still trying to throw the football.

And we just had, we had great games with Dallas. You know, the Hail Mary pass, I think that actually started the instant replay. It was such a bad call. Everybody saw that Drew Pearson pushed Nate Wright down—it was a great play by him, that was the only thing he could do. They were beat. And there again, we win that game, and everybody says that that's the best team we ever had—well, I don't know if it is or not, because we'll never know. And it was so flagrant that they had to do something.

My greatest college day—oh, boy, I don't know. I always used to like going back to Michigan. And I remember I caught a pass against Michigan [Ed. note: Krause played for Iowa], and I ran for about a 50-yard touchdown, and there were actually eight guys missed me. Eight guys on the Michigan football team had a chance to tackle me, and I just kind of weaved through the whole team to score the touchdown. That was a pretty good game for me, because being from Michigan, I used to like to go back there.

Sure, in a way I missed receiving. But, you know, I played defensive back almost as a wide receiver. I mean, if that ball went up, it was mine, just as well as it was the wide receiver's. I always had—I don't know if it was the luxury or what—I always knew, or I had a sense to know when I should go for the interception or whether I should knock it down or make the tackle.

And believe me, that's a tough deal. Some guys just have absolutely—some guys just don't know how to go for the football. You know, they'll go for the wide receiver and tackle him and everything, but they just won't make a play on the ball. And I was blessed with that success, I guess, to figure out that I could go after that football.

I think it was a God-given gift. I don't think it was something you could really teach. It was, I always felt, through my professional career, that I knew what the quarterback was trying to do against the defense. There was just something about it that, in a split second, I could tell what they were trying to do. Especially a quarterback that's trying to attack a defense in its weakest spot, or whatever. I felt that it was a battle between me and the quarterback, and what they were trying to do to us, and I always had a pretty good sense on that. And a lot of times I won.

As far as I'm concerned, you take a John Unitas, as a quarterback, I mean, all-around quarterback—he was a true master. Then as far as I'm concerned, Sonny Jurgensen was probably the best pure passer of the football. So, different types of quarterbacks were gonna try and beat you different ways. And as a field general, hey, Johnny Unitas was absolutely the best.

Something about Namath—Namath threw a lot of interceptions, because he had such faith in his arm, he was a gambler. And as far as I'm concerned, I didn't play against him that much, but Joe would not come to my mind. I like Joe, Joe and I are good friends, and I showed him around my freshman year in college when he was in high school, so we've known each other for a long time. You know, he came to Iowa as a recruit.

But Joe tried to—he had a great arm, but he tried to force the ball a lot, so he was gonna throw a lot of interceptions. But there again, here's a Hall of Fame quarterback—my goodness, if you become a Hall of Fame quarterback, you're a pretty good quarterback. You had to know what they were trying to do to us as a team, and all of 'em were different.

So it all depends on what offensive help they had, too, as far as running backs and receivers. I mean, playing against a Bart Starr—Bart Starr had a Jimmy Taylor, Paul Hornung, he had a Donny Anderson. He had a running game to go with him.

Donny Anderson, he was telling me a story. He and I, Donny and I are pretty good friends, and Donny Anderson said Lombardi would come to Bart and say, Bart, do not throw the ball near Krause. And Bart always would say—he took it as a challenge—Well, I'm gonna beat Krause. And then I'd pick him off or something, to stop a drive or something, and Bart wouldn't go near Vince when he came off the field, he was so furious, because Vince would be cussing him out.

I would have to say that types of receivers were tougher. You take a guy, you know, I played against Paul Warfield, or Bob Hayes, some of these guys like this—they didn't scare me as much as the guys that would catch the ball anywhere. I mean, you knew Bob Hayes was not going to catch too many balls across the middle, that type of receiver, because our linebackers back then, they were gonna take your head off. I mean, they were flat looking for those guys coming across the middle, which . . . you know, today you can't touch 'em.

A guy like a Gary Collins for Cleveland, a Charlie Taylor from the Washington Redskins, Charlie Sanders, the tight end from Detroit—those types of receivers, they'd catch the ball anywhere on the football field. Those were the tough guys. John Mackey, absolutely, they would catch it anywhere. Those are the guys that would give you the trouble, because basically you knew where a lot of the other guys were gonna run their patterns. You know, Pete Retzlaff from Philadelphia—my goodness, he was all over the football field.

And we had, when I was in Washington we had a strong safety named Jim Steffen. Well, whenever we were going to play Philadelphia, he wouldn't sleep the whole week. He was scared to death of Retzlaff, because he just didn't know where he was gonna be. And they had a guy named Harold Carmichael, 6'9". Those were the types of receivers that were really tough on us.

There again, you had to know what their offenses were gonna try to do to you, and in what situations they were gonna try to do 'em. And then you would maybe have some help from the inside, or from the outside, or whatever, you know? Certain plays, you had to know what that offensive quarterback was trying to do to you with the field position that he had. And I think, I knew a lot of that better than the offenses that I was competing against.

I knew the game—I knew the game itself. You know, I have a tough time with the athletes of today, because there are so many specialized guys. They play two, three plays and go out and everything. In the '60s and '70s, the players that played knew the game better—the whole game. Because they were playing all the time, they played the whole game. They weren't out there for just passes or they weren't just out for the running game, or they weren't nickel backs or whatever.

We played the whole game, and we understood what they were trying to do to us. Nowadays, those players, my goodness, they don't play the whole game. And the coaches are almost overcoaching them, you know. They're telling them exactly what to do in exact situations and everything, and they're not letting 'em really play. That's the way I look at the game.

I would say that I think the league is diluted right now, compared to, say, the '70s, because the best athletes were always playing. And the best athletes were always out there no matter what situation they were in. We took pride in the fact that we were gonna help our buddies, you know, and if eleven guys do their job on the defense, we're gonna beat the offense.

I don't know, I just don't think there's much loyalty. You watch a game, say he gets a sack or he makes a tackle, and he's out there celebrating like he's just been named to the Hall of Fame. And to me, I can live without that.

My goodness, and then a guy'll say, the commentator will say, well, this guy is the greatest running back or the greatest wide receiver—well, he may be good, but for me to call a guy great, he's gonna have to do it for ten, eleven, twelve years, year after year after year after year. Like [Chris] Carter of the Vikings—this guy, I mean, he's a great receiver, he's proved it over and over and over. And a guy may have a great year, a guy may have two great years, but I would say, well, he's a pretty good athlete, but until he does it year after year, I'm not gonna call anybody great.

I get so sick and tired of watching these guys jump up and down after they just make a typical play. I intercept a great pass, stops a drive—I walk off the football field, Bud Grant doesn't say one thing. That's the deal. Or if Carl Eller got a sack, you don't jump up and down there, you walk off the field, the coaches expect that, that's what you're supposed to be doing.

You want me to relive one, or change it? If I was gonna relive a game—a game—and we could change that game, I really would have liked to have been on one Super Bowl winner. If I could relive a game and not have it changed or anything, probably it would be the Hall of Fame deal. Because, my goodness, that's the ultimate, that's the pinnacle, I mean, you can't get any better than that. As a football player, you can't get any better than being in the Hall of Fame. That's the pinnacle that everybody wants to end up at.

I think the year Alan Page won the Most Valuable Player award in the National Football League as a defensive lineman, he had to be the greatest teammate I played with. He was so dominating that it was incredible.

I would say that the greatest opponent I played against was Jimmy Brown. Jimmy Brown was probably . . . I never feared playing football or playing against anybody, but I think he's probably the only one that I didn't like playing against. I mean, the guy was unbelievable. You really didn't want to go out there and play against Jimmy Brown.

The whole package—physically he was great, but my goodness, he would run over you, through you, around you, I mean, he did it all. I would say Jimmy Brown is the best running back that I ever played against. I didn't fear Johnny Unitas, but it was almost fear from Jimmy Brown. I mean, there was a lot of guys that did not want to play against Jimmy Brown. We loved playing Johnny Unitas, we loved playing against some of these other guys, for the challenge. But, boy, I'll tell you what, Jimmy Brown put the fear in you.

## Steve Largent

*As a receiver, Steve Largent was a veritable magician, a wide-out with a knack for getting open and making circus catches. Largent starred for the Seattle Seahawks in the '80s, and the climax of his career came when he helped trigger the Seahawks' upset playoff victory against the Miami Dolphins in 1983. Largent was also a model of consistency, breaking Harold Carmichael's record for consecutive games in which he caught a ball, a mark that stood until Jerry Rice broke Largent's mark in the mid-'90s. Largent now makes his moves as a congressional representative from Oklahoma, where he grew up and went to college.*

I would say in the National Football League there were two.

One was a game that we won in Miami. It was the divisional championship game against Miami. We were the wild-card team—we won the wild-card game against the Broncos, I believe. That meant that we went to play the team with the best record in the AFC that year, which was the Miami Dolphins.

It was Dan Marino's rookie season, and we went down

there as heavy underdogs and upset the Dolphins. This was in 1983. It was the first year the Seahawks had ever made the playoffs, the first time I was ever in the playoffs. It was a game where I didn't catch a pass until about the last four minutes of the game. And then, that's because basically we were just trying to keep their offense off the field and run the ball and use a real ball-control-type passing game.

So what happened was in the fourth quarter, the Dolphins intercepted one of our passes and took it back and scored, and we were behind for the first time. And so we got the ball right after they had scored, and I caught two passes in that drive that got us down to about the 1 yard line, where Curt Warner then punched it over. We scored to go back ahead and then ended up getting a couple of fumbles on kickoffs, and that sealed the game.

But I remember that game because we were underdogs. It was the first time we were in the playoffs, and winning a game of that magnitude the way we did. And then that plane ride back to Seattle, which is a very long trip, was one of the greatest experiences I had in professional football. It was just totally wild. We couldn't believe that we had won the game. So it was a very fun trip home.

There was only a couple of minutes left in the game, probably about four, five, six minutes. So we were behind and we were forced to throw, and I remember one of the first plays in the drive they threw a pass at me over the middle and we picked up 20, 30 yards. It got us out to mid-field. And one of the next plays that we ran was a corner route, and I actually drew double coverage, and the guy on the outside that was responsible for the deep half, he bit on the post move that I gave him. But anyway, he bit, and he really wasn't supposed to because he had inside help. And so when he did I broke back to the outside and caught this pass that literally took us down to the 1 yard line. And then, like I said, Curt Warner scored.

Well, everybody was a little nervous about Dave's throwing [Dave Krieg] at that point because he'd thrown this one up for grabs. But no, we knew what we had to do, and we had a lot of confidence and we'd been ahead the whole game. Now the pressure was on us, and of course the crowd there—this was at the Orange Bowl at the time—went crazy. It was a great deal. Marino was incredible, like he always was. He had Duper and Clayton and they had caught just a ton of touchdowns that entire season and they did so in this game.

It was a great experience. And you learn that when you finally get in there that that's what it's all about. And once we had that first taste, it was hard to really . . . they call it the second season, and it is. It was a great experience for our franchise and for that team.

Well, our defense played an outstanding game. We had a great game plan. It was really well coordinated with what we were doing offensively and defensively, and everything worked. We didn't turn the ball over, we didn't have a lot of penalties. We were able to keep Marino sitting on the bench, because our offense was pretty effective at moving the ball and picking up third downs, and that's what we had to do. You go do that in a hostile environment in a pressure situation? It is just the greatest feeling.

The second NFL experience was very memorable for me. It would be 1986, I believe it was October, when I broke Harold Carmichael's record for consecutive games with a catch. It's one of those NFL records that's predictable, unlike when are you going to hit a home run or when are you going to catch this certain pass.

That's exactly what it was like, Cal Ripken's streak, and I was at that game. So everybody was coming with full anticipation of this happening, and there was a big media hype about it, and so there was just a lot of pressure and a lot of relief once I caught that pass. But the whole thing was just a really cool experience. We played the Chargers in the King Dome. It couldn't have been better.

I want to say it happened in the first part of the second quarter or at the end of the first quarter. It was a third-down play, and Dave Krieg was quarterbacking, and he threw a great pass and it really was an important play, because it was a third down and it enabled us to keep a drive alive. It wasn't just a little quick screen to extend the streak. We never did that, and I was proud of that.

They stopped the game, they gave me the ball, and Harold Carmichael was there and came down the field and shook my hand. So it was just a really neat thing. Everybody was relieved. I was relieved, my teammates were relieved, Dave Krieg was relieved, and the Seahawk fans were relieved. I think they held their collective breath every time I was thrown a ball, because they were into this record much more than I was.

There actually was a playoff game where I didn't catch a pass. They don't count playoff games, they play regular season. And it's only the games you play in. So I'd been injured, only not that much, and so didn't play in some games. But it was just consecutive games that you play in, and I can't remember there being many one-catch games.

My greatest individual game? You know, we went and played in Denver one year. And it would have been '84, '85, something like that, and it was at Mile High Stadium. And every time we went there it was always a very difficult game. I don't think we won a lot of games in Mile High Stadium. And so we went back there, and I think the Broncos were the AFC West champions from the previous year. And we went into that game, and I want to say these were nationally televised games.

And so it was a very important AFC West game, and we won in there, and I remember the first play of the game was a pass to Darryl Turner. It was a bomb, we hit an 80-yard touchdown strike on the first play of the game. And then from then on we just continued to throw. We threw the ball a lot, and I think I ended up with nine catches or something like that for 150–160 yards. So to do that in a big divisional game on their field was very gratifying. The Broncos always were tough. It sounds trite to say it's a team effort, but it really is. I mean if you don't have the pass protection, the quarterback, the other receivers running a coordinated pattern, it doesn't work.

The greatest circus catch I ever made was on a pass over Lester Hayes back in the late '70s or early '80s. I went up over his back and was actually suspended in the air on top of him and came down in the corner of the end zone and that would be one. I didn't believe it. You just stick your hands up and it sticks. It really is one of those things where, when it happens it happens in slow motion and it really does feel like a dream.

College? Well, we played in the Missouri Valley [Conference], first in Tulsa, and one year we played Drake who—I'm not sure if they have a football team anymore, but this time they had a fairly good team with a good record. They had one defensive back, cornerback, who was very good. He had sort of popped off about the fact that nobody had scored a touchdown on him all season, and this was probably November. By the time we played it was cold. And so we went up to Drake and we had a very good team, a very well-balanced team too. We went up there and I caught five touchdowns at Drake on this guy. So I'll always remember that.

Going into the Hall of Fame, it was really just . . . it was a very intense weekend because they keep you hopping. A lot of times you don't get to appreciate it until you reflect back on it. And sometimes, not even until you come back for somebody else's can you really appreciate it. I still say it's like a dream for me to be included in what I think is the most exclusive Hall in professional athletics. I went in with Kellen

Winslow, Henry Jordan, Leroy Selmon. I remember my speech was very short, and it was very hot and Kellen Winslow's speech was very long. We were all ready for him to finish.

If I could relive one, I would say back to Miami. That was just a tremendous game going into a hostile setting, 5,000 miles from home and coming away with a victory. I just don't think there's anything that's sweeter than that. Being inducted into the Hall of Fame is sort of lucky. In other words it's something that happens because of something you did at least five years ago, and such a tremendous honor. You can't . . . it's indescribable. But actually being in battle with your teammates, and like I said going into enemy territory and pulling it out against all odds, that's as good as it gets.

This would be a long book if I went into all of that, Bob, in terms of how it affected who I am now. I think other than just the pragmatic stuff of how to be understanding of the influence you have being a person in public—being a public figure and using that platform wisely, and for good. I think the whole team concept, understanding in the House of Representatives you don't get anything accomplished without 218 votes, and so I like that part of it. Football really is a relationship driven—if you're successful it's relationship driven in terms of trust in your teammates for fulfilling responsibilities and being accountable, and it's the same way in Congress.

Well, in professional athletics, a lot of people say, you've got to be a disciplined person to do that. It's not true. Because most of the discipline is asserted by a coach or a trainer or somebody else. So you just follow the regimen and someone is there to give you your hotel key and hand you equipment and wipe your face off and give you Gatorade. They do everything for you, so you don't have to really be disciplined. You just have to be able to follow orders.

But in what I'm doing now, the workload is very intense, the learning curve is steep, and you really do have to be self-disciplined. There's really not anybody other than your constituents looking over your shoulder.

What's interesting was that when I first came to the NFL there really wasn't anybody, especially in the off season, telling you to work out, lift weights, stay in shape, to push you, to stretch you. Today they do. So you'd really have to have some discipline about that—you know, I kind of came in when the attitude was, you get in shape in training camp. And now, if you go to training camp with that attitude, you'll be gone. So there really is a year-round mentality that wasn't there when I came in. So I've always been a fairly self-disciplined person except for what I eat.

I think I really got [my work ethic] more from my grandparents, who I lived with for years. And I started working in my grandpa's shop when I was in seventh grade.

I think the best football player I ever played with was Kenny Easley. He was just a tremendous athlete. He was tenacious and mean and unbelievably talented as a football player. He had a knack for making big plays, and he really led by example. He ended up only playing about six or seven years.

The greatest player I played against was . . . a bunch of guys come to mind. I'll give you a list, including Dan Fouts and John Jefferson at San Diego, Dan Marino at Miami, John Elway at Denver, Jerry Rice, Lawrence Taylor. A guy who has to be in the top three—Earl Campbell of Houston. No doubt about that. And Walter Payton.

I think day in and day out, the guys that would get me up off of the bench when we were over there trying to suck down some oxygen, to watch him play, was Dan Fouts. I think the fact of his toughness, and also his leadership. He had an incredibly strong arm, his passing arm, and a great sense of timing. But all the other things added to that made him incredible.

*John Mackey was the prototypical tight end, a savage blocker and a great receiver who became a particularly devastating force after he caught the ball when he got loose in any NFL secondary. Mackey's greatest day came when the Baltimore Colts redeemed themselves after losing against the New York Jets in Super Bowl III, and it was Mackey's catch of a tipped ball against the Dallas Cowboys that turned the tide in a 16–13 victory the Colts won on a last-second field goal by Jim O'Brien.*

Every day I woke up and went to practice was the greatest day, because I know I could do my job. That's the key.

And the matter of after you play and you win, it's extra special. But if you lose it was because you didn't do your job, it was horrible. It was a great day when we won Super Bowl V, and I know why we lost Super Bowl III—they didn't beat us, we beat ourselves. We announced the victory party the Wednesday before we played. We cut up the shares at the pregame meal.

And what it was, that's the only time we ever had our families on the road with us. That was the only time we had our families on the road, and I'll never forget because my son, who is now married, with three daughters, he came running up to me and said, Daddy, is he important? And I said, What do you mean, is he important? And he said, That man, they want him to write on a piece of paper. [I said,] It's called an autograph. But does he play football? That's Frank Sinatra, [I said]. Who is he?

That was also when my wife says to me, How do I get to the game? I said, I don't care if you go. Well, the next year that we went back the wives came in the day of the game and you only saw them that day if you wanted to. That's when we beat Dallas.

That was fun, because I ran 75 yards for a touchdown. But everybody tried to tell me, You won the game, and I told him or her, I didn't win it. You don't understand that if the line didn't block and Unitas couldn't throw, if it wasn't tipped twice it would have been illegal, and once I catch it and they don't block I don't go 75 yards. So it was a team effort; it's never "I." I've learned that if you say, I won the game, it means you can't see. If you say, It was me, it means you were missing everything. But if you say we, it means win and enjoy.

Our approach in that game was just that we got ready to kick ass rather than being a 19-point favorite celebrating before we went out there, just assuming that it was an automatic win. So it was an attitude adjustment.

We didn't do anything different. You go through studies, find out what works, and then you put a game plan together and then it's about executing. It's not about playing it in your mind and winning before you get on the field. It's about thinking what you have to do and executing it. So that's how it worked.

We practiced the way we always did, and we didn't assume we were going to win because all we had to do was show up.

We were working together as a team, because we did the things that we normally did when we won instead of just saying, Oh, we're going to win, knowing that you're automatically going to win because you're a 19-point favorite. We got different results.

Well, we never gave up even though we won on the last field goal. At the end, we just never gave up and that was our attitude, the game isn't over until it ends, because we pulled out a lot of games in the last two minutes. When you got guys like Unitas, man, shit, you don't ever give up.

I saw the pass coming in my direction, and my job was to catch it and run. I didn't have anything I was thinking about, it was just to catch it and run. Then, once you get into the end zone, it's up to the ref and the rest of them to make the determination. Because I didn't know it had been tipped twice, and it was this and all that. All I knew was that anytime a ball comes in your direction, you catch it and run. Matchup wise, it didn't matter, I didn't care. They had eleven-on-eleven and my job was to kick ass. That's the only thing. It was eleven-on-eleven. Do your job.

The only thing we were thinking on the field goal was that we had to make sure nobody blocked it, and that we gave him the protection and to make sure that no one got a hand up. And so that's what we were thinking, and we didn't even look up to see if it went through, because we were just doing our job. But after it went through, it felt good because we'd gotten there. As a matter of fact, we would have won Super Bowl III if they'd brought Unitas in sooner, because if you notice as soon as they brought him in, we scored a touchdown, but time had run out. But the coach didn't want to bring him in because he'd been injured and because the other quarterback had taken us there and he didn't want to pull him.

Well, we just—there was no big celebration or anything, because we had our families with us and we just went and spent time with our families, man. We didn't go for no great party, although we did have one. Carroll Rosenbloom had a party at his house and a lot of the guys went there and got caught speeding trying to get there. It was crazy. But when we got to the party, it was crazy.

No, nothing that stands out. All I know is that when you win, we did what we were supposed to do, and when you lose, after being a 19-point favorite, you need your ass kicked.

The Hall of Fame induction? Well, it was good to go in. Especially after it took so long to get there. I went in with Al Davis and Lem Barney and John Riggins. But I was voted the best tight end in the first fifty years, and I didn't go in until after my fifth year after I retired, the reason was that I had been president of the union and sued them and won free agency and that was my punishment.

But it didn't bother me. Every year I used to get a call— How does it feel to be voted the best and you're not in? And I just said, I thought I was in.

It was a good week. My best friend, Jack Kemp, introduced me, and it was a lot of fun because I had a lot of family and my kids there, and it was an honor. All I know is that I talked about my players, my coaches, and my parents because they were the ones that got me there. Without Mom and Dad, you ain't born. If they don't give you the right background, you don't end up playing in the NFL.

My father was a minister, and I went to church, and he said either do it my way or hit the highway. And the key was respect. You couldn't be disrespectful to anyone, and we were raised at a time when the whole community raised you, so if your parents saw me doing something wrong, they'd kick my butt and then tell my parents and they would thank them and then they would kick it. Today, you get sued. It was that kind of thing, you couldn't be disrespectful.

As a matter of fact, I had five brothers and a sister and three adopted brothers, because my father adopted every kid that was in the community that was having problems and stuff. And he would adopt them and then he turned them all around. I remember the first time, the first kid that was adopted, he came and my mother walked in the room and my father said, Stand up. And he said, Shut the f—— up.

And my father stood up and said, I'm leaving the room. Teach him how to talk to your mother. My oldest brother knocked him from the table. And my other brother punched him in the mouth. And I stood up and said, You don't have to be a punk, you can fight, and I beat the hell out of him. Now he's married, graduated from college, he's got three boys.

And I guarantee you, man, when you say hello to his sons, they're the most respectful kids you ever want to see. I trained my son the same way, because one time he talked back to his momma and I knocked him out. And the reason I know he learned, because every time—he's got three girls and when they disagree with me they say, Granddaddy, I respectfully disagree. You know, it was my way or the highway back then.

The union victory was important when you look back, but at the time I was just doing my job. Therefore, it's not something I look back at, other than at that particular time I did the thing that was right to do, based on the situation that was going on, because it was my job to do what was right for the players.

And they said, That's what took you so long to get into the Hall of Fame. Years after I got in I got a call. They said, John, how does it feel now that you're in? And I said, Well, I'm a little disappointed. And they said, Why? And I said, Now I never get a call. I used to get a call when I wasn't in. I was president of the union and it was my job to do what's right for the players. And that's why I took it to court, and we won, so evidently the court thought it was the right thing to do, so we won free agency. And I had my punishment, but who cares?

I had a lot of good times in college, because my roommate was Ernie Davis. I blocked for him and he scored, that was wonderful. I became number 88, because when I got there, I wanted to wear number 44 because Jim Brown wore number 44, and most people don't realize that 44 people from his hometown paid his way.

When I got there, coach told me I couldn't wear 44 because Ernie had it. And I said, Well, I'll play another position, and then when Ernie graduates, I won't sit on the bench. And he said, Then you've got to play another position. And I said, tight end—if you give me number 88, because I was twice as good as number 44.

Every time I threw a block and he ran all the way, that was the greatest college day. Oh, yeah, because I did my job and he did his. I don't look at any one moment. I enjoyed the fact that we went undefeated in '59 when we won the Cotton Bowl. Syracuse went to the Cotton Bowl and kicked butt.

If I'd been a running back, I would've been trying to be like Jim Brown, so I probably would've been punishing some people. I mean I—it didn't matter, Jim was my idol. I would be trying to punish them like he did.

## Wellington and Tim Mara

*Wellington Mara*

*They were enshrined together in 1997 as the first father-son combination ever to go into the Hall of Fame, and together their lives encompass the entire history of the NFL. Tim Mara brought pro football to New York when he bought the Giants for $500 in 1925, and as time went on he converted the franchise into a family operation, turning the reins over to his sons Wellington and Jack. Together they made the New York Giants into one of the league's elite franchises. In this interview, Wellington Mara reflected on his own greatest day in football as well as that of his father.*

He was a fan. He had never seen a football game before he started the team in 1925, so he didn't pretend to be an expert—he enjoyed the victories even more, he didn't analyze why we did it. I don't know, I think he felt elated that we were making progress, and I think his big ambition . . . I remember the very first time we ever heard the mention of pro football. He told this story many times—we were standing outside of church, Sunday morning of the first game we ever played in '25. I remember my father saying to a couple of his friends, we're gonna try and put pro football all over New York today.

And I think he thought in '38 and '56, he thought we had taken great strides toward that, and then '58 I think he thought we had arrived. He was right, we had arrived.

He had the same sense of distance. I always said that the way things worked was that I ran the personnel and my brother Jack ran the business affairs, and my father ran us. He oversaw both of us.

I think he would pick the founding of the team as his greatest day. I think the fact that he founded the team, and he stayed with it through some very bad times, and came out on top, and achieved what he had set out to do, to put pro football over in New York.

He went into the office of Billy Gibson, who was Gene Tunney's manager at that point in time. They were trying to get some big fights for Gene Tunney, who was an up-and-coming young light heavyweight who was growing into a heavyweight. They felt that my father had some political affiliations that would get them a championship fight. He went in to discuss that with them. Well, they wanted to discuss it with him, I guess, and Howie Moss, who was a retired army doctor, a surgeon, I think, was in the office at the time, trying to get Billy Gibson interested in putting a pro football team in New York.

My father answered that, and at that time to join the league it was a $500 fee, and my father said that an empty store with chairs in it is worth $500 in New York. And as far as staying with it, the amount of money involved then was peanuts compared to today, but it was a lot of money in those days.

He was an optimist as an owner. He was tough, he wasn't gonna let a couple of setbacks turn him away from his goal, and I guess he just stayed with it. He kept saying, it's bound to get better, it's bound to get better.

I think he was content to hire a coach and let the coach run the team.

I think winning the championship in 1938 was big, because first of all, we beat Washington to qualify for the playoff the last day of the season. The year before we had lost something like 42–14 to that same team, and we had a very young team. In '37, we had a twenty-five-man roster, and seventeen of our players were first-year players, so it was a very young team.

And the following season, I think they played the whole season pointing toward that last game with Washington in the Polo Grounds. And Steve Owen, of course, never let them forget what Washington had done to them the year before. I remember the week before that game, he had an ability to get under people's skins and exhort them to greater efforts, and he used every bit of that ability on the players for that game, so that it's not often that you have a feeling that they're gonna play well and that's fulfilled, but that was one.

The whole week I had a feeling they were gonna do well, and of course the day of the game, I think the final score was 36 or 38 to nothing, and Hank Soar, who was a halfback on that team, ran for a touchdown on the very first offensive play, and it was just never a contest.

That was also the year, because he had so many players, that Steve used to alternate teams. He'd have one team play the first and third periods and the other one play the second and fourth periods. Except for Mel Hein, he played every play in every period. It just was coming more or less as a revenge of the '37 game. It was a big moment, I remember just feeling like on top of the world.

Going back, I remember the next night I was going down to Madison Square Garden to a hockey game, and I remember riding the subway and the shuttle and all, I even enjoyed the subway ride. It was just a great feeling.

Another day like that would be when we beat the Bears in 1956 for the championship. There again, the feeling in the locker room before the game was electric. Guys came in, they could hardly wait to get the uniform on and get down on the field. Those are the two times that I think I really felt that in the locker room, the '38 game and the '56 game.

Of course, we beat the Bears by a big score. There again it was a game where it wasn't as close as the score indicated, we just completely overwhelmed them. I felt good about that because, after the game, my brother Jack, my older brother, came up and congratulated me, because in those days I was the general manager, the personnel director, and three or four other things.

That kind of motivated the deals that had put that team together. I felt that that was kind of a peak period for me, because I haven't felt that close to a successful team since then, and I haven't been involved in as many facets of the game for thirty years, so it was kind of a feat. Of course, the playoff games and the Super Bowl games, I'm not gonna take anything away from them, but those two other games I felt more personally involved.

They used to have a thing, well, about what do you do— owners own and managers manage, and coaches coach and players play, and I've been fulfilling the task of an owner for a long time. I used to be a general manager and it's a whole different feeling—I had a little more detachment in those days.

*In today's game, the benchmark of greatness for most pass rushers in a season is a double-digit sack total. Gino Marchetti, though, was a pioneer, the man who defined great defensive line play in the 1950s with his combination of speed, outstanding footwork, and raw power. The fact that Marchetti lived by a different standard was reflected in his choice of a greatest day, a single game in which he got a season's worth of sacks and put Detroit Lions quarterback Bobby Lane through a very long day.*

I think my personal best day was in Memorial Stadium against the Detroit Lions when I sacked Bobby Lane, I think eight times during the game. It was 1957 or '56, I really don't exactly remember. But, I guess personally, that might have been my second-greatest individual game.

It started pretty early. I really, for some reason, felt very fast that day, and very, very quick. And the tackle, I don't remember the tackle I played against. It was a big, tough guy from Notre Dame. I can't think of it. It was a long time ago,

I think he passed on. I was just able to do anything that I came up with, I was able to get by. In other words, I could go outside of him, get the quarterback, or I could go outside, then go inside and I got the quarterback. I just bowled him right over. It was one of those days, I think, that everything just clicked for me.

Yeah, they had a back on me, but sometimes what happens is that when you—and this happened to me a couple of times—when you can beat the tackle quickly, then that puts you in a better position to take on the fullback that comes over to help. So I was able to beat the tackle very quickly, and when the fullback came over I was able to gather myself and able to handle him.

A lot of times when you see the tackle quick and you're coming in with some force, they want to get you low. So the best thing that I have found, I used to be able to leapfrog him. I was able to jump over him, because they'd come at my ankles or my knees, and they just could never do that because of the quickness and agility that I had.

They tried trapping, but the best thing I was proud of, probably more so than rushing the passer, was my ability to play the run. I was very tough to trap, because I recognized it immediately and I was able to close distance between my position and the guard who was coming to knock me out. I was able to handle that very well.

And screens and draws, I reacted to draws, but screens, to me, I never looked for them or played for them. If you're going to be a pass rusher or an aggressive defensive line, if you sit there waiting for screens and draws, that'll just tell the offensive tackles that you're really never going to be aggressive against them to try to get the passer. So I always tried to play aggressive.

If they screen, my job was to keep going and raise my hands and try to cut the vision of the quarterback, but never to stop halfway through and react to the screen. That way you don't accomplish anything. You want to force the bad throw. That was primarily what we were supposed to do.

Well, sometimes Lane really got pissed off, and he had the ball and I heard him tell his tackle, he got so mad at his tackle he said, Goddammit! If you can't block him, let him come through, I'll block him. He said some things to me, but you know, we were at the Pro Bowl, and I played a couple of games with him—he was a real intense type of guy, so he talked a little but not a hell of a lot. He was just, more or less, you know, maybe next time I'll cover the ball more, or you'll get hurt or something. More so like that than anything else.

That was the best part of the game. I don't remember if we won the game. Tell you the truth, it was so long ago. I think we did win. But anytime you sack a guy, it helps the defense. Other times you get sacks because of your ability to get around the tackle, plus the coverage in the back. If you don't get coverage, then you'll never get a sack.

I guess the best part of the evening, or the best part of the day when we were reviewing the films, they all laughed and really got a kick out of what I was able to do to that tackle. They found it very amusing. Well, we all enjoyed watching each other. Art Donovan had some moves and Joyce and Braase, so we always enjoyed, tried to learn from each other, how they did different things.

But my best day was when we had a game in San Francisco, a game which we had to win in '58, in a little town called Antioch, which is about thirty-five miles from San Francisco. And I never really had the type of day there that I felt I would've really liked to have had. When you have a great day you say, God, I'd like to have it at home in front of my home fans. So that particular day, I must have had four sacks, six or seven rushes or hurries, what they call making a quarterback hurry, and we had a grading system, where coaches used to grade players so much.

And I had played in sixty-seven plays, and had played at 100 percent level, which meant, actually, that I never got blocked. So I was . . . I really felt good after that game because I was able to have that type of afternoon in San Francisco in front of my family, which is something I always—anybody would like to have. And I tried to have it before, but it never did happen. The tackle was, I remember his name was Thomas—Brodie was the quarterback, this must have been '58 or '59.

I hit it one other time, 100 percent. I think it was 1960 against the Chicago Bears in Chicago. Mostly, I always graded up anyway. I'd probably get graded up an average of 95 percent.

We won the championship—no, we won the division, we went out to San Francisco in 1957. We were, if we won the game—we'd be the Western Division champions, and we lost on a fourth-down play where Brodie had McElhenny in the end zone, and they beat us, 17–14. I don't believe in revenge, But this one was just—it was probably our turn. I think we won by 17 points. It really wasn't all that close.

It was really just a general defensive effort. I can't say there was a play that really turned things around, I just think we really jumped on them from the start, and we just kept on them.

We won that division championship, eventually, and we were all happy as hell. And the owner, Carroll Rosenbloom, who was a great owner, had arranged—by the time we won the game and went into the locker room and by the time we were dressed, he had said that he was having a party for us at the hotel we were staying. I was able to bring my friends and my family to that party, which was real nice, because I was able to spend some time with my family, and we were flying out the next day to Los Angeles.

Not only that, but it was nice to have me be with my friends, and have them meet my fellow teammates. They really enjoyed it. I'd introduce them, and they'd say, That's Johnny Unitas! They'd get all excited, more excited than me—the whole ball of wax.

I think the greatest game as a team that I think we played, was in 1958. I got my two games mixed up. The one in San Francisco was prior, but 1958—Jesus, all these years are creeping up on me. Well, we played San Francisco, it might've been '59. They were leading us 27–6 at halftime. And then we went into the locker room and I remember we had on the board, Must score or hold them scoreless. And we did that.

We came out the second half and we had the best second half of football, I think, that could ever be played. We scored four touchdowns, we held them scoreless, Lenny Moore was awesome, Raymond Berry, John, I mean we just kicked their living butt. Not only that, but we got the championship too right after that game, because the Chicago Bears had beaten Detroit in Chicago, which gave us the Western Division championship.

I've been in lots of locker rooms before the game when the team is quiet, studying, and God almighty, now everybody's concentrating. We had a week's good practice and you say, Wow, let's go get them now. We go out on the field and get the shit kicked out of us. And there's times when I've been in our locker room, everybody comes in laughing, telling jokes, had a week of poor practice, and you're afraid to start the game because you don't know what's going to happen. And you go out there and play a hell of a game.

So what happened that second half. We were embarrassed, and we realized the importance of that game, and we just said, Let's hold them defensively. We've got this defensively, let's work as hard as we can to do that, and the offense got in their part of the meeting room, and they said the same thing—that they were going to hold the ball. We gave them a chance to score, and we win it, and that's what happened.

I think the first half was not being up as much as we should have been on the importance of the game. It was an important game for us, and we went out there and I think the first part of the game, everything they did worked, every defense we called they seemed to have a play that worked against it, and they just drove down the field two or three times, which never happened to our team. They really controlled the ball on us in the first half. And with the changes we made at halftime we were able to stop all that.

Well, we went to the hotel and had a big party, you know, threw another big party for the team. Champagne and everything, but I didn't drink any because I don't like champagne. I was drinking beer. Family, not my family, but my wife and kids were all there. It was pretty nice. I think that what makes those things so good is that, I always believe there is more pressure on those guys getting to the Super Bowl than the Super Bowl game itself. I think the pressure of getting there is awesome.

I think once you get there, the championship game is like no pressure at all. You want to win but you don't feel like, Goddammit, this is it, you go nuts thinking about the game. The championship game is just to get there. That's the tough part.

Well, the Hall of Fame to me is—it's something you never thought you'd be there. I never thought I'd play professional football, because in high school I was no good. I never thought I'd be in a position to go into the Hall of Fame. But I did, and I think the thing that makes that experience so wonderful is that they bring your family in, they take good care of your family, your family is able to go to all the events and get good seats, they treat your family as good as they do you. So I think that experience was really nice.

But I did miss something, which is, I never went through the Hall of Fame. So I just went back there this last July when they invited all the old legends there. I went up a day early, and my wife and I drove down, and I went just to see the

Hall without all the people around. That's why I would never go before, because walking in there, you'd never get past the autographs.

So her and I we drove there one afternoon, we snuck in, and I tell you, when I walked down that Hall of Fame where it has all the displays of Van Brocklin and Nagurski, all these guys that I played against, seeing their display on the walls and the lighting of the room and the soft music, I tell you, it really sent a chill down my back and there I am. I think that part of it I probably enjoyed more this time than I did twenty-eight years ago.

Well, I think all of your friends being there, but I think one thing that really struck me, I was standing there waiting to get into the car for the parade, and this couple come with their cars and they had a sign, We Love Gino. Anyway, so I talked to them, and they drove down from Utah just to see me inducted. And I said, You drove all this way? And they said, Yeah, listen, we've been your fans for so long that we just wouldn't miss this great day. And to me that hit home. Hell, I wouldn't drive 100 miles to see the president of the United States. I think that sent it all home to me.

The '58 game, I think people—they call that the greatest game, and I think the reason it got the name the greatest game, primarily, was because it was played in New York City. If it was played in Baltimore, St. Louis, you wouldn't have got that kind of coverage. We all recognized that.

I don't think it was the best game. I think what made it—I think it was the most important game ever played, because right after that game the following season, I mean, you could see the stands start filling up. You could see football start growing. You could see that you were in demand, where in years prior to that you weren't. You could just see the whole picture of the National Football League get bigger and bigger. I think that Baltimore played a big part in it. Trouble is, they don't have a team in Baltimore anymore.

The greatest college game, I think, I played with a small college. And I think we had 1,400 students in San Francisco. And we played Stanford, and Stanford whipped us terribly because we went over there, we were kind of scared playing the Pac-10, and we went in there, and the first play they ran, it was a perfect play, they ran 65 yards for a touchdown. It was all downhill after that.

But then later on, we got a chance that same year to play the University of California. We went over there and they beat us 13–7. And to me that was the greatest game in San Francisco where we played, because they went to the Rose Bowl and all that kind of good stuff. They were really lucky, they beat us on a fumble, but anyway we ended up 13–7.

I never know what kind of day I had. I think we played well. We were ready for them. We had nine guys who went on to play pro football, and the best football player never played was Burt Toller. He got invited to the College All-Star Game with me, and during that game we played the Rams. You remember the College All-Star Game? We'd play the champions of the NFL. He tore his knee up something awful and never recovered from that. In them days, a knee injury, it's not like today where they can go in and do all this stuff and make it like new, but his was torn so bad he was never able to play again.

I think he'd be one of the top linebackers who ever played. Even though with us he was an offensive tackle, he played linebacker, but he was probably the best tackler I'd ever seen—fast, quick, had everything going for him. When he was drafted he was really a junior, that's what the NFL thought of him.

I think the two greatest guys I've ever played against are St. Clair, Forrest Gregg from Green Bay, and big Bob from the 49ers. Forrest Gregg was the smallest guy I ever played in front of. That's the reason why they talk about weight, it don't mean nothing. He was very quick, he was very agile, and he had great balance. I fake him in or out, I used to do it occasionally, but he won a lot of those battles.

And St. Clair was a different problem. St. Clair was so tall, and he had good balance, and he wouldn't shut up. I used to tell him, You block out the whole sun. Those were probably the two guys. As far as who I played with, God, I couldn't name those. You got Johnny Unitas, Lenny Moore, Raymond Berry, Ollie Matson, just so many. Art Donovan, he's probably the best guy I ever played in the line with, and Matson was great, too. But some of those guys are really, really nice people, so to say that Lenny Moore was better than Ollie Matson, I couldn't do that.

# Bill Parcells

*In the early '80s, Bill Parcells built the Giants defense into a great unit that became the foundation of one of the teams of the decade, a club that would battle the 49ers, Redskins, and Bears for supremacy in the NFC. After taking over as head coach in 1983, Parcells led the team to Super Bowl victories in 1986 and 1990. He later went on to take the New England Patriots to the Super Bowl in 1995 and the New York Jets to the 1998 AFC Championship game before he retired from coaching to become general manager of the Jets. For his greatest game, Parcells chose the 1990 NFC Championship game against the 49ers, a gritty 15–13 victory that the Giants won on a Matt Bahr field goal as time ran out.*

I'd say it would have to be the second championship game, in San Francisco, against the 49ers. We had started off the season real well. I think our record was 10–0, and then we lost our quarterback in the eleventh game, and we lost a couple of games. We finished the season winning two games, but we didn't look very good, and we had our backup quarterback, Jeff Hostetler, playing, and no one had ever won the Super Bowl with a backup quarterback.

And the first round of the playoffs—I know I'm telling you about the deal, but here's the background—we beat the Bears by 30 or 31–3, you'd have to check the score. And then, because we had home field, we had to go to San Francisco for the second time that season. They had beaten us in San Francisco on a Monday night, 7–3, and now we were kind of replaying them.

Now this San Francisco team was the team that was going for the three-peat. They had won two. They were gonna be the greatest team in history to win three in a row and that kind of thing. And, you know, we just went there, and it was a tremendously hard-hitting, tough, well-contested game with a lot of great players playing in it. And they had some great players, and we had some great players, and with four seconds to go we kicked the field goal to beat them, 15–13.

And that was euphoria for me.

It was very bright and sunny—we had had a tremendous rivalry with the 49ers dating back to the middle '80s, '84, '85, '86. We played them in the playoffs all those years. And, you know, we were pretty familiar with their players. They had a nucleus of guys on their team that had lasted a long time that were proven, winning-type players. And we had a pretty good nucleus ourselves, of ours, that had won.

And the day was just . . . warm, not hot, a very sunny, beautiful California day, January day, you know? The place was all full of red, you know, obviously. You walk out the tunnel from the locker room and you have to kind of pass through and go almost underneath the stands. You come kind of out an alleyway out onto the field, and you know, there's some pretty good verbal abuse going on there.

The game was just hotly contested. They were ahead 3–0, you know, I don't know whether we tied it up. But we kicked four field goals and missed one, and I think they scored one touchdown and kicked two field goals.

I know we ran a fake punt to get one of our field goals, to get in a position to do that. And we dropped a touchdown pass very early in the game that was in the end zone that would have been a real good start for us, but we had to settle for a field goal instead.

You know, they had taken possession of the game and were trying to run the clock out. Had they run a couple more plays, they would have run the clock out—the Roger Craig fumble. We recovered it, and then we had to go a few yards to get into field-goal range—we didn't have to go a lot, but I know we faced—we threw a 13-yard pass in that time right there, and the field goal wound up being a 41-yard field goal, you know, so the ball is probably on about the 24 yard line.

And, you know, that's still a pretty tough kick on grass, especially with their turf. We had a great kicker, Matt Bahr. He just made it, and it was just kind of a pandemonium thing on our sideline. It was very quiet in the rest of the place. You know, I could just recall, talking to some of—just a little bit, congratulating some of their players on a great run, Ronnie Lott, some of those guys.

And then we just got to the dressing room, they present you with the NFC trophy, and it's a very small dressing room there in San Francisco. They presented us with the trophy, and we went right from there, we got on the bus and we went to Tampa for the Super Bowl, and we're getting ready to play Buffalo now.

The decision I made that I think was the biggest gamble was the fake punt. I don't know where exactly that yardage was, we weren't on the plus side of the 50. You know, it was around midfield, maybe just shy—that was a big play for us.

We knew something—we looked at it in the game a couple of times. We knew that, this fake we had, they had lined up the same way they'd been lining up most of the time, and if they lined up where they had previously lined up in the game, it would work. They just didn't have quite enough guys . . .

and actually, I think they only had ten men on the field during the fake, too.

Well, the one that we played the next week was pretty emotional, too. It was the same kind of thing, but I think that, had we lost to Buffalo, I would have felt that the superior team lost. This game with San Francisco, I felt like the sides were very even. They had scored . . . we played twice during the season, and at the end of the day we scored 18 points and they scored 20, or 19, or something like that, you know? They had a touchdown and 12, and we had 15 and 3, so we had 18, so in eight quarters of football that season, the score was 19–18. I mean, that's indicative of the teams' strength.

Now, the other thing that I think I would be remiss if I didn't mention—one of the reasons that it was a great game was that there were so many great players playing in the game, you know what I mean? When you start looking back at the Rices and Montanas and Lotts and some of their defensive players, Charles Haley, you know, guys like that, and all our guys, our defensive guys, O. J. Anderson and Mark Bavaro and Marshall and Taylor and Banks—I mean, we had some real upscale players, too.

And I think that's . . . hey, it was a great day.

Certainly, they had their share [of Hall of Famers]. A couple of them were already in, one of ours is in.

I think people had a tremendous tendency to underrate our team. Because our team, I think, that year, was one of the best teams ever. Now, I'm very prejudiced—but our team had played in a lot of close games, and always, most of the time managed to win. It was kind of a very resilient team mentally.

I know I'm using coaches' phrases here, but now, don't forget, this team won the Super Bowl with their backup quarterback. They knocked the team out that was gonna be the team of the decade, the team of history, San Francisco. And then they went and they beat the team with the offense of the '90s. They were averaging 39 points a game, the Buffalo Bills, or 35 points a game, I'm not sure, you'd have to check that. I know it was in the middle thirties, at least.

And that—you know, it was just a team that was a lot better than anybody gave it credit for, because defensively, we were strong. And you were gonna have to really play well on offense to beat us.

I think, you know, we had some good battles, and I've gotten to know their players now since it's over with. I know Montana pretty well, and Ronnie I always knew, and some of their guys, and there's just a tremendous respect on both sides.

A guy who might be able to help you on that game . . . Jerry Markbreit was the referee. He told me it was the greatest game he ever officiated, at that point. Now, I don't know if he would ever remember saying that, but he told me, Hey, that's the greatest game I've ever officiated. He said, Hey, that was some game right there. It really was, though.

It was so hard-hitting and so physical, and just so . . . every inch counted. I mean, it was really like a military adventure, you know. You're just trying to gain a little ground, and there weren't hardly any big plays. It was just, slug it out.

There are some other games that I could put close to the category. The first Super Bowl was a very one-sided game, you know, in the second half. The last Super Bowl, for me, or the last one we won, was a game very similar to San Francisco, but it was a much more unsettling-type game. They had a wide-open attack, and it wasn't—it was just, we couldn't afford to make a mistake, you know, and they were a fast-paced-type thing.

So, that game, I thought we strategically played very well, and I think that's one of the things I liked about the team— it understood how it had to play to be effective. No matter who we were playing, whether it be San Francisco or Buffalo, they could adapt to whatever I told them, as far as, hey, this is what we have to do to win here, you know, we're gonna try to do it this way.

Now, I played in a great game in Washington in '89, the opening game of the season, and we kicked a 52-yard field goal to beat them after we'd been way ahead. And they came back and caught us, and then they went ahead, and then we tied 'em, and then we beat 'em, you know? It was unbelievable—and it was one of the most dramatic, eerie, foggy, like a cemetery-type feeling, that was what that was like.

But this game, to me, I think if you said, hey, Bill, one game, what's the most vivid in your mind, I would say that that game was.

You know, you never assume, when you start out coaching and these things, college and the rest . . . Canton, Ohio, is the furthest thing from your mind. You never in your wildest dreams, ever dream that something like that could happen.

You know, I think I just happened to be in the right place at the right time with some good players. You've gotta be pretty lucky. I know I had some great battles with Walsh, and Seifert, and my biggest rival, of course, was Joe Gibbs. You know, when I think back on my football career, I think of Washington and San Francisco as the teams that—maybe it was just . . . you know, the last few years for me, it's been the Dolphins and the Bills and those kinds of teams, but I just think the fiercest rivalries that I've ever been involved with were those two.

The other thing, too—and I would be remiss if I didn't mention this—the Redskins had a lot of great players playing on their team, too. So I think, you know, the Art Monks and the Russ Grimms and the Rigginses, you know, Darrell Greens, and the guys that they had that are gonna go in the Hall of Fame—that's what made those games great. And, hey, that was a battle now—trust me. Those games, they were something to behold.

# Pete Pihos

*During his ten-year Hall of Fame career with the Philadelphia Eagles in the late '40s and early '50s, Pete Pihos earned a reputation as one of the greatest ends ever to play the game, a fabulous two-way player who was an All-Pro player on both sides of the ball. In 1948, Pihos was an integral part of Philadelphia's NFL title win against the Chicago Cardinals in the infamous "Snow Bowl," and the following year he caught a 31-yard touchdown pass in the championship game as the Eagles beat the Los Angeles Rams 14–0. But his greatest day came during his first pro game against the Washington Redskins, when he scored two touchdowns to help the Eagles to a victory over Slingin' Sammy Baugh.*

I started as a pro and did very well—in fact, I didn't play in any exhibition games in 1947. The first year we were going to play the Redskins with Sammy Baugh, and I'm a rookie. Well this all happened, I scored two touchdowns and took one to the 2-foot line. In other words, I had a big jump and we won. We won 45–42. At one time it was 45–21 and Sammy Baugh got hot and we were lucky to get 45.

And then in '53, '54, and '55, I led the league in pass receiving for a tight end with over sixty. Back then we only played twelve games. And Jerry Rice, he had sixty-four, but he had sixteen games. But God's been good to me and all the players we get coming out. We're all trying to do the best we can.

The greatest day out of all that as a pro? I decided, by talking with Joe DiMaggio in 1955, he said, Pete, quit while you're on top. And I said, Well, I'll finish this season. And I led the league in pass receiving again and I was a tight end, and I made a whole bunch of money, and I won't tell you how much because it was a lot. And God was good to me, and I finished up and told them that I quit. And from then on it was fun.

I think the greatest day for Pete Pihos was playing the first game against the Washington Redskins, to score two touchdowns and take one to the 1-foot line.

I was very successful. But the first six years we had to play both offense and defense. But then, when it became around '53, '54 and '55, I finished up with sixty-four catches in '53, sixty-two in '54, sixty-three in '55, and quit.

It seemed like I was a lucky rookie when I caught those passes and went for touchdowns. Took one to the 1-foot line, and I was pretty high, but then again, we didn't win the championship in '47, we won it in '48 and '49, and Sammy Baugh, when we played in '47—we were playing them now in Washington and he was the guy who punted, and I took the ball off his foot and went on for a touchdown. But that was how we won. He was a great, great player.

What happened was that Pete Pihos started to play harder. He was a rookie, and it was a big, big game. The players all played exhibition games, but I told them I didn't want to go play in a certain game like the rest of them did. It was the All-Star game in Chicago. And I said, No, I've already been through all that. So then they put me in, and I wouldn't go play the exhibition game so I had to wait 'til I was—I didn't know what the hell they were going to do but they told me, you'll start on offense in the first quarter.

Well, I just wanted to play well and play my position. We had great football players in those first four years—first three, I mean, I'll say it like that. But we had fun, and being a dumb Greek I learned to do a lot more.

We just got hot. It was something if you were going to win, even though we won the championship in our conference, but then we played the Chicago Cardinals for the championship. They beat us 28–21. The next year we beat them 7–0 in Philly, and it was snowing, yes, it was bad.

But then we played the Rams, and we beat them 16–0, and I scored a touchdown. But to me, I just wanted—I finished up, and Joe DiMaggio said, Pete, quit while you're on top. You've been fantastic, and you can play and no one's going to say, he ain't worth a damn.

He was such a great guy. He came out in 1955 on Dean Martin and Jerry Lewis just like I did. And he was great, and what a dumb Greek I was—when my mother died and I was in Daytona Beach, and guess who was sick in Hollywood? Joe. And I didn't get going fast enough to say, Hey, buddy, how are you doing? Because I was close enough. And it made me kick myself in the ass.

In college, the first two years I was pretty up—'41, '42, and '43, I was pretty successful, because back then we had to play both ways. And I was very, very good on the '42 team because I was just a sophomore and didn't play when we were freshman. And I, I just played to win and I did well with my schoolwork and all that, making A's and B's. But Indiana was a great school for Pete Pihos. Bill McMillan was great. And whatever I did, I did with his plays.

We played in an All-Star Game in San Francisco, and then when we came out, I had to go to New Orleans to get into the infantry. And I went into the infantry with General Patton and I became a lieutenant and I scored on honors. I don't want to tell you how much I did, or who I killed or what. But to me, General Patton was great. We would have meetings on Monday, where we were going to go and what we were going to do, and Tuesday morning he'd be there, five o'clock in the morning at the point where we were supposed to be.

I think I played well, and I had my teammates that were good, Steve Van Buren, and I'm going to go to the Eagles game with him this year because he keeps saying he's got prostate cancer and—if he's got it, I want to make sure we can get rid of it. And I'm going to be meeting him somewhere these next two or three weeks. He's great, and so are the other guys, but most of them died. What can I do? It's me, it's my seventy-seventh year.

I played well, I thought, and Joe DiMaggio had a lot to say when he said Pete, quit while you're on top, and I decided to do it. And just remember—know how much I got paid? Take a guess—$150,000 in '55. I played offense. Charlie Trippi and I both started out in 1947, $25,000 apiece. We did that for the first six years. And then it came to a little bit more.

The greatest day for Pete Pihos was 1947, that first game, because here I am a young guy, and I go there and play great and score. And Sammy Baugh was a great player, so playing against him and all that, you had to be good. And then when we played Charlie Trippi and his bunch. We were playing the Cardinals in Chicago and they beat us 28–21. And the next year we beat them, and the third year we beat them. Then when I started playing offense only, it was a lot of work. But I played a lot of people and had fun.

Going into the Hall? It was great. I was there and made my hellos and all that. I had Howie Brown [induct me]. He was one of my teammates at Indiana and he was also with the Detroit Lions, and he was a leader for me and all I could say is, I thank you very much. When you're being honored, the guy who brought you in does more talking than the player. But we had four good guys: Jack Christiansen, Tom

Fears, Hugh McElhenny, and myself. That was a great bunch of guys. The only thing wrong is Christiansen died four years ago, Tom died a year ago, and the rest of us are in good shape.

I'd relive any one of them, but the first one that set me up made me realize what I can do.

The greatest player I ever played with was Van Buren. He was great. He was the best when it came to a player. We'd have to make holes and he'd run just as hard as anybody else. And he was always a teammate, that's what counted. I can't remember all the guys, but we had guys that were just good on defense. And they had to be, or they wouldn't be there. I'm going to go see Steve sometime in the next two months, because I want to make sure he's not sick. He says he's got prostate cancer, but then somebody else says no. He's well, but I'm going to go there on my own to get him and take him to the doctor.

The greatest opponent was the Chicago Cardinals—Charlie Trippi was great. And we had Tom Fears, believe it or not, he was a great offensive end, and he did well. But Steve Van Buren I felt was the best guy I had ever been with.

Trippi was a guy that—we both gave the game a certain thing, and we were the guys getting $25,000 instead of the other guys getting $5–6,000. And we both got that. And I didn't play in any exhibition game that year. And that way, I didn't play any exhibition games until we came to the league games, so I had to start the damn season in my first quarter. But I was lucky because I scored two and set up a third one.

## Gale Sayers

*In 1965, Gale Sayers began a seven-year career in which he electrified the league with his amazing running ability, which featured darting cutbacks, frightening bursts of speed, and the occasional display of power during the few times when he got caught up in defensive traffic. Sayers's most incredible game was his six-touchdown effort against the 49ers late in his rookie year, but to get to that game he had to go through his greatest day, when he proved he belonged in the NFL.*

Probably my greatest day would be the third game of the season my rookie year against the Green Bay Packers. We lost the ball game 23–14, but the reason I say that is because I think that was when George Halas, who was the coach at that time, and my teammates at the time, they accepted me as a member of the Chicago Bears football team. I can think of other great days, but in my mind that day that I now belonged on the Chicago Bears and I played in the National Football League. I scored two touchdowns in that ball game and we didn't win the ball game, but I just really felt then that I was now a part of the National Football League.

Well, I heard that George Halas didn't like starting rookies. He felt they had to duly earn their way on the football team. But training camp was kind of unusual because I played in the College All-Star Game. I was a member of the College All-Star team. And that particular year and that particular game I did not play because Otto Graham, who was the head coach of that team, he thought that I was dogging it and I got hurt in a scrimmage, and he came out in the papers and he said Gale Sayers would never make it as a pro football player.

And so I had that label on me coming into training camp, but George Halas said, Gale, we're going to judge you by what you do from now on, not what you did in the past. And so training camp went along well, and I had a pretty decent exhibition season in a couple games. I scored on a punt return and a kickoff return, scored a couple of touchdowns from the line of scrimmage against some teams, but again, our first ball game was against the 49ers in San Francisco, and they beat us something like 52–14.

I played a little bit in that ball game, and then we played the Rams in L.A. the next weekend, at the Coliseum. We lost that ball game big, too. I did score a touchdown in that game. I didn't score any in the 49er game. Jon Arnett, he was the starting running back at that time in both those games, and George Halas, he had a way of never letting you know when you would start. You come back in from pregame practice, he would come back in and he would announce the starting team. You didn't know on Friday that you were going to start, or Thursday. You knew on Sunday right before the kickoff.

I still felt that Jon Arnett would start the ball game against the Green Bay Packers because it was the third ball game of the season, so I'm out there doing my thing and I'm always prepared to play. We come back into the locker room and he calls out the starting team and announces my name. I'm quite sure that many people were shocked, so I was there and, again, we lost the ball game, but that's where my career started, really, right there. After that we lost the first three ball games and then we won the next nine of ten ball games and were second to Green Bay in the divisional race.

The game was in Green Bay, I think a very exciting ball game. I've always felt once the kickoff is done and you're in the first play and you get hit, the butterflies are gone and you do your job. I scored two touchdowns in the ball game, one on about a 15-yard run and one on about a 65-yard pass play, and what I remember about the game was that it was a rivalry against the Green Bay Packers. They were the champs of the league, and we wanted to win that ball game, but it didn't happen.

They got out front and they stayed out front. It was 23–14, and the Bears, we played well. I think we came of age during that ball game. I remember after the ball game, Paul Hornung, he came up to me and said, Gale, if you continue to do what you're doing and work hard, you'll be one of the better running backs in this league. And that really stuck with me coming from somebody who'd been in the league, and played for a number of years, and saying that to me. That really made me work that much harder. That's when my career took off, really, in Green Bay on that day.

Well, I don't think Green Bay really expected me to do as well as I did against them. I'm pretty sure they didn't know anything about me. They knew that the Bears drafted me number one, and Vince Lombardi was like George Halas, he didn't like to start rookies either. I don't think they expected too much of me. But I think I surprised them with my quickness and speed, and the next ball game, three weeks later, they got on me pretty good as far as saying different things, trying to upset me. That happened rarely at Wrigley Field.

All of them were talking, Ray Nitschke and Willie Davis, Herb Adderley and Willie Wood. They were all talking the next time we played them, because I had probably another four or five touchdowns with several teams, so they knew I was for real. They thought this was one where they could upset me by talking to me, but I came to play, I didn't come to talk.

But that first game, I played the whole game. I was out on a couple plays, but I played the entire game and I scored a touchdown in the second quarter and at halftime it was 17–7. And then later in the game I scored on a 65-yard touchdown pass play. I think the whole game, I probably gained about 80 to 85 yards in that particular game, so I felt that I belonged in the National Football League at that time.

I always prepared myself to go out there and play, and I think that we as a team took into the rest of the season that we could play with the world champions. We proved that on that particular day. They beat us by ten points or whatever it may be, but they were in a dogfight. I think Dick Butkus came of age in that particular game too. We both were rookies, and he was playing middle linebacker and he had a great game.

I think we just came together, the young players and the older players came together, and we felt that we could play and be a force in our division. We proved that and, as I say, we won the next nine or ten ball games. We proved that we could be a force. I think as a team we came together and everything jelled.

I think the first ball game, Bill Wade, who led the Bears to a championship in 1963, he was the starting quarterback. Then Coach Halas put in Rudy Bukich, who was a great quarterback. He had a great arm and he could throw it and he could run a little better than Bill Wade. And Rudy had a good ball game in that particular game also, so I think that game turned the whole season around. We had the people that we needed to start in that game in order to be in that game, so it turned everything around.

My teammates, I think they knew in training camp. I think they knew that I could play. But I had that rap of "Gale Sayers loafed" and things like that, but they knew in training camp that I had more quickness and I had more speed and I could see things better than other running backs we had on our team. I really believe they probably thought, it's just a matter of time that he's going to play, whether it's the third ball game or the tenth ball game, he would be in there, because I had that kind of talent.

There wasn't nothing said after that ball game—Coach Halas congratulated me on a good ball game, but, again, we lost the ball game. The team had a good game and we came together but we still lost. We were 0–3. We had to go from there. There wasn't anything that anyone said, Sayers is the man, or anything like that. We were ready to play.

Probably the turning point in camp was when we played the Rams in Nashville in an exhibition game, and that particular ball game the first time they play a lot of rookies because they're trying to figure out who's going to be on the team. In that particular ball game the first time they punted to the Bears I fumbled the punt. And Coach really got on me when I came to the sidelines, and then several series later, they punted again to us and I ran it back for like 67 yards for a touchdown.

Then the second half they scored and they kicked off to us, and I ran back a 95-yard kick on them. And I threw a 25-yard pass for a touchdown to one of our wide receivers. So I think they knew that I could play, and again, I'm a rookie, and I still have a lot of things to learn, but it was just a matter of time when I would play. I really felt that game proved that I could play in the National Football League, but yet and still George Halas again, he didn't start me until the third ball game because he wasn't real comfortable starting rookies. So I didn't start until the third ball game, and the rest is history.

What Otto Graham said made headlines in the *Chicago Tribune* and the other papers here in Chicago, but when I met George Halas, he said, Gale, I saw the things in the paper, and I will judge you by what you do from today forward, and that's all I needed to know. I didn't give a damn about what my teammates thought about me, or anything else, all I needed to know was that George Halas said that he'd judge me by what I did from the day I came to camp forward. And so I worked from there.

It was ten years later when I saw Graham again. He was at the Coast Guard Academy, and I spoke at the Coast Guard Academy and we talked about his comments, but it was no big deal. He felt that way and he thought that I was dogging it, and he had a right to feel that way. Wasn't no problem with me. I proved that I did belong in the National Football League.

I love George Halas. He was there when I first came to the Bears. It was almost like a father/son relationship. We got along very, very well, and all he asked his players to do—he was a tough coach, no doubt about it—but all he asked his players to do was, give me 100 percent and I'll leave you alone.

And a lot of players didn't give him 100 percent and he got on them. I can't think of any time he ever got on me about doing something wrong. I may have fumbled here or there, but he knew I was out there to play. Every day in practice it was full speed, every game was full speed, and he knew that. I don't care where the ball was placed, 40 yard line going in, 50 yard line going in, if I got the ball, I'm full speed to the goal line. Because if you don't practice that, if you've never been there, how're you going to get there when you break one?

And if it's on our 40, I'm going 60 yards to the goal line, and that's in training camp and that's every day and it's hot. Halas stopped practice one day, he said, hey, if Gale Sayers can run 40 yards to the goal line or 50 yards to the goal line, everybody can run 50 yards to the goal line. They were on my ass, because they jumped me, slow down or do something different. But that's the way I had to prepare myself for a game.

We had a great relationship. He was a great coach and a

great person. He cared about his players, and cared about what happened to them after their playing days were over, and he cared about their families. He was a man, when I first came to the league, sixty-nine years of age, and I could not believe it, I thought he was old at that time, I don't think that now. He was an old man out there limping around, sixty-nine years old, and that means he was the first one on the field and the last one off the field, and we had some cold days in Chicago—he was out there.

I would run through a wall for George Halas, because here's a man that old out there coaching football and you have kids twenty-one, twenty-two, twenty-three out there saying, Coach, I got a cold, I've got to go in. He didn't miss a practice and he stayed out there. I don't care how cold it was, he stayed out there and I couldn't believe it. And if he could do that, why couldn't I do it?

It'd be very difficult for him to coach today, like Mike Ditka and his troubles with the Bears. We played injured. It was stupid, and today the kids out there, they don't do that, they get a charley horse, they get a sprained ankle—I can't play. We took a shot and we went out and played. Gale Sayers on one leg is better than a second-string back on three legs.

And back before in the '50s and '40s and '30s, those players, very few pads and leather helmets. Tough people. People say, are the players of today tougher? Well, I ran back punt returns, kickoff returns, from the line of scrimmage, and passes, and these kids today, they run two or three times and say, I'm tired. They think they've done something and do dances.

It's a different game today, it really is, and they talk about how there's so much situational play on third and 3, you bring in somebody who can catch a pass, nickel defense, and all that kind of stuff, and players are not playing as much as we played. And I think this is why many people are getting hurt today because they're not getting into shape. They think, I'm on the team to play, so why do I need to be in shape?

I had to be in shape, because many times during the course of the week we'd script what plays we were going to have, and the first three plays, I'm carrying the football. And this is going to be after I run a kickoff back 30 or 40 yards and I got to get back in the huddle, and I know the first three plays I'm going to have to carry the football, so I had to be in shape.

But George Halas was a great individual. A lot of people talk about him, but he did so much for so many people.

I like the Green Bay game better than the six-touchdown game because it was earlier in the season. The six-touchdown game was the tenth ball game of the season, the eleventh ball game of the season, and again, I was accepted at that time. People knew of Gale Sayers at that time.

I had some great Pro Bowl games during my short career, and there's no doubt about it that the Hall of Fame is probably the best thing that happened to me because I only played sixty-eight ball games. And for somebody to make the Hall of Fame in that short period of time is something that I never thought was going to happen. I never even dreamed about being in the Hall of Fame, and suddenly I get a call—Hey, Gale, you're in the Hall of Fame. I just think that those things were after being accepted in the league or by the Chicago Bear team. If you don't get accepted by the team or the league, you're not going to play. Those things couldn't have happened if I hadn't been accepted by the league or the team.

My college greatest day was probably my sophomore year against Oklahoma State University. I set the Big 8 rushing record of 283 yards in that particular ball game. The thing about that ball game was we were behind 17–7 at halftime and it was a tough ball game for us, but the thing that I remember was that I gained 283 yards on twenty-two carries.

The other thing that I remember about the game, I scored two other touchdowns in the ball game, one from 50 yards, and one of 65 yards, that they called back. Those two, I felt were the best runs of the whole game. I had to do some things on those particular two runs to get the touchdown. And that's what I remember of that game. They called those two runs back, and those were probably the best two runs of the whole game that I did. I did score one on a 96-yard run from scrimmage that particular ball game, but the other two I felt were better runs.

So, yeah, it could have been a 300-yard game. And another thing I remember too, about the game, in the fourth quarter, I guess somebody said, Gale needs only ten yards more to break the record. Hopson or somebody held the record. But anyway, in the middle of the fourth quarter a fight broke out after they hit me out of bounds. And then it was second down and I got up and the coach took me out of the game, and someone said I needed ten more yards to break the record, so I went back in the ball game and I gained 15 yards, and the referee said to the coach, hey, this kid was kicked out of the game, so he can't come back in.

So anyway, they let it go, because . . . I don't know why my coach didn't know I was kicked out of the game. And I came back in and gained 15 yards or so, and they let it go and I broke the record. Again, that was a good ball game. I had an NCAA-record 99-yard run against Nebraska my junior year, but we lost that ball game. But I think that I remember that ball game my sophomore year the most.

I've gotten a lot of compliments from different opponents, so I would have to think about which one stands out the most. Many opponents, they've come up to me and said that I've seen them all. They were older players, Hall of Famers, Jim Brown and O. J. and Eric Dickerson, even Barry Sanders, they've said, you were the best. So I've heard that many, many times, things like, Your style was so unique, you know Barry Sanders, he does a lot of stuff, he couldn't do what you could do. But as I said, I've always remembered what Paul Hornung said to me after the Green Bay game.

*The football gods broke the mold when they created Bob St. Clair, a 6'9", 265 pound lineman who spent the 1950s opening holes for San Francisco's Million Dollar backfield of Hugh McElhenny, Joe Perry, and Y. A. Tittle. The multidimensional St. Clair also pioneered the art of blocking punts and field goals, a skill that helped ensure his long-overdue election to the Hall of Fame in 1989. St. Clair was also a fan favorite who went on to have an intriguing life after football, as he was elected mayor of Daly City, California, before "retiring" to the life of a dairy farmer. His nickname during his playing days was the Geek, a moniker he earned for his habit of eating raw meat during training camp.*

I have two of them, Bob. My first probably, one of my greatest moments, was when I ran down Emlen Tunnell of the New York Giants. We were playing an exhibition game in Washington, Huskies Stadium, in Everett or Seattle or wherever that stadium is. And we were down about the 5 yard line.

And Y. A. Tittle threw a sideline pass. It was a little flat pass, and it was intercepted by Emlen. I was blocking. Tunnell was on the right side. I blocked to the right, and I saw him intercept it. And I started chasing him, and I chased him from behind, 60 yards, and I caught him. I was pretty fast.

Of course, I needed an oxygen mask to get off the field. That was probably one of my greatest thrills, was to be able to catch him because when I was chasing him—I'm 6'9" at the time, and my long strides, and he kept looking and he kind of turned around and said to himself, Well, shit, some lineman is running after me. And all of a sudden I kept gaining on him and gaining on him and gaining on him, and I finally leaped and caught him, and that was probably one of my greatest moments.

There was great joy in 49er land after that.

I'm not sure when it was. To tell you the truth, this was so long ago, and criminies, it was back in the '50s, the early '50s.

I was fast for a big guy. I could run the 100 in 11 flat, which was—someone like me, I ran high hurdles in high school and all of that kind of jazz. I could run. I played end in college, but that was the extent of it.

Well, your greatest day was like I just told you, it was something like that, or in 1956, in a twelve-game season, I blocked ten field goal and punt combinations.

Oh! I know another one, too. I broke my shoulder in the beginning of the 1957 season, the first game against the Rams. And I was out—they operated on it and put a screw in it—and I was out for six weeks. And on the seventh week they took the pin out and everything and I worked out with my shoulder enough, and they built a harness and everything else for it, and we were playing the Giants in New York. So I was in San Francisco and I flew back on a Friday night and we were staying in Upstate New York, Bear Mountain, in the facilities up there.

What happened is I came in and I busted into their meeting

because I was their captain, and I said, Moses has returned
from forty days and forty nights to lead you into the Promised
Land. And we were underdogs, the Giants were favored by
14 points, and we beat them. I don't remember the exact
score. And the team gave me the game ball. I still have that.
That's probably one of my greatest games.

But another great moment, too, was naturally the thrill of
a lifetime when I was inducted into the Hall of Fame. Nothing
compares to that. For an offensive lineman, nothing compares
to being enshrined in Canton, Ohio.

Oh, my God, just the idea of being an offensive lineman,
you never ever get any recognition hardly at all. And to be so
honored, to be picked to be in the Hall of Fame with such
great athletes of the past. As a kid, I only dreamed about
playing the game with them on that same level. [Charlie]
Trippi, and Otto Graham and on and on and on, and Bronco
Nagurski, you know, Red Grange. And then here's old Bobby
St. Clair from the neighborhood.

I went in with the big guys—Tom Landry, Franco Harris
and Jack Lambert, and Ted Hendricks and Bob Griese. Yeah,
it was so much fun.

I was so nervous. My presenter was Dave Baronio, who
was the first newspaper sports writer that ever presented anybody. He was just a real close friend of mine, and all my
coaches had passed away. But he was such a good friend, and
very knowledgeable, and he had gone to bat for me for years
to try to get me in. I picked him.

The thing I remember about the speech is, actually, before
the speech I wrote it on scratch paper, a couple of little pieces
of scratch paper, because, I tell you the truth, I was just going
to go up there and wing it. I didn't know, exactly. I'd never
seen the ceremony before or anything.

And all of a sudden I see, the night before—I was asking
Ted and these other guys. Bob Griese, for instance, he had a
regular written speech and all neat and under a cover. I said,

oh, my God. And then Tom had basically the same thing, everything was prepared for him.

So on the day of the ceremony and the parade, immediately after I rode in the car, I told the driver, I want to go right back to the Hall right this second. And I went in to the director's office and sat down and just wrote the speech out. I just wrote highlights and so forth. And that's the way I gave the speech. It was just so exciting for me to get up there.

I think the highlight of the speech was when I equated it to—I was asked how it felt to be in the Hall of Fame—and I equated it to the movie *Rocky* where Sylvester Stallone was running through the streets, and after weeks of practice he would hardly ever be able to walk up the steps on the monument there, and, at the end of a week, because of his practicing, he ran up to the top and flung his arms out and said, I made it! And this was the highlight of my speech. I did the same thing. I raised my arms and I said, I made it!

You know, offensive linemen aren't the first to be considered. And being that we hadn't won any championships when I played, that was probably the main deterrent. But when they took the whole Million Dollar backfield, I think Baronio made them aware of the fact that—he said, hey, look, these guys ran for 1,000 yards each, etc. etc., and they wouldn't be in the Hall of Fame if it weren't for guys like St. Clair. And I was in a lot of Pro Bowls, as well.

And I think that one statistic about me playing on defense and blocking all of those field goals throughout my whole career. They didn't keep a record of it in those days. But they did in 1956 for some reason, and I blocked ten of them in twelve games. And I think that was the turning point right there. They said, Whoa! Wait a minute! How the hell did he do that?

I was a center, I went through the middle. My technique was—in the beginning when they kicked the first one, I didn't even try to block it, I just ducked my head like a bull and just rammed the center as he centered the ball. And he wasn't expecting it, naturally, and I just ran over the top of him with my cleats and everything else, not trying to block it.

And then, the very next one they tried, that center would look up at me and look back and look up, and the minute he snapped the ball he was expecting the same thing. And he would go right to the ground on all fours, and that's when I leapfrogged over him. And once I hit the ground, especially if I landed on my feet on the other side, I had it. Because I went straight up and, bingo, I had it. We basically did the same thing with Leo Nomellini. He and I had some stunts, with Leo up the middle.

But I lost those five teeth on one play against the Rams in 1954. I lost them blocking a punt. I got in there so quickly that when Norm Van Brocklin was coming, I leaped at him and knocked the ball away from his foot before he had a chance to kick it. And he kicked me instead. It was my upper teeth, and they put cotton in it. We were on the 5 yard line, and we were behind, we scored, and then I came out.

By that time the air started getting in there and woo . . . ! Then they had to shoot me up with Novocain and everything else. Oh, God, they were all crooked and cracked and everything else, so when I got back they put in some temporaries and things like that. Then I was able to wear a helmet with one bar, so I did that.

I played mostly offense, but when I was playing defense, they would try to double-team me and things like that, move people in and everything, leaving less resistance on the outside positions so they couldn't give away too much. Actually, it just made you work that much harder to try to beat both of them. I knew I could beat one, but try to beat two is a real challenge.

I don't know what my greatest college day was. I can't remember that. I scored some touchdowns. In high school my greatest day was in the championship game. We were on the

20 yard line and I received what they called a tackle-eligible pass, and I carried about five guys down the field and into the end zone. By then I was 6'5 and 225 pounds, something like that.

The way I got into politics was after my career, I just got asked to go on the school board for some part of the community when I lived in Daly City, California. And I said no, I didn't have the time to do that, but of course then one of the politicians who was a city councilman in the city was having a fight with the other board members and so forth, and he asked me if I'd run with him.

I was the captain of the 49ers, and naturally had name identification, and then I decided to run for it, and when I do make up my mind for something like that I have great tenacity. And I went door to door and worked my ass off and I was elected. And then later, I became the mayor. That was a nonpartisan office—I was a Democrat at the time, however.

In fact, Jack Kennedy asked me to help run the campaign in northern California. I was the athletic chairman for Jack Kennedy's election. I didn't see him as much as I saw Ted. He did come out and worked with his brother in San Francisco quite a bit.

How do I compare it? I really don't know how to answer that. Politics was such a challenge, a whole new field for me, and I was the youngest man they ever had as mayor in Daly City. I learned as I went along to compromise. I think the biggest thing was compromise, which is a difference between football—you don't compromise at all. There is no compromise. You don't leave any wounded or anything.

The stories about me with the meat? When I was about the age of five that I can remember, my grandmother, who was chopping meat at the chopping block in the kitchen where we lived in San Francisco. She would be throwing me scraps of meat, almost like I'd sit up like the dog and I'd get some meat. And I just acquired a real taste for eating the meat raw instead of cooked. And then, as the years went by, I just kept that particular appetite. It never bothered my stomach, no, not at all. Chicken livers one time did me in. I never ate those raw again.

The whole meat thing was when training camp started. Every year I would have raw liver put on the plate, and I would hide it with a napkin and walk over to where the rookies were sitting. Being the captain of the team, I can see the expression on their faces, you know, geez, why is the captain sitting with us? Usually we sit alone.

And I sat down and pulled the damn napkin off, and started to cut a piece of raw liver and put it in my mouth, and I crunch it, and let a little blood trickle down my chin. And these guys would look at me, I'm telling you, and their eyes, my God, they just said excuse me, and they all left. That night when they called home I bet they said, I don't know if I can make this team! One guy is crazy!

My greatest opponent is easy. That was Gino Marchetti, from the Baltimore Colts, who was also my teammate on the USF Dons team, the 1951 championship team we had. And there's no question about that. He was the greatest I'd ever played against over a period of time. Deacon Jones would come in second; I only got to play against him when he was just starting.

The greatest thing about Marchetti was his speed, and he had great feet. He moved side to side real well. He was very fast. He was as fast as a back for 40 yards. He could really move. He was a big man, but he was the one who gave me the most trouble. Of course, he gave everybody trouble. I didn't have as much trouble with anybody else as I did with him.

I really don't know who won those battles the most often. I probably have an advantage because I knew that . . . I cheated a lot. Well, holding him and stuff, and everything was legal in those days. I had to come up with these inventive ideas on how to stop him, and then my roommate wouldn't speak to me for a week.

My greatest teammate? That's an unfair question because I have such fond memories of all of them. The Million Dollar backfield. Bruno Banducci, my first guard who really helped me tremendously. You know, everybody, Bob Toneff, there's so many, R. C. Owens. We were just so close.

*Don Shula started his football career in the early '50s, playing as a cornerback and a running back for the Cleveland Browns and then the Baltimore Colts. But he made his mark on the game as a coach, guiding the Colts to a 73–26–4 mark and a berth in Super Bowl III. The pinnacle of his career came a few years later, when he avenged the sting of that initial loss to the Jets by guiding the Miami Dolphins to an undefeated season and then winning the Super Bowl against the Washington Redskins. When he retired in the late '90s, Shula had more career victories than any coach in NFL history (347), and he took a total of six teams to the Super Bowl before entering the Hall of Fame.*

OK, reflecting back, my greatest day had to be winning the Super Bowl, completing the 17–0 perfect season. The reason is that I had been 0–2 in my previous two Super Bowl appearances as a coach. The first one was the loss to the Jets, the embarrassing loss to the Jets. We were 17-point favorites and they won. Namath made the prediction that made him famous, and we were the team on the other end of the score. And that was tough to live with.

That was followed up by my second Super Bowl appearance with the Dolphins. Although we had a great year, we ended up playing poorly against Dallas in a Super Bowl in New Orleans. So that made my record 0–2 in Super Bowl appearances. The next year when we had the great team and the undefeated season, we were 16–0, and I was faced with the reality, the possibility that if we lose, 16–1, that the season is a complete failure and that I'm now 0–3 in Super Bowls. Wouldn't say very nice things about my coaching abilities.

So all of that led up to the Super Bowl, my third Super Bowl, and that's why winning made it so important. From a personal standpoint, I wanted to win the Super Bowl. From a team standpoint, I wanted to be the first team in the history of the National Football League that had gone undefeated. And as it turns out it hadn't been done before that, and it hasn't been done since then. It makes the accomplishment that much more important in my mind.

The first Super Bowl, we'd have our press conferences—this is Super Bowl III—we'd have our press conferences after practice in the lobby of the hotel. And there would be a few writers gathered around, and that was the media attention we got. And it built more after that to where it was in Los Angeles in that Super Bowl.

Yeah, it would be in the first Super Bowl that I coached, the families came in on a Friday night, and that was hectic because teams didn't know how to anticipate or control these situations, and it was hectic. The players were distracted from their preparation with all of their friends and relatives coming in and looking for accommodations and tickets and all of the things that go with it. Now, all teams are much more organized, and they have special departments that just take care of situations like that.

Against Washington, George Allen was coaching the Redskins, and he was a very thorough coach, and we knew that he was going to be doing everything he could to get his team ready. We wanted to do everything we could and more to make sure that our preparation was the best. We knew that he spent time and sent people to study how the sun was going to set over the stadium, the Coliseum in Los Angeles, and where the shadows were going to be at different parts of the game. And that's something that we were interested in also, because that could affect what goal you want to defend.

We felt that we were strong in all areas. Our biggest strength was ball control on offense. We just . . . in many games that year we'd win the toss, get the ball, have an eight- or nine-minute drive, score a touchdown, go ahead 7–0, our defense would hold them, their offense would be three-and out, and we'd get the ball and repeat. When the first quarter was over we were ahead 14–0 and the other team had the ball for three or six plays. Our time of possessions was just a real trademark of that football team.

The other trademark was once we got down near the goal line, we didn't settle for field goals. We invariably had the answers and came up with the touchdown, either with Csonka bullying over for the touchdown, or the play-action pass with Griese hitting Warfield.

We certainly weren't going to go away from the things that got us there. We just had such a well-rounded football team, we felt that if we played our game, we'd be tough to beat. So we had that ball control and that time of possession, and that made it tough on other teams' offenses.

The stadium . . . there was an excitement and adrenaline flow, a nervousness that comes from getting ready for the big game, and it was accentuated on my part because of my past experiences being 0–2 in the Super Bowl. The dreaded thought of not winning the big game. Getting to the stadium and the time before—Super Bowl Sunday is such a huge, unique time because of the excitement, the experiences, the adrenaline that goes with such a big game.

And you don't have to worry about your team being ready,

because they sense the importance of the ball game and know how hard you've worked to get there. And especially our football team, having been there the year before and going away with a negative experience. That's when you realize that there's only one winner. In the time leading up to the Super Bowl, both teams are treated exactly the same, given the same amount of press coverage, and talked about in glowing terms. But after the game, there's only one team that's talked about and that's the winner. We wanted to make sure that this second time around we were going to be the winner.

We knew that we were a very good football team because we'd been to the Super Bowl the year before, and although it was a negative experience, we still felt we were a very good team, and then we proved it through the year by not losing any ball games. So we had that sense of confidence that we knew that if we played our game that we were going to be the winners.

We dominated the ball game. We're ahead 14–0 and it could have been 21–0. We had a touchdown called back. We had a touchdown pass to Warfield called back. And that would have put us ahead 21–0, but with a 14–0 lead I decided late in the ball game I would go for the field goal to put the game totally out of reach and make it 17–0 with . . . you can check the time with the minutes remaining.

And instead of us kicking a field goal to make it 17–0, that's when Garo's famous . . . I've called it many things right after it happened. Then the realization that after playing so well that the Redskins were back in the game 14–7. Fortunately, we got the ball and kept it, and that ended the threat of them being able to take it to overtime.

It was a bizarre play, it's hard to believe it could ever happen in a professional football game. It was just such a shock, and I think all of us on the sidelines, when it happened realized the magnitude of the play, and that the Redskins, who hadn't done anything the whole ball game, were back with a chance to tie. So immediately, we had to keep that from happening. All of my concentration and attention was on doing that. Looking for the onside kick, and then getting the ball and making some first downs to run out the clock. It wasn't panic, it was more a feeling of embarrassment to know that we had let them back into the ball game by just a poor play on our part.

The realization that we had done something no other team had ever done, to go undefeated, and that pride was what took over, and also personally the satisfaction of finally winning a Super Bowl in my third attempt, which was very, very big in my career. Looking back, I still would have hated to be 0–3 in Super Bowls.

It was just total . . . it was probably even more satisfying to us because we had been through it the other end the year before. Getting there and not winning and knowing the feeling of being in the loser's locker room. That's what made winning so important to us and the satisfaction of winning that much more enjoyable. We had a party that night; a party was planned and all of the friends and relatives showed up, and it was just an evening that you'll always remember.

When I reflect back, that was a very businesslike team. It was a very intelligent football team, and we were sometimes characterized as a team that was not an exciting team because of the way that we dominated games. We took pride in that approach. It was a very professional approach, and it was a very thorough approach as to how to win a football game.

That's what I tried to convey to you, that sense of relief. I not only was proud and happy to be the coach of the first undefeated team and up to now the only undefeated team, but also a coach now that had finally won the big game. You could win a lot of games and have the most victories, which I have, but those things wouldn't be as near important to me as they are now if I hadn't have won that Super Bowl and been the coach in the Super Bowl in the perfect season.

Of course, afterwards, when you realize that you know you are the first team that has gone undefeated, and then through the years each year that team is . . . the accomplishments of that team are relived. Because anytime a team looks like they might have a chance of running the table or going undefeated, the conversation immediately goes back to our team. We are resurrected every year until somebody gets beat.

The Bears in '85, first of all, were a great football team, and if we hadn't upset them in that Monday-night game, they could have conceivably been an undefeated team—they were that good. But we dominated that night, and, again, that makes that accomplishment more important in my reflections of my coaching career. And of course Denver two years ago. They were 13–0 and they really looked strong. Elway and Terrell Davis and the defense, and Shanahan the coach—everything was pointed to them possibly being able to win them all. And then of course they were upset by the Giants and then the Dolphins beat them the next week.

Well, going into the Hall is the ultimate recognition of a career, and that's something that everybody would like to . . . I don't want to say everybody. It's certainly something I cherish, because it's the final recognition or the stamp on your coaching career. So that was, of course, a very, very big day for me. It didn't really have the same importance to me as winning the Super Bowl and being the coach of the only undefeated Super Bowl season.

If I could relive one, it would be that [Super Bowl]. And of course the next would be the final recognition. But that final recognition comes in large part because of the accomplishments, which were the undefeated season, the perfect season, and the Super Bowl win.

My greatest day as a player? You know, I played seven years and had twenty-one career interceptions, but the interception I remember most was when it was called back against the Bears in the game that Dub Jones had six touchdowns, and I had the seventh touchdown in that game. It was a 96-yard interception return for a touchdown and it was called back because of a roughing-the-passer penalty. I think at that time it would be and might still be the longest interception of a touchdown in Cleveland Browns history. That was 1951. My reaction was one of total anger and disgust, and when I got to the end zone and I saw the flag, I walked all the way back to where the flag was thrown, realizing what a great play had been taken away from me.

I think when I was a rookie with the Browns, Tommy James was the starting corner and he got hurt and I was the only rookie to make the team. Tommy James got hurt and I went on and played the rest of the year until we got into the championship game.

My greatest day in college was the Syracuse game. I don't know if you're familiar with this, but we scheduled Syracuse in Cleveland Stadium, and Paul Brown and his entire coaching staff were there to look at Syracuse players. Although we grew up and John Carroll [the college Shula attended] was right in the Cleveland Browns' backyard, nobody expected us to win. We were a very small school and the headlines in the Syracuse paper when the game was scheduled was, "Syracuse schedules John Carroll . . . Who is John Carroll?"

And they came to play in Cleveland Stadium and we beat them and I got drafted. I had 125 yards rushing that night against Syracuse, and my teammate Carl Taseff had a big night. We both got drafted by the Browns. That was amazing, two guys from a small school both being drafted by the Browns. The Syracuse defense had Carl Carrolelis, Jim Ringo played for them. Ben Schwartzwalder was the coach. They were a big-time football team, and of course, we were just a small college that played a pretty good schedule. We played Xavier and Toledo and Bowling Green and teams like that.

I would have to say, looking back, the greatest coach I coached against was Lombardi. I had the opportunity to coach against Halas, and then Lombardi later, and Chuck Noll, who won four Super Bowls, but Lombardi at that one stage was the one that was winning all the games.

When I think about coaching against a player, I think about Butkus. I think he had to be the greatest defensive player I coached against. And then the greatest player I ever coached, it's just so hard, because now you've got Marino who's broken all the records and Unitas, a Hall of Fame quarterback, and Griese, a Hall of Fame quarterback, Csonka, a Hall of Famer. Along with Butkus, you can also say Namath in that one big game, the Super Bowl upset.

The best teammate? Gino Marchetti, when I first went up, was a guy that revolutionized how to rush the passer—Hall of Fame pass rusher. The other guy . . . Otto Graham, offensively.

And then playing against . . . that's going way back. When I first broke in, the Rams had Waterfield and Van Brocklin, and Tom Pierce and Elroy Hirsch. They were pretty good players.

# Bart Starr

*The championship game in 1958 between the Giants and the Colts may have put football on the map, but it was Green Bay's great run in the '60s that cemented the sport's reputation. The defining moment of the decade, of course, was the Ice Bowl, which took place on December 31, 1967, when the Packers beat the Dallas Cowboys 21–17 in subzero temperatures to become the first team in pro football history to win three consecutive championships. Here, Bart Starr narrates his greatest day, from the crucial pass to Chuck Mercein on the final drive to the quarterback sneak that has become one of the most familiar replays in NFL history.*

That's difficult to pick just one, for obvious reasons. If I were limited to just one, I would pick the Ice Bowl, the reason being it enabled us to win three consecutive championships, something no other team had ever done. And, additionally, that year was a very demanding, taxing year on us. We had a number of injuries. Everybody wanted a little extra piece of us that year because of our past championships and the fact that we were going for three consecutive ones. That just primed everyone to literally be at their best all year long. The combination of the two took its toll. We were a very tired team after the Ice Bowl was over.

Actually, we were healthy going into the Ice Bowl, even though it was a very demanding year for us. But we were very excited and challenged by the opportunity of winning three consecutive championships, and I picked that particular game because of what it meant to us. No other team had ever done that, no other team has done it since. All of us wear that particular championship ring for that reason. All those who were there at that time.

It was a very, very meaningful game. I've had tremendous respect as I've reflected on it over the years for the Cowboys and how well they played under such brutal conditions. I think that the key to the game was the team, the total team strength, which we had, and experience. The Cowboys were an outstanding team and they played well the year before in the championship in Dallas. But I think we simply had more team experience than they did and that ultimately was the defining factor.

We didn't change that much [in our game plan for the weather], we just had to be aware of some of the things that we were doing relative to the conditions as it went forward. It's ironic, because the day before when we had our pregame workout on Saturday, it was cold. I think the high that day was 0 degrees. It was very cold, but the field was in excellent condition for that time of year. But as you know, it simply went down from that and became colder during the night and that heating system apparently couldn't handle it, so the ground was becoming harder by the hour from then on.

Started out it was decent, but as the game progressed the ground conditions were poorer, so you had to be aware of certain things that you were doing. Your double-type move on routes and things like that had to be certainly factored in, and certain running plays, but generally speaking, we didn't make that many adjustments. We just tried to execute our game plan as best we could, and went about things as we normally do.

We had great respect for the Cowboys, as I said, because they had an outstanding team. We saw it the year before. They had turned around and repeated and had come back. It's just that the conditions were so brutal it affected everybody. In fact, I remember before the ball game, some person saying to [Max] McGee about how tough this was going to be on the Cowboys, and his response was, and I'm paraphrasing, "The Cowboys? It's going to be tough on everyone." He was exactly correct because, unless you were there, it's very, very difficult to state and to have someone understand how brutally cold it was.

We obviously started out in good shape. The game then was evened up, brought back to even by the Cowboys' play, and so we go into the final quarter and the game is in their favor. And the last drive was a great example of the team structure, which we had. I remember stepping into the huddle as though it were yesterday, and looking into the eyes of our players, my teammates, and I was about to say something and I could see in their eyes I didn't need to say anything. They knew exactly what we had to do. And so nothing was said, we just called the first play and started the drive.

I thought the greatest play I ever called was at a time when we really needed something like this, and I thought the timing was such that it was the right thing to do. All the way back to the huddle about halfway into the drive I asked Bob Skoronski if he could cut off their defensive right end if I ran this play and he said "yes." And so I called a play to Chuck Mercein that was just called a "31 give."

George Andre was the defensive end. And you'd have to look at a diagram of how the defensive lineman of the Cowboys was there in order to appreciate this, because the tackle

is well up tight on our left guard and inside and Andre backed
off the line of scrimmage and almost head-up with Skoronski
so that he can cover to the inside when this tackle chases our
guard if a guard pulls. It's a very, very good strong defensive
system, which Coach Landry had developed against a particular formation.

Well, we run the play. When he said yes, he could, I called
the play, our left guard pulls and [Bob] Lilly, he chases at
such an angle it created a great hole in there. And Bob gets
his block on Andre and Mercein runs right up the field, and
I think if the footing had been better he might have run for a
score. It turned out to be exactly what we thought it would
be and I'm grateful that we had the play there in reserve and
used it at that time, and grateful to Bob that he made the
block that he did.

Typically, when I asked him if he could get that block, he
would've told me if the footing was such that he couldn't get
there to make it. In a situation like that, that particular play
absolutely demanded a crucial block by a person, because
you're just letting one other player just move and flow to your
movement in order to open the hole there in the first place.
But, at any rate, Skoronski did a great job and the play got
us down in great position. He made it, and the rest is history.
Mercein runs it down and puts us in position to score.

I don't think we had any moments of doubt. I think what
we were disappointed in is that I fumbled the ball and gave
them a turnover, and Willie Wood fumbled and gave them a
turnover. You can't commit crucial turnovers like that in a
ball game of that magnitude. I was sacked and I fumbled the
ball in the process, turning and twisting, and those were the
only I think big disappointments that we had—that we turned
that ball over like that. In a game like that, as I said, it's
absolutely imperative that you not do that.

Our lead play in a goal-line situation like that was called a
"wedge play," and we had run it down on the goal line twice

with Donny Anderson carrying the ball, and he couldn't get his footing to get in there and was slipping and sliding. The ground down there was very hard because the scoreboard at the south end of the field had cast a giant shadow on the field for some time, and I think that made it even harder.

So it was very, very slick, and after the second one was run I took our final time-out, and I asked the linemen if they could get their footing for one more wedge play and they said "yes." And so I ran to the sidelines and mentioned to Coach Lombardi that there was nothing wrong with the play, the backs couldn't get to the line of scrimmage, they were sliding in an effort to get there and slipping. I said, "The linemen said they can get their footing to run it," and I said, "Coach, I can sneak it in because I'm upright, I can shuffle my feet and lunge in." And you've heard this, I'm sure, in the past, but typically Coach Lombardi, at a crucial time like this—and it is brutally cold at this point in the game—all he said was, "Run it and let's get the hell out of here."

We had the ultimate confidence in the play—it was getting someone to the line of scrimmage and to the hole when it was open to get it in there. And so that's how we chose to go with that. I didn't think about anything except scoring. That's all I had on my mind. And they blocked it and they did a great job with it.

Well, it hit me immediately because when I ran the play into the end zone and then scored, I just felt that the drive had accomplished exactly what we needed to do, and that was score the touchdown. And we were obviously very thrilled, and we kicked the extra point and they got it one more quick time and the game's over.

We rapidly tried to thaw out. I was thrilled to get inside. What an exciting time, because you've seen the photos of people all over the stadium tearing the goalposts down. It was just the climax to a very, very rewarding year of effort, and all of us were just beyond words, thrilled and excited.

We ate dinner that night with teammates. We thawed out after a while. [Getting around] was not that big a problem because there wasn't that much snow, it was just cold. There was snow certainly, but not to the degree that you couldn't get around. Up there they—to the credit of the state of Wisconsin, I think the farther north you go in the state the better they remove snow. So that is not a problem, it's just cold.

[What sticks out is] the awareness of the great people that were part of your organization and your team. We truly had some exceptionally devoted, committed, special people. When we meet today, we don't shake hands, we hug. That was the kind of team we had under Coach Lombardi and his staff, and we had built. And I can just remember the numbers of hugs that we had with one another after the ball game and how exciting it was. It's just so rewarding, it's very, very difficult, literally, to put it in just a few words.

Obviously our other championship games were very, very meaningful. Anytime you win a championship game for the first time, it's such an exhilarating feeling, and it is hard to describe. But then to have come back and won two after that, so that we had three in a row. We won five in seven years and we're very, very honored and grateful and humbled by that. But to win three consecutive ones and going through what I explained to you earlier about the trials of that third consecutive year, it made it so special it's hard to describe.

If I had to pick one, I would pick that one, but the other ones, they're right there paralleling it. They're hardly a step behind it, and I'm grateful for being a member of a wonderful team, an organization that was a part of all those things, too.

When you're inducted in the Hall of Fame, I think the greatest feeling or piece of appreciation that a player would have is to recognize how his teammates helped him get there, and the value of that. I'm there because of great teammates, it's that simple.

My greatest college day? Good question. I guess it was being a freshman on a team [Ed. note: Alabama], which had a super, colossal, successful day against Syracuse in the Orange Bowl in 1953.

Gosh, there's not a lot to say. As a freshman I was a backup quarterback, so I sat there and admired the play of the ones who were playing in front of us for a lot of the game. We got a chance to play in the second half because they had run up a lot of points and I'd never been in a situation or atmosphere like that before, so it was a great thrill.

One of our receivers was setting a record for number of receptions in the Orange Bowl at that time, and I don't recall the exact number nor how it was stated. I'm trying to remember [who it was]—I don't even remember now. You might look it up. I want to say his name was Joe Cummings, but I'm not sure. On second thought I think it was someone else. He was a senior and I don't remember his name.

Anyway, they were asking us to throw him a couple more passes so he could get that, and we'd thrown a couple and he dropped them. He came back to the huddle and I said, "Will you please catch one and get this over with?" It was really funny. It was obviously a great thrill for a freshman, in his initial year there with the team and inexperienced. You're in awe when you get into a situation like that.

I would put it back to the team concept, because here I was a freshman and part of a great organization there, a wonderfully strong team which had earned the right to go and play in the Orange Bowl. I had looked to the sophomores and the juniors and the seniors for guidance and leadership throughout that year and had developed some great relationships with the upperclassmen. In fact a couple remain very close today, because they befriended this nervous young freshman when I reported that fall. So I'll always remember all of them, but particularly those couple, three or four teammates.

Well, three of my closest friends coming out of that team were Tommy Lewis, and Harry Lee, and a fellow named Hootie Ingram. There were others with whom we were very close, but if I were limited to two or three picks I would certainly name those guys because they were the ones who had befriended me more as an older brother when I reported there, and it was a very special relationship.

You're posing great questions, you really are, and they're difficult to answer because you have so many memories of the experiences. And again, unless you've been there and you've experienced the relationships that are developed between people, it's tough to narrow them down. I think what I'll always remember most about the days at Green Bay, in this order, are the arrival of Coach Lombardi, the staff that he assembled, how he brought this group of men together. We had some very good players.

To the Packers' credit, they made some good draft choices. What we lacked was leadership and Coach Lombardi provided that the day he walked in the door. And that's what I remember most about it, because he was such an exceptional leader and was able to bring us together in a way that we created a team whose record speaks for itself. I'd like to leave it that way, because I think that's the best way you do something, is you do it through performance. In my opinion that's always been the greatest form of leadership is through example.

Obviously the situation may be duplicated again. I just think it'd be a long time before it happens again. It's such a thrilling period in your life that you are so grateful for and honored by, you feel richly, richly blessed just to have been there and been a member of it.

There's one other thing that I'd like to mention if I may. My wife and I just celebrated our forty-sixth wedding anniversary, and the greatest years of our lives were spent in Green Bay, Wisconsin, with our sons and our family and our friends. It is a fabulous place to raise a family and it will always be our adopted home, and I think that needs to be stated too about the community, because, unless you live there, not played there, you really can't begin to appreciate what a special place it is. Perhaps you do get a little smarter as you get older, as you reflect on it. It was, it was just truly special.

I would like to mention one other name, when you asked me about names in college. Another one of those who was very nice to me and like an older brother, so to speak, was a fellow named Dan Law. I'll always remember those people for that because I think each of us—you do every day in your life, I do today—we have the chance to impact on the life of someone else by how we conduct ourselves with that person, and those guys were just superb to me. You don't hear enough about those, when people are helping someone else. And that's how I'd like to leave it.

*For most kickers, the ultimate moment usually boils down to the game winner, a pressure kick with little or no time on the clock and everything on the line. But Jan Stenerud was more than just a great pressure kicker—the Hall of Famer was a pioneer, one of the first soccer-style kickers to enter the game in the 1960s and an integral part of Kansas City's ability to dominate opponents using a field-position game that combined his stellar kicking with a great defense and a ground-control offense. Stenerud's ultimate day came during the Chiefs' Super Bowl win in 1970, when he kicked three field goals and kept the Vikings pinned in their half of the field as Kansas City bested Minnesota by a score of 23–14.*

I would pick the Super Bowl, because of the magnitude of the game. I can still remember when I looked at Alan Page at the coin-toss ceremonies at the Super Bowl.

I can remember in those days, you kicked from the 40 yard line. So, in the opening kickoff, the ball sails well out of the end zone. And they start deep in the hole. They move far to get close enough for a field goal, but they don't try it. And we get the ball and I kick a 48-yard field goal, which cleared pretty good. And I kicked the next ball out of the end zone.

And [Page] said at the press conference, when I kicked the field goal from midfield and kicked the kickoff clearly out of the park that the defense felt like they were playing on a 50-yard field. Now that is self-serving to say those things. I remember Carl Eller said that after the game, too. So that was important. I kicked another couple of field goals, that made it 9–0, and so there's no question that I was a significant part of the outcome, but it sounds selfish to talk that way.

It was a significant day for me, there's no question about that, and there is no question that it helped us win. Then if I talk through it, the other ones will came to mind. In mud, it was probably more difficult up in Milwaukee with the Packers playing against the Buffalo Bills and we won the game, and it was a more difficult thing that I did that day, but that was a regular-season game, it wasn't a Super Bowl game. It was a thrill to maybe tell the coach, Look, there'll be a 53- or 54-yard field goal and I'm forty-two years old, and there's seven seconds left, time for a play but let's not do it, I can make it—and then go in and kick it.

And then John McKay, who didn't want to look at me when I was down in Tampa in 1980, he hired [Garo] Yepremian instead of me, and I knew that I could kick ten yards further than him at the time. And he didn't come out and look at me, and every time we played against Tampa Bay, I had to kick more field goals, the last-second field goals to beat him. And then in Minnesota, the same division, I remember on the way home, he resigned effective at the end of the season. So that was thrilling for me, but it doesn't have an impact, so the more I talk about this, it has to be Super Bowl IV.

I know that Minnesota was favored anyway by 12–14 points, and we knew we were good, but I also remember leading up to the game all my thoughts were, I don't care how I do as long as we win. That's the only thing that went through my mind. That's how every player felt in those days. As long as we win, it doesn't matter what I do. You want to do a good job, but you don't look at your own stats. The only stat that counted was the final score.

We played down in New Orleans, and it was a cold day. The temperature was in the forties. It was rainy and cold the night before, and there were holes in the tarp. I know two of my field goals were kicked out of mud holes. I do remember the pregame, I was horrible. It was blustery and windy and I was probably excited and nervous and it scared me how bad I was, so that made me concentrate even more in the game. But also they allowed so many people on the field pregame. They had NFL films all over the place, there were television cameras all over the field, so it was kind of a strange circus thing.

I remember lining up for the opening kickoff, I thought, I can't be overanxious and top the ball, I've got to hit it clean and hard, which I did, which I was supposed to do. And I kicked it out of the end zone, and then when I kicked my 48-yard field goal I didn't think the distance was no problem whatsoever. It was an easy kick from a distance standpoint. And then the next one out of the end zone, then the second or third field goal—I think they were both in the second quarter, I'm not even sure. They were both out of mud holes, so I was very concerned about my footing. The only thing I could do, I put the longest fleece I could find on my left foot, for footing, because they knew in the pregame there were a lot of muddy spots on the field. It was blustery and windy that day.

I don't think there was any extra pressure in that game, because when you look at pro football in the late '60s, we went through a period, in my opinion, where there were a lot of low-scoring games. The defenses dominated football in those days, and if you had a good defense and a good kicking game, you had a good chance. And I think every football rule that's been changed lately—and of course they make changes all the time—it was to enhance the offense in football and give them a better chance to score. Which is probably true for most football fans from an entertainment standpoint, it probably has increased.

That season I think I kicked nearly thirty field goals in fourteen games, and we didn't have a high-scoring team. I know we won two games where I kicked five field goals per game. I thought I'd get an opportunity. It was a matter of getting it down.

I was able to be so intense that day. Regardless if I was going to be doing poorly or well, it wouldn't affect me one way or the other. I said, oh, good, great kick, but I wasn't relaxed for one second. I was totally determined the whole day long, didn't matter what the circumstances were.

Because, I remember the great old actor, Pat O'Brian was on the sidelines and he asked me for my warm-up, my little raincoat, kind of a windbreaker-type warm-up. And I gave it to him right after the game. But he asked me with two minutes to go, and the score was 23–7 then. The game was over, and I said, You've got to wait till the game is over. I had walked away from him. There was no way that anybody or anything could distract me that day. That's how intense I was on concentrating the whole time, no ups or downs, staying in the focus.

As a kicker, I am a spectator, but by the same token, if we had a turnover, I can't stand there screaming and yelling, jump up and down, you know, putting my head down if we fumble the ball or whatever. I'm well aware of what's going on in the game, but I never get caught up in anything. But I knew we were very good. The Minnesota Vikings were very good. I knew we were tremendously well prepared to play and that we had many talented people.

I did have a sense of the flow of the game, but it's like a golfer, I guess. You've got to stay level. You cannot enjoy the good things as much as you like to, nor can you let adversity get you too bad. And I tried to stay that way during the game and stay that way during the season, during the week. Which means you don't get quite as much enjoyment out of the game as you should perhaps.

Lenny [Dawson] held for me during the field goals, and I could hear his reaction. He said, that's it, great. I knew that I was doing my job, but so was everybody else. So it was just kind of a satisfying feeling, but don't let yourself for a minute think that you're so great, or the next kick—who knows what's going to happen?

I was only in my third year, and I felt relief and a lot of elation when the game was over. But I remember thinking more in terms of how tremendous it would be for people like Lenny or Jerry Mays and Ed Budde, Fred Arbanas and Buck Buchanan and Bobby Bell. They could have gone to the other league. They were good enough to play anywhere. And they had a choice, and also a couple had been turned down by the other league, too. And then to play for the AFL and for our team to win the Super Bowl

Because I was thinking, as happy as I was about winning, I remember thinking a lot about how much a tremendous satisfaction it was for them, who really had a choice, and also a couple of those had been turned down by the other league. For them to dominate the game and win, I felt they must be like, it can't get any better than that. That's how I felt, I think, and more so for them than for myself.

Keep in mind that they were favored. I mean, we respected them, but we had a pretty quiet confidence, we knew we were good, too. That is the only time I can remember, in nineteen years of pro football, before and after, that I was aware of the point spread. We thought it was crazy—we felt a very good chance going into the game. The Jets had won the Super

Bowl the year before, and they scored six points against us in Shea Stadium in the playoff game, they had a great offense. Oakland scored seven points against us in Oakland, so I think most of us felt, yeah, the Vikings are good, but can they score any more than those other two teams did against us?

Well, in the locker room afterward people were running around, hugging each other, everybody loved each other, we win the big game and we were a close team anyway and it was a tremendous satisfaction. And we went down to—I can't remember what hotel—and we had a team party, in a hotel down in the French Quarter, we had a team party. Of course we stayed up, and walked—Bourbon Street was just a little bit cleaner then than now. There were more nightclubs for jazz music and jazz bands playing. So I think it was just basically bouncing from one to the other.

I think what I remember the most is the Kansas City fans, the people who were down there walking around with us. They were part of us, they were the businessman-type of a fan, and that sounds bad because I'm going to knock some of today's fans, they are kind of tattoo-ish types.

There were people that we knew, lawyers and businessmen we knew that had come down to watch the game that we had known, because the business community was involved. When the Chiefs moved to town, some of the business leaders were involved in getting their people and their companies to sell season tickets. These were very much respected businessmen that we had gotten to know that were down there. So it was fun to see them and to share it with them as well as teammates. I remember a lot of them, too, were walking around French Quarter at night, because all of us in those days worked in the off season and these were businessmen that most of us had met.

I worked at a bank the first five, six years in Kansas City. So did a lot of my teammates, because they worked in the insurance business or whatever they were involved in, so they knew a lot of the businessmen in Kansas City. A lot of them were down there, actually, for the game.

For the ring ceremonies, by the way, we got those in the mail in the summertime. With a little note from Hank [Stram] that says, Congratulations, we're world champs, take care of yourself with class and dignity, or something to that extent.

Hank did a lot for my confidence, I think. He made me think that I was pretty good. Just always encouraging me and patting me on the back when things were going well. I think he gave me the feeling that he thought I was as good as anybody. He knew I took the misses hard, I think, and he would encourage me even then because I think he felt I was a person that had felt responsible for things. I can't recall him ever really getting on me.

I do have some individual games. I do remember getting a thrill up in Minnesota when I was about forty. It was in 1984, I was almost forty-two years old. I was ankle-deep in mud on the infield that hadn't been sodded because it'd rained all morning. I can remember telling Les Steckel, when he was the coach up in Minnesota in my next-to-last year, we were losing on third down. I had to go in and start running another play, and I said—I had a 54-yard attempt—I can make it, which I didn't know for sure, but I made it and we won the game.

That was only time I called it, because you're not 100 percent sure if you're going to make it. Things can happen. It can be a little bit poor timing of the snap or the hold may be wrong. You can mishit it.

So that was fun, but oh, gosh, I had to dig into this for a long time to really dig up some of these games. Frankly, I don't remember a heck of a lot of them. In Kansas City, early 1969, five field goals against the Buffalo Bills on a cold December day, and some of them were long, a couple around 50-yard range, because in those days it was a bonus when you made a 50-yard kick.

I just talked to somebody on the phone not so long ago,

and they were talking about the difference between kicking now and thirty years ago. A lot of the reason the kickers are so much better today, first of all they are talented as a group, you kick in better conditions, most of the time the footing is usually pretty good, you kick from eight yards back instead of seven, so the balls aren't blocked as many times. You don't have as many 59-yard attempts into the wind, because if you did that, then the ball went to the 20 yard line.

But the biggest difference is, nowadays you can kick with a center or a holder thirty or forty kicks, at least four or five days a week, where we kicked maybe a half dozen kicks a week. So many quality reps, because I went through that. I kicked less than 70 percent when I had my most talent in my early years. Then I kicked well over 80 percent up in Green Bay in the '80s. And that is because of those reasons I gave you, but the main reason is you practice so much more with the same center and holder.

In the late '70s, they started hiring special-teams coaches and they'd give you things to do. And then you start getting the punters who became holders. He had time to stand out there a half hour everyday and kick field goals with you.

I think Hank was my best special-teams coach, truly outstanding. He knew everything. The only thing we didn't do, we didn't have the reps because we were in Kansas City. We were probably doing as well as anybody else, or at least as well in those days. They did have a routine, you know. I kicked on my own across the one practice field, head to the end zone, put the ball in the grass and kick it across the other side, ran over and kicked it back all alone. But at the end of practice a couple of times a week, we tried a few field goals, the center and the holder, that was it.

Whereas later, you kicked thirty–forty kicks at least four days a week with the same center and same holder. That's the biggest difference. That's why my stats are a lot better when I was forty years old, because I wasn't nearly as talented.

I didn't learn to prepare for pressure until late in my career, and I kind of figured it out on my own. I remember in Green Bay, it was Bart Starr's last season or my last season, 1983. We kicked field goals for five games that were won in overtime or in the last play of the game. And we never failed.

I didn't know until about my fifteenth year in the league, to prepare myself mentally. Early in my career I kind of got by on some talent and I kind of winged it, but late in my career, all season long, I would tell myself every day in practice, or sitting in my car or sometimes at home, trying to get the situation in my mind, that the game is close, that we're either tied or one or two points down. You make it feel like you feel on the sideline in a close game and expecting the coach to say, OK, field-goal team. Try to go over that situation, maybe 100 times in my mind during the week.

So then, what happened on Sunday, you were not in a state of shock, you'd gone through it. Still, a little different when it counts for real, but at least that was how I prepared myself the last five or six years.

I didn't prepare myself that way early on. You either make it or you didn't, and I didn't prepare myself as well. By that time, I knew how to do that, but I figured it out on my own. When I tell young kids now, you know, the good kickers, kicking in the NFL, it's not necessarily fun, because to be good at it, you've got to put this pressure on yourself even all day during the week and go through this stuff. And that's what you have to do.

In Green Bay, it was very difficult, the conditions. First of all, you go on the field before the game the minute the bus gets to the stadium, check out the field conditions. Then the only thing you can do really is adjust your cleats, and that still doesn't help. You've still got to find a way to adjust your swing or your kick. And you had to do that in Green Bay.

Ideally you like to kick a 25-yard field goal as hard as you kick a 50-yard field goal, but when the conditions are bad you've got to just find a way. So you had to make adjustments. You don't kick as hard, you don't plant as hard, you kind of more tiptoe into it instead of doing your normal stuff because the field dictates that you won't have the footing. It becomes more difficult.

I always stayed in pretty good shape. I ran a lot, ran the stadium steps. I was in good shape. That's the only thing you can do.

I pick the Super Bowl because, when you win the Super Bowl, it's more fun to share good times with people than to do it alone, so to speak. You can share it with all of your teammates and the whole city. Whereas, you go into the Hall of Fame, the only people that really share it with you, maybe you and your family. It's like going to a big party. It seems like more people enjoy each other's company and celebrate with people, instead of celebrating alone, that's all. So from a satisfaction point of view, the Hall of Fame gave me every bit as much satisfaction, but it's more fun to celebrate an event with a lot of people.

I never thought of myself as a pioneer, but I knew what was going to happen, because people like myself that actually come to this country on a skiing scholarship, and end up kicking in the Super Bowl. You see a couple of other people who are foreign-born, you know darn good and well that some parents are going to say, see these kids, they come from another part of the world, they didn't play football, they're in the NFL or the AFL. So I'm sure they encouraged the kids. Also, even then, millions of people playing soccer, you knew that was going to happen. No question about that. But I didn't look at myself as a pioneer. I was just busy trying to survive.

I kicked in college in my senior year, and my greatest day still remains a 59-yard field goal. It actually opened the scoring. It was in a game against the Montana State. It was my senior year, my first year playing football, and we played against the Grizzlies, it was a windy day. And Jim Sweeney, who later became the head coach at Fresno for many years, he was the coach at Montana, he put me in for a 59-yard field goal, and it clears by at least 10 yards, but the wind is blowing pretty hard.

And the next kickoff, the other team sends the guy right after my knees, so I'm like a matador out there trying to avoid this guy, but I can see my kickoff actually sail over the end-zone seats, which was over 90 yards in the air. But that was also up in Montana where you have altitude, and the college football goes a little more than the pro football anyway.

And that turned out to be—we didn't find out until almost a week later—I think the headlines were in the Bozeman paper the following Friday, "Bobcat Kicker sets NCAA Record." That was the longest kick in the history of football, pro football as well as collegiate football. So that game—and Montana State against Montana, believe it or not, that ranks with the Auburn-Alabama game down in Alabama, you see—so that's the biggest game of the year. There were probably about eight or nine thousand people there.

We won 24–7. But it was not a big impact, but see how it goes thirty years later. People come up to me and say, I remember that 59-yard field goal when you beat the Grizzlies in the last play of the game. That's how history changes it. It was not the last play of the game. It was in the middle of the first quarter which made it 3–0, but that's how time can change things.

It was kind of a big surprise, but see, I'd kick off into the seats all the time. And so I got the feeling, maybe I didn't know any better. I got a feeling that they enjoyed even the kickoff, because I kicked to the goal, and so most of them were never fielded. It went over the end zone seats. So the crowd roared a little bit. It was kind of a phenomenon at the time, I suppose, but boy, there's a lot involved in going 100 yards. You just don't think it was real.

It was cold and miserable, it was, and I wasn't aware of

anything else. You grow up in Minnesota here, that's how it is, that's how the winters are and you live in it and you enjoy it and you do the best you can in it. Now when I go out on those fields I think, how the hell did I kick on this? But that's the way it was, and you did it.

*The physical and mental toughness of the Green Bay Packers came through at many different levels and positions—throughout the defense, in the precision blocking schemes of the undersized offensive line, and through the methodical, surgically precise play calling of Bart Starr. But when the Packers needed tough yardage, they called on the man who in many ways was the heart and soul of the NFL's greatest dynasty: Hall of Fame fullback Jim Taylor.*

The Packers? That's your goal, and you hope to get an opportunity to get drafted, or have an opportunity to play professional football. I didn't really know where Green Bay was. I tell you, I knew Abner Wembley, one of the assistant coaches at LSU, had played there, or been up there in some of his professional career. And so he had probably put in a good word in the scouting, and so I was drafted number two behind Dan Currie, who was number one. I was number two, and I think Nitschke was number three and Jerry Kramer was number four. The year before was the last of the bonus picks, when they'd let the worst team in the league get a bonus pick, and this is when Ron Kramer and Paul Hornung were picked.

The team started to look like an influx of personnel, because the year Hornung came out they won two ball games out of twelve. My rookie year we won one of ten and tied one. That was the worst in Packer history. It was Blackbourn who coached with Hornung, and then Scooter McLean from Detroit or somewhere distant, and he coached the one year, and then Lombardi came the next year.

Well, he comes in, and he kind of knew—he was an assistant for many years—knew what he wanted to do and knew how he wanted the setup to be for championship-caliber football. He tried to be very simple and have a minimum of rules and not a whole lot of plays, and he was a very strong disciplinarian. It was like a love/hate relationship with the players, that type of approach, kind of like a fatherly type or motivator, and some of the players after a year or two, they left. They didn't accept his type of approach. And I know a couple of players retired or were traded, this type of thing, so you knew where you stood. There wasn't any guesswork. You knew what page you was on.

It was like, he was a very strong motivator, and he would motivate Bart Starr with a little lower temperament because of his personality. Myself or Fuzzy Thurston or Jerry Kramer and other players, he could motivate and fire up by threatening you, and knowing you and cussing you and intimidating you, this type of approach. You couldn't do this to Bart or to other different temperamental types or personality.

So what he did was to figure out and know—his was kind of like a psychologist-type approach. Let's just take as an example, the twenty-two players. The black players, and Willie Wood and Herb Adderley and Willie Davis and things, color was no barrier. He was consistent with everybody. Not prejudiced and not partial or any of that. This is what you admired about him. I don't know if you've read or heard some of these things from other articles and from other players, if you've interviewed some of them.

Well, it came down to a couple of championship games, I guess. I felt good or bad or made a play or two that may have altered part of the outcome. I think the game in Cleveland, I think a couple of people had mentioned to me about catching a short pass, juking a couple of players and getting in the end zone and scoring. They thought that was an outstanding play.

Oddly, I reflect back on the '62 championship. I look back and see some clips or plays of it. I ended up with thirty-one carries in that game, which is a career high for me. And there was only one touchdown scored, and I scored it with a rushing touchdown. Only ended up with 85 or 90 yards in rushing. Then the wind-chill factor was probably about thirty below, and I was carrying the ball and being banged out of bounds during the game, because you couldn't cut and get up the field, because after the first half of the first quarter it froze over. In Yankee Stadium that wind was just blowing, and just awful.

And I was banged out of bounds in that game because of not being able to cut up the field. I had thirty-one carries, and that time, I think at halftime I had about six stitches put in my elbow, and I'd bitten my tongue and was bleeding— couldn't stop the bleeding from the mouth, so it was real brutal. We didn't have gloves back then, and it was just a real tough, tough, brutal ball game.

We reverted back to what we had done all year, which is ball possession. Had to do more of that because of the frozen field, and then they couldn't cut, too, and you tried to go one direction and you couldn't cut very well much. I tell one little story about this. I don't know how it came about. One of the plays going into the end zone, we were about 12 or 14 yards out, I'd run an off-tackle play, and Sam Huff came in there and busted me for no gain or stopped me, and he gave me this, You stink, Taylor.

And I went back to the huddle, and we huddled up, and next play I ran to an off-tackle play, and all the pursuit came, and they were skating across there. And I cut back some kind of way and broke in the end zone and scored the only rushing touchdown, and I held up the ball and said, How do I smell from here, Sam? I had the last laugh, because I think Kramer kicked three field goals and we won 16–7.

I think it was early in the fourth quarter, somewhere in there. I think it was in the fourth quarter, we were still in the balance. I think we were leading 9–7, you know, not scoring much. Finally I think that was when it was scored. I don't know, you'd have to go back and see the play-by-play. It was a brutal ball game, you know. It's just a tough one and really cold and frigid and hard fought, and we just prepared the same way.

And here you don't know your weather conditions three or four days before. The whole week before in our preparation we just stayed with that ball possession, which we had to revert to more. I never carried the ball thirty-one times in all the years I played. So it was really up to me, or I was going to get the football because I could. In the regular games I'd carry twenty-five times a game and Hornung was ten or twelve carries. Bart throws twelve or fifteen passes, that was basically our offense.

As cold and tough and bad as it was, Hornung didn't play. We had Elijah Pitts and Tom Moore and some other people that played, and he didn't kick. The swirling wind, you couldn't throw the ball. I bet Bart Starr's longest pass was 20–25 yards maybe. That was it. He couldn't get the ball down the field because of the swirling wind.

Tittle was more the quarterback and Alex Webster and Gifford, and their regular people. Their strong, solid defense, which was good for them. They didn't have the ball possession or the good runners—Webster and whoever the other runners were—and so, yeah, it was rougher on them. And we just tried to move it down and stay on the field. Our philosophy was move the chains, first down, first down, and they can't score when we got the ball. And that was our basic philosophy anyway with our good solid attempts that we had.

We hardly ever blitzed on defense, and Nitschke and the good linebackers in the front four, and our solid defensive people with Adderley and Wood and Bob Jeter and Bob Brown, and the other people that were real consistent and solid.

Well, 16–7 is not going to be a lot of scoring in those weather conditions, ground conditions and everything else. We felt good. Any points that you could get on that board, and you're leading 16–7—they need two scores or something, and in those conditions it was almost impossible. So we were very fortunate. We'd gotten down in there and didn't score, but we'd had the three field goals. I don't remember the distances or anything. Here again, we kind of possessed the football to even get it into position to get you three field goals, and you end up with the one touchdown.

We felt good. We felt what got us there was going to continue us to finish it up in that third or fourth quarter and win us the championship, because all year long that was what we did. And that's what you go to, is what got you there, so that was our philosophy anyway. Actually the bad weather played more into our hands than theirs because of our ball possession.

Well, the year before we beat the Giants 37–0 in Green Bay. So we felt that we had a good team, and we went back, and I think it was the day after Christmas or something, and we went back and celebrated in Green Bay, or flew back that night—with the cold weather you were just ready to get the game over with and get somewhere warm and celebrate at that time.

That would be our second NFL Championship. We got beat in '60 by Philadelphia.

I don't remember a whole lot about us beating Cleveland in '65, I know our defense held Jim Brown down. We just kind of hung in there. I think we beat them 27–13 or something. It was just another ball game that we did the things it took to win. And our defense played sound and we moved the ball on the ground, and I don't remember my stats or anything about it. They held Jim Brown because he's better than half their offense, and they held him down or contained him to a point, and we won the '65 championship game.

Lombardi had a lot to do with that. We had our own self-confidence and self-esteem, and knew that we could compete and excel when we started it in '60 when we got to the first championship. We got beat there, but I think you learn a lot from losing, and we started to grow and to build and our '61 season was what, 12–2 or 13–1. In the '62 season we carried on over, and then we hit a little bump in the road and got beat by the Bears for the '63 year.

Then the '64 year Cleveland or somebody came and beat us going down the stretch, and so it gave you the sense of reality that you're not invincible, that you're not unbeatable type of thing. You had to work so much harder to accomplish and to get back to the level of your superiority and your outstanding play. So we returned in '65 and '66.

Well, when you lose you go back and you find out where you broke down at, and where you weren't hungry enough, you didn't do the things that it took to win. Go back and evaluate and say, Where was the breakdown? Where's the weaknesses? You go back and work toward and work on, and you get a little tougher and you get a little hungry, and whatever it takes to get back to our '61 and '62 seasons that we were very dominant.

I don't recall exactly any one or two things. It's just that you condition yourself. You get a little older, and you've really got to work on your conditioning and will to win, just some things, your determination, your attitude, some things that help to put you up where you want to compete at an 85–

95 percent. Maybe you've had a little lapse and you've slipped back and you're not as hungry. You've got a ring or two on your finger and you want to get back in that arena again.

The Pro Bowl, it's just another game. You work hard, and whatever the outcome is if you're voted to go to the Pro Bowl—and this is your ultimate goal in essence, in the back of your mind is that you want to be the best football player you can be. Whatever that takes. And if you're voted into that or whatever, you're not concerned one way or another. It's not in any contract that you got a bonus or this or that. We played football back then almost for the love of the game. We didn't play for big money. Don't get me into that.

The Hall of Fame, it was something that you don't live to, it's not your last breath to hope or wish to. Here again, you're trying to be the best football player I can be with the Green Bay Packers while I was on that football team. If it brought you the acknowledgment and the accomplishments of being All-Pro in 1962, and being the first Packer to go into the Hall of Fame, so be it.

It ain't like I'm trying to break records, is what a lot of today's generation and players are all about. I never tried to break a record in my life when I was a football player with the Green Bay Packers. You say that today's football players are better? They step out of bounds, and not too many who are worried about getting hurt or getting hit, and the agents say, Don't do that, don't stick in there, don't block anybody.

Lenny Ford's daughter was my inductee, for he had passed away, and Ray Flaherty was the other, which was a coach, and he played some with the Redskins. He just passed away at age ninety, just a year or so ago. There was only three of us that were inducted in 1976, and I called Marie Lombardi to be my inductee. It was like, here again, it's just another honor, and you've received many, many, many through your career and you have an inner feeling, I've accomplished that. Fine and good.

You don't stand up and rave and do this, you did your job

almost type of thing, and you just have to, one of the fortunate and lucky ones to get to the top type of thing. It's almost like when I was voted the MVP in 1962, the Jim Thorpe Award. It's how you just take it with a grain of salt. You're not raving with, Well, I'm a big superstar, or any of this. What you see is what you get. As a team person, there's a team camaraderie that those other ten people helped me accomplish—some of my own talents and my own abilities.

I'd had a good many people that—I was living in New Orleans then, and a lot of my friends, and I think my mother was there, and you just tried to thank people who had helped you along the way, coaches and everyone that's ever been a part of you to accomplish that.

Oh, I don't know which one I'd relive, they all have some memory of enjoyment or satisfaction type of thing. I don't— they all run together type of thing—I guess probably the Pro Football Hall of Fame, being the first Packer. We've got ten players, you know, five on defense and five on offense. Lombardi had gone in in '71. I got '70, and then they went the next year and inducted him.

You're talking about the college level, too, huh? I was looking at some clippings or whatever some months ago and we might have been playing Tulane, and I scored quite a few of the points there, which was an in-state rivalry. This would be probably the last game of the season, either my junior or senior year, I don't exactly recall. I kicked extra points at LSU, kicked off and what have you. We played both ways in those days. I played middle linebacker, and I was a defensive tackle. From time to time I would go to defense during games, and we rushed between the tackles.

And you know, you'd throw only eight or ten passes a ball game. We ended up a 6–5 team, somewhere in there, maybe a .500 team. You're playing sixty minutes and you're playing every down. You've got to be well conditioned back then. It was exciting, and I enjoyed it. I guess that maybe jumps out at me a little bit. I might have scored all the points in the ball game. I scored the three touchdowns and kicked the extra point or field goal or whatever. Something to that effect.

Well, Tulane is an in-state rivalry. They didn't have real good football teams for years and years and years. They're more scholastic, academic, you know? They would be our last game of the season out of the Southeastern Conference, because they're not in the conference, they're independent, have always been.

We were 5–4 or 6–4, something like that. We were never in contention the two years of my junior and senior year.

Greatest teammate? That's almost impossible. Different eras, different players, different everything. I would venture to say Ray Nitschke, an outstanding football player, and then when he leads his career of a role model and a real role model for professional football. The opponent? Probably Dick Butkus. Well, all your middle linebackers were the ones, you know, the toughest on me, and that's their job.

I know Butkus. We'd view films and he'd block one and get up and be blocked again, and the play was going way across the field. I mean he just really had some determination to get to the football. Not once or twice, you saw it many times. Joe Schmidt was a good linebacker. It was hard with the old Bears and Bill George and Nitschke, a lot of great linebackers.

Sam Huff, he had a good press agent, you know? I saw him in camp, and I see him from time to time and I joke with him, and we're all the time joking. In the championship ball game we had a few words on the sidelines. He would get me piling on or maybe taking some cheap shots after the ball is out of bounds on a play, and he's still trying to rough you up, and I said, Why don't you do it before the whistle's blown? You're not tough enough, but after the whistle you've got the cheap shots.

So I just—I tell these guys the way it is. They don't want

to hear it, but we can go back and look at those films and it would be just like when you hit the quarterback. All bets are off, the whistle's blown, and the guy's taking cheap shots. They know when they should pull off and when they shouldn't, and we're all out there doing a job and trying to play within the realm of the officials and the rules and stuff, so in that ball game there, you can go back and see five yards out of bounds, and they're still trying to drive an elbow or shoulder into you. They won't hit you in the field of play.

I never talked about it—I just wanted to get back to the play and let's do it again. I want to catch up with him. Forget all that talk, I like action. Forget all the jaw-jabbers. It's like today's athletes, they're just full of so much conversation, instead of, keep your mouth shut and do your job. Well, that's today's athletes, that's what the media and some of the people want—whatever, I don't know, I don't get involved. I don't even put up with it. I don't even watch a game. If they're not going to play, that's it.

# Lawrence Taylor

*As a football player, Lawrence Taylor was a veritable force of nature, a linebacker who combined the ferocity of Dick Butkus and the speed, focus, and tenacity of Mike Singletary into a unique style that was totally individual. For his greatest day, the man who led the great Giant defenses of the '80s and became known simply as "LT" chose a game against the New Orleans Saints in 1987. In that game he took the concept of playing in pain to a whole new level and earned the nickname that would stay with him for the rest of his career.*

It was a Sunday-night football game. We were playing New Orleans. That's the game where I had a real bad shoulder, where I shouldn't have been playing the game, but I played anyway.

What I do remember about the game is that, if I'm not mistaken, I think the final score was something like 10–3 or 7–3. They put a harness on me, a shoulder harness, because my shoulder was really . . . the muscle was just about ripped off. I do remember that. Every series, when we came out on defense they had to redo the harness on me, because it was very, very painful.

Anyway, I remember having something like three sacks and twelve tackles. And that was probably the only time that Bill Parcells actually came up to me after the game and told me that I was great. We've always had this thing where Bill doesn't have to tell me I'm playing well or that I played well. We don't have to give each other compliments. We know when we were doing the job, getting the job done. But that was probably the first time, and maybe the only time, that he ever came up to me personally and actually face-to-face said that I actually had a great game, and that I played great.

I guess that was a big moment for me, to know that throughout the adversity, I had just stepped into another realm as far as defense goes, taking it to another level. There's no way I should have been playing, and I remember my little girl crying, telling me to leave the game, to get out. This was in New Orleans, probably in midseason. It was a Sunday-night football game. ESPN was doing the game. All that stuff was just a blur to me.

You know what, I remember that because of Ricky Jackson, who's probably my best friend as far as players go. They had a pretty good team. Bobby Hebert was the quarterback, and I remember going against this guy called [Dave] Dombrowski. He was their tackle, this guy was like 300 pounds. This was one of those games we had to win, and I was just so focused. They had a good club, and the linebacking corps was awesome.

I just remember that Dombrowski—it just seemed like every other play I was getting hit, and it just sent me to my knees. Harry Carson was telling me to get the hell out of the game. But I was just killing Dombrowski, just hitting him with one hand and driving his ass back into the quarterback. It was one of my finest hours as a defensive player, I would say.

They were doubling me all over the field . . . I got through it. I had three sacks and twelve tackles. I must have done pretty well. I know one play when they were driving, I came around the corner and caused a fumble.

Actually, I think a week or two weeks before we had played Dallas, the quarterback cut back and I tried to reach out and catch him. I grabbed him, but the way he was going and the way I was going was awkward, and I ripped the tendons in my shoulder. The blow was . . . right now, even today, if you were to touch my pec [pectoral muscle], I don't have a pec there anymore, there's one tendon. It disintegrated.

I remember Phil Simms saying that he watched the game and his eyes were focused on me, and he was just amazed that I was still going, playing through the pain and stuff. And after the game, he said he realized that he had just witnessed something that was truly great.

There'd been a couple of times when I'd just tell myself . . . I think it's all like a buildup. Even though sometimes when you hurt so bad, but because you've got a reputation of playing through pain, you just make yourself go out there anyway, even though you know you shouldn't be out there. And that was one of the times I knew I shouldn't be out there, and there was another time, too, when I broke my ankle.

I kept going, trying to live up to that Superman myth, that indestructible type of myth. And who knows if that was the smartest thing to do, because it took me a lot longer, it took me some time to recover. After that game all it did was get worse, and it took me time to recover from that. Even though it was maybe my finest moment as a defensive player, you have to really think about it and say what was the logic in doing it that way, was it really the smartest thing to do.

Ricky Jackson still talks about that day . . . and I'm quite sure from the articles, that's when they truly started calling me Superman and stuff. I'm quite sure that has to do something. Your offense has to think about it when you can't even get a man with one arm. I do remember Dombrowski, and the coaches . . . how do you give a guy—you double-team him, how do you send a person more help when he's already got another guy helping him on a guy that's got one arm? That's gotta be demeaning to a team.

We won that game. I also remember Wellington Mara walking into the locker room and walking up to my cubicle, and looking me square in the face, and giving me a hug, and saying, you had a great game. The thing is, you never realize when you're playing, it's all a blur to you. You're just going out there and playing the game and playing as hard as you can. You really don't realize what you've done on the field until after it's all over.

The great thing is not when other people just tell you what you've done . . . when your teammates come up to you, and your coach comes up to you and looks you square in the face, man, and says, hey, you did one hell of a job. And you know he means it. So it's not just one of those things [where people say] aw, good game, good game, even if you got beat 50–0. Nobody wants to hear that. If we win 50–0 and I played poorly, I don't want to hear anybody say, good game, either, if I haven't played well. That was one time when "good game" was said, and I knew it was meant. I felt very very proud of myself and of what I had done.

A lot of people want to talk about the Joe Theismann thing. A lot of people want to talk about the interception on Thanksgiving Day, and other things I've done. But to me that was my greatest moment, knowing that I had really gone against the odds and put something together that was truly great. Because I felt . . . I almost felt like I was truly invincible then.

*The Giants took a lot of heat back in 1961 when they traded guard Leo Cordileone and a number one draft pick to the San Francisco 49ers for a thirty-five-year-old quarterback whose best days seemed to be behind him. But Y. A. Tittle went on to become one of the most prolific quarterbacks in the team's history, leading the Giants to two Eastern Conference Championships and setting a slew of offensive records along the way. Tittle defined his greatest day in several different ways, working through the trade that brought him to New York to his record-setting day against the Washington Redskins in which Tittle and 'Skins QB Norm Snead tore apart the offensive record books, then celebrated with an appearance on* The Ed Sullivan Show.

My best day in football was when I was traded to the Giants. But my best playing day was against the Washington Redskins.

I have to clarify that, because I had so many nice, good memorable days . . . that was my best record-breaking day as a professional. I had two professional record-breaking days: One was my first game with the Baltimore Colts. I broke in with the All-American Conference, and my first game against the New York Yankees in Baltimore. I broke all the All-American Conference records in my first game as a rookie.

That sent me on my way, because I got a lot of press after that. Not that the records were big, but the All-American Conference had only been in existence for three years. I broke a whole bunch of conference records. And so that was a big day for me.

My other big day prior to that was against Tulane as a college player, and I broke all the Southeastern Conference records against Tulane. I think I hit nineteen out of twenty-one or something like that. So my three record-breaking days were Tulane in 1944, my freshman year at LSU; I was a freshman and they allowed freshman to play. I broke the record there. That was my biggest day in college, against Tulane, and my next biggest day was with Baltimore, against the Yankees as a rookie.

And then I had some good days in San Francisco. . . . I can't recall any win that sticks out the most. But my most memorable moment was the last game in 1961 when the Giants had cinched the championship game and the fans were counting 10, 9, 8. . . . That was my first championship game. I didn't have that good a day. A tie cinched the title for us. The great moment was that 10, 9, I'm over the center waiting for the ball to . . . not to snap the ball, just waiting for the crowd and the time to run out. That was my biggest thrill.

It was against the Cleveland Browns in 1961, the crowd roaring in Yankee Stadium, that constant roar as the crowd counted down. Can you imagine Yankee Stadium, how loud it is? They started chanting and cheering for the last ten seconds, that was my greatest thrill.

There's a good funny story I can tell you about my first game with the Giants that's sort of interesting. My trade came during training camp in 1961 when I was with the 49ers, and we played the Giants in an exhibition game in Portland. There'd been a lot of trade rumors for many months prior to the opening of training camp, because we were gonna use a shotgun offense as a full offense, meaning we were going to run off it. They had drafted Billy Kilmer from UCLA, who was a single-wing tailback, passed and ran—at thirty-five years old, I wasn't going to be running off tackle.

So when I was traded there was a big controversy. I report to Salem, Oregon, where the Giants were training. After they played us in the first exhibition in Portland they stayed over and trained there. I reported to training camp there on Tuesday. I was told by the 49ers that I'd been traded to New York. I came back home and delayed a day, trying to decide whether I would quit after fourteen years or go ahead and go.

And I got a call from Frank Gifford, and he said that he thought that I would be competing with Charlie [Conerly] for the job. I wouldn't just be second string. He was working in some kind of capacity with the Giants that I would be given a fair shot. So anyway, now the big trade is made, and I go up to Giant camp. I've been there only a day and a half, two days, and they're on the way to play the Los Angeles Rams on a Thursday night or Friday.

And [Allie] Sherman wanted to know whether I was gonna play, and this is my most embarrassing moment. I said, of course, I'll play. They gave me a few plays to run, and I could make up a few in the huddle, whatever. I had played fourteen years so I could just diagram pass plays by saying, Shofner run a post, or Joe Walton run a square-out, and I'll hit you— kind of like sandlot ball.

So I go down there. I'm their big trade. They'd gotten rid of their first-round choice, and now they're looking forward to seeing me play. And we get there, and Charlie Conerly goes the first half, and the start of the fourth quarter Sherman says, OK, are you ready to go, and I said, yes, I'm ready.

I got warmed up and I go into the game, and I wasn't used to Ray Wietecha's snap, the snap from center. So he sort of hit me, I thought, in the wrong spot in my hands, and the ball fumbled around on the ground, and I fall on the ball, and Jack Pardee, their defensive linebacker, hits me in the back with his knee.

Well, he hit me in a very interesting spot. I played one play, I fumble the ball, they have traded their first draft choice for a bald-headed old man, quite controversial. Why would you trade a first draft choice for a bald-headed has-been, over-the-hill, and on the first play he fumbles the ball?

And then, I get up, and I go back in the huddle, and I can't talk—I got hit in the back, and I can't talk. These guys are saying, call the play, and I couldn't talk. These players are saying, Jesus Christ, come on, Goddammit, we better call a time-out—call the play. Hell, I couldn't breathe.

So I signaled to the referee, and I turned to the sideline, and I gave my arm signal, like, come get me. And these guys on the sideline—Sherman and the coaches had their hands on their hips, they didn't see what happened to me, all I did was fumble the ball. I got up and got in the huddle and couldn't call the play, and I said, come get me. I couldn't talk, I couldn't even talk to the referee . . . I couldn't talk.

I get over to the sideline, and they said, what is it? And I'm holding my back, and now these ballplayers are saying, what's wrong with this guy? I got in the huddle, and they're thinking, geez, he's been in the league fourteen years, I thought this guy would at least not be scared stiff with stage fright so bad he couldn't even talk. No one saw him hit me.

So I go back to the sideline, and I'm sitting there, and they take me back on the airplane, and they X-ray me, my ribs cracked, three of 'em, the transverse processes, those little things that stick out the side of your back. So I've got three of 'em cracked in two. Now I'm out six weeks, and probably the most miserable time of my life was sitting there during all of training camp, watching these guys looking at me, thinking they'd lost their first draft choice, got this bald-headed guy, and he played one play. That's my worst experience.

The Redskin game in 1962 was probably my best game in football. I threw for over 500 yards, which was just a few yards short of [Norm] Van Brocklin's record, and seven touchdowns, which is still a record. It's tied by others, but seven touchdowns in one game for 505 yards, which was my biggest day with the Giants.

It was played at Yankee Stadium. The ironic part of this story was that I wasn't really supposed to play, because the week before I played in a very, very tough game against Detroit. At that time they had a very strong defensive team, Joe Schmidt and those guys. I got hit in the arm, in the muscle of my right arm, and I had a blood contusion there. In fact it's still there, I have a knot there.

So I couldn't throw all week—not that I was hurt that badly, but just with this blood contusion I couldn't throw. So I didn't throw Tuesday, Wednesday, Thursday, or Friday or Saturday before the Redskin game. I didn't throw anything on Saturday, so Sherman suggested that I warm up the next day and tell him if I could play.

So I warmed up prior to the game. I threw little quick slants, nothing very deep, but I'd already learned a long time ago you don't ever say you can't play—there's always a John Brodie or somebody else ready to get in there. I said, OK, I'll give it a go, and we played the 'Skins, and at that time they were leading the league, and we were I think two games behind.

Anyway, I threw my first eight passes, and they were all incomplete. I knew one more incompleted pass, and I'd be taken out probably, because I was so ineffective. Then I hit thirteen in a row, and had my biggest day, went on for 505 yards and seven touchdowns.

And I had a chance to get number eight. We were down

there on the 5 yard line with about thirty seconds to go, and all the guys in the huddle were saying, go for it, go for it, throw the eighth ball, and I thought that would be in pretty poor taste. We already had the game won, 49 to 20-something, and we had to play them again in RFK. With thirty seconds to go there was no way for them to catch us, so we just ran the clock out. It would have been 100 percent showboating for me to throw a pass like that with only fifteen or twenty seconds left in the ball game.

I did hit every receiver, just about. I know that Morrison caught one, Shofner caught one, I think Joe Walton maybe caught three, I'm not positive about that, and I'm not sure about Gifford. It was a combination of Shofner, Morrison, and Joe Walton, and maybe Gifford, I think—he did, he caught one across the middle, he was wide open on a post pattern.

At the time the Washington Redskins were leading the league in pass defense, so we expected a real tough ball game. It was Norm Snead. He threw four touchdown passes that day, I threw seven, he threw for 400 yards himself—it was a track meet.

We didn't pull away until the end of the ball game. Every time we'd score a touchdown, Bobby Mitchell would catch one for the Redskins and run it [into the end zone]. So we didn't really pull away until close to the end.

I was never one who was aware of what was happening [with the crowd]. I'd been booed so many times out at San Francisco with some of the days I've had in the past, the crowd noise—I didn't hear 'em. I wasn't aware of how many until midway in the fourth quarter, that I could really break a record . . . which I didn't, I tied a record.

We won the division, and lost to Green Bay in the Frost Bowl, subfreezing weather and windy weather in Yankee Stadium. I led the league in passing, and in touchdown passes. I had thirty-three that year. That was a record also, at that time. The next year I had thirty-six. That was a record the next year.

After the ball game, that's another interesting part. After that big day of mine, we had already preplanned, I was supposed to go on *The Ed Sullivan Show*. So I went on *The Ed Sullivan Show* with Norm Snead. He was single, and he didn't have his wife with him, but he went out with my wife and my children.

He's a wonderful person—I came back later on, I coached him when I was with New York, for Alex Webster. I coached Norm to the division passing title. I take part credit for it. It was '72 or something like that.

They bring you up onstage and introduce you, and then they have those different skits, if you remember *The Ed Sullivan Show*. It was a big thing for us, my wife and children were back there, they all go on *The Ed Sullivan Show* with Norm Snead. They all stood up in the audience and they were introduced, so they liked that.

I'm sure he must have said something about the record, because we combined for more yardage in any one game at the same time. I think Norm had 400 something, and I had 500 something. That was the most yardage gained in a professional football game at that time between teams, and it was second to Van Brocklin . . . see how stupid I was? If I'd have known that Van Brocklin had 507, all I could have done was hit another 15-yard pass, and I'd have had all the records.

I did throw a football through a hoop one time on *The Johnny Carson Show*. He had me interviewed. It was just a typical interview, and then he said, I think I can outthrow you. And I said, what do you mean? And he said, I think I'm a better passer than you are. I said . . . OK, maybe so, how're we gonna prove it?

So they pulled up another little screen that they had covered up there, and there was a Volkswagon tire. And he said, I'm gonna throw through that Volkswagon tire, and we're gonna have a contest.

He hit the first lady in the audience, knocked her glasses off. I thought he was probably gonna get sued, he missed the thing by about eight yards. And I probably threw the best pass of my life. I could never do it again. It went from one end of the station to the other. It hit and ricocheted and went right through it. And he said, Gee do it again! That's easy.

And I thought, how could I have undignified myself by doing something so stupid. If I'd thrown twenty more times I couldn't have done it. I accidentally did it the first time, and I told him it was a piece of cake.

*Most great players make it a habit to turn up on great teams, but few stars made a career out of winning the way Paul Warfield did. Warfield started his athletic career under the tutelage of Woody Hayes at Ohio State, then went on to establish himself with the Cleveland Browns, where he became one of the NFL's best receivers. Warfield capped his great career after joining the Miami Dolphins in the late '60s, where he became a vital cog on the club that went undefeated and won the Super Bowl against the Washington Redskins in 1972.*

Let's discuss that just a little bit more. I guess my thoughts would go along whether are you looking toward a statistical day, or if we're discussing what I considered to be my greatest day, a combination of productivity, or the game itself?

Well, I guess I would have to define it in terms of—it would probably be productivity along the lines of a statistically . . . but I think in my own mind, I wouldn't necessary count it as the greatest day, but my very first year playing with the Cleveland Browns, I was having, in my mind, a productive and good rookie season.

But one game stood out in which it was a productive day. I didn't set any records or anything as far as that was concerned, club or league records with receptions, but I scored two touchdowns and I was well over 100 yards, probably somewhere between 120–130 yards on receptions. But it occurred against the best team in football. And that's the reason why it was significant. It told me that not only could I compete in this league at the highest level, that I could compete the very best team and do that. So that's why it stood out.

I would say it was certainly into the midpoint of the year, but as I was saying, it was a good season for me up to that point, and I was in the running for Rookie of the Year honors. But for my own personal satisfaction and my own level of confidence, when you do certain things against . . . I don't want to say the lower echelon players, or when you do things against good players, but when you do things against the very best personnel, the very best coach, the very best team in football at that time, then for me that was validation that I could play certainly on this level, that I could play with the very best and I could raise the level of my game above the very best. It was against the Green Bay Packers, and it was in Milwaukee, as a matter of fact.

Well, I guess I'd have to go back to much earlier to that ball game when we played against the Packers in a preseason game. I just joined the Cleveland Browns returning from the Chicago College All-Star Game that was still being played at that time. It was the annual summer classic. Ironically, the collegiate stars that year played against the Bears, who had beaten out Green Bay the year before, and the Bears went on to win the then-NFL title.

After I played that College All-Star Game I joined the Browns. And then two or three preseason games down the line we played the Packers in the final preseason game of the year. And I had a good ball game, and I was somewhat impressive in that preseason game against the Packers, and one particular play I remember running a pattern against their defender. I believe his name was Jesse Whittenton. And I ran a pattern against him, and it was a classic pattern in which I turned the defender completely around in a circle and gave him an outside fake, which he spun his body around too far to defend against me on the outside. Then I broke instantly to the inside. Technically, I mean, I was as wide open as you'll ever dream of being.

And as the ball was coming in the air—and this would have been an 80-yard reception for a touchdown—for some reason, I didn't have a lot of confidence where I was thinking, and the thought entered my mind as the ball was descending, what if I didn't catch it? Exactly—it was one of those "oops" moments, and I dropped it and there was 85,000 people there and the national television audience watching that ball game that night, and you can imagine how I felt.

That was against Green Bay. It would've certainly have boosted my confidence. I did everything technically right as I was taught in the pattern, the throw was perfect, but I didn't concentrate to the fullest and I dropped the football.

I didn't let that get me down, so as we swing back to the point when we're playing Green Bay when it really counted during the regular season, and playing against the same defender out there again, and their ballclub, I did make it count. I had a very successful day all in all. What even boosted my confidence even more was the fact that when our writers— the Cleveland writers—went into the Green Bay locker room, when Vince Lombardi, the legendary Packer coach was holding court, when asked about me his comment was very short but direct.

He said, I would say he was a mild sensation.

So coming from Lombardi that also boosted my confidence that I had really arrived to the point where I could be considered the top player. And so that ball game, although two touchdowns doesn't represent four or six or a record performance, leaguewise, or didn't even break the individual club performance. But against the individual team of perhaps that decade of the '60s, against their personnel, when they were at their powers and their peak, because they went on to win three straight NFL championships from that point on.

The secondary—Willie Wood was on the other side, he was a free safety, and Herb Adderley played the other corner. Whittenton, if my memory serves me correctly, was an older player, but had been a Pro Bowl performer at the corner. So it's not extraordinarily glamorous or whatever, but for my money and for my personal confidence and for what had helped me along the way to perhaps subsequently to be selected for the Pro Football Hall of Fame, it meant everything to me to have that kind of acknowledgment from Lombardi. To have been able to succeed against the top team in the league, it just gave me the level of confidence that what I knew I could do I could do against anybody at anytime.

From a team context, the 17–0 season altogether, and winning the final game in Los Angeles to complete and cap that historic season. It meant in the true tradition, and I'm a traditionalist in this sense. I believe football is a team sport and a team game, and whatever it takes to win is a philosophy that I believed in, and my career was based mainly offensively. Whatever it took, whether running the football or throwing the football or certainly a combination of the two, and when I think about the 17–0 team and many of the teams that we had, it was a very unselfish team, individual players recognized as stars but a whole sense or embodiment of commitment as to win and do whatever it would take to win.

Built into that framework, if I didn't believe that then I would have been a very unhappy player at Miami, because they simply didn't throw the football. Well, you know, I likened my existence to that of a thoroughbred. A pass receiver wants to catch passes. A thoroughbred wants to really sprint in any mile race or whatever. Yes, it was frustrating, but I learned my lessons well in the foundation of my football background and experience that dated back to grade school, and that was you win as a team.

Yes, the level of frustration would build to an extent that I would go home after some ball games greatly disappointed because I knew there were things that I could do or could have done maybe different to score one way or the other. The object is to win the game, not to necessarily satisfy individuals. And so the only disappointing point for me was that I would have to go out there and work hard and on individual execution as a pass receiver one would feel much like an understudy and never get a chance to do that. So, that was the frustration, but I would justify it all in, look, we won the game and that's the most important thing.

Now, ironically, when I see a lot of offensive performers today and not necessarily pass receivers, but rushers or pass receivers or a combination of the two, they're saying they're unhappy when they win. I don't understand, because you know, winning supersedes everything.

And that's what you're out there for, and so it's just kind of interesting. That was the overriding theme of the Miami Dolphins football club. Now we used the rushing game offensively more so than the passing game, but that was a philosophy that was geared toward taking time off the clock, and our team was a magnificent team for doing that. We would just have control of the football because of our ability to rush and take time off the clock. But not only did we have the ability to take time off the clock in rushing and moving the ball down the field on long drives of 50 or more yards, or up to 60–70 yards and take six or eight minutes off the clock, but we could finish. We had the killer instinct. We could finish with seven points more often than not on the scoreboard.

Again, it was the fact that you had eleven members of the

offensive team, and Bob Griese was a wonderful passer. His passing statistics had to suffer also because we were rushing the football, but we were all geared to win.

You know, I could only set the scene this way: One year before we had been humiliated by the Dallas Cowboys in New Orleans. And we were a young football team, essentially, that had accomplished a lot and probably got to the Super Bowl a year too early and were really just outclassed by an outstanding Dallas team. So the loser of the Super Bowl feels a sense of humiliation, unfortunately, but that's just the way it is, and we all vowed that we'd be back to redeem ourselves in that game. But how many times have you heard that story from other teams?

Well, we decided that we'd do something about this, so that was the impetus if not the drive or the momentum if not the goal that we set—to get back to the Super Bowl to win. The longer focus was so great the following year that a wonderful thing happened. We won all of our ball games up to that point and didn't lose any. But that was really the ball game that we were, more so than ever, geared to play.

And we played against a fine Washington team. We had complete control of the ball game. The score should have been 21–0 at halftime, as a matter of fact. I caught a TD pass that would have made it 21–0, but that pass was called back because of an infraction. My feeling was, as the clock was counting down to the final seconds—the offense was on the field—it was then for the very first time that I felt a great sense of relief. It seemed like I had been so focused and I can say the same for my teammates, so focused on getting back to that game and winning that game to show the critics who said that we're just another team, because that was only two years into the complete merger and consolidation of both leagues.

And while I had background from the old NFL team, it was basically an AFL club at that time, so it was a sense that we were able to redeem ourselves. In the early years of play over there in the AFC, the feeling was that the old NFL that was, the NFC was far superior, and that changed very quickly when you went into that string of consecutive NFC wins, but there was a short period right after when once we claimed the title in '72, from about '72 up to right up to '80, where AFC teams dominated, and we were the start of that.

It was really that ball game and, as I said, when the clock was counting down, and I looked up and it began to resonate with me and they were flashing on the scoreboard at the Los Angeles Coliseum, "Dolphins Are Super." It was flashing, and it all really sort of came together at that point for me. I felt like a great weight was lifted, that we had redeemed ourselves, that we had proven that we were a championship team. Even the 17–0 at that time had no significance.

The 17–0 during the undefeated season, when we were putting it together, never really registered in my mind, simply because our focus was, number one, we had to win our divisional title. Then we had to win the American Conference title and the championship game and then we could get to where we wanted to, which was the Super Bowl, and show all of our critics and the pundits that this was a good football team.

There was a team party, obviously, and we all attended the team party and the festive occasion. Everybody was in a mood of celebration and happiness and jubilant. I stopped by the team affair for a very short time, and then subsequently I was leaving to go to San Diego, but particularly on the field for me, that moment I don't think I've ever felt anything like it before. Because again, personally, I felt like there was something that the team needed to prove, and there were so many distractions and so many critics that had indicated—there were even things that were said about our ball club that we were entering into our second Super Bowl that we were just another ball club.

The feeling was that the Washington Redskins was a far superior ball club, George Allen's club, and they would beat us handily. So even as we were going into that ball game after getting back for the second consecutive year, which many teams didn't do, we had something to prove. So it was like we continually had to prove ourselves from the point that we lost to the Dallas Cowboys the year before, all during that season, in the playoffs, and even in that final game.

So finally after we won that ball game, it was there for everyone to see that we were the champions, and I don't—as I said, for me personally the 17–0 didn't register. I don't believe that the 17–0 registered on anybody. The press was aware of it, but it was not as big a deal as it is today, simply because teams are—that is a mark that they are trying to reach and surpass. While a couple of teams have come close, nobody has yet equaled it or gone beyond it.

Let me tell you a little bit about going into the Hall—it has a little bit of irony to it in my mind, and it has a great deal of significance because I chose my high school coach, the late Gene Slaughter, to be my presenter, and I chose him specifically because he's the reason I played football.

Years ago, when I was a youngster in junior high school, he'd just been named the new head football coach at the high school. He came over to my junior high and talked to football players who were going to be going into the high school system the following year, and he was trying to encourage us to come out for the football program and telling us in very strong terms that the football program was going to be something special, and that we had a chance to be a part of that.

Well, I wasn't quite sure I wanted to play football in high school, because I was a better baseball player, and I was an outstanding track and field performer. High school represented a new world that I would have to go up to, and there were other young men who I knew about who were simply better football players than I was. So I wanted to go up to high school thinking that if I'm going to go out for a sport or two, it's going to be something that I know I can compete in and do well.

So I wasn't sure I was going to play football—but after Gene Slaughter spoke to our group, I was absolutely certain that I was going to play football. It was something he said, the way he said it. I'd never heard a message like that before, and at the time I was only fourteen years old, just to satisfy him, and it was really rewarding for the two of us, but he was the reason why I played football. And so ultimately the reason I was in Canton that day, so I felt that he should be the one who should present me.

As far as the Pro Football Hall of Fame is concerned, I never dreamed that my football career professionally would lead me there. I tried to play at the top level and play the very best I could play every Sunday I played. I've had a discussion about the Hall of Fame with Brooks Robinson and I asked Brooks—Brooks, did you ever think Brooks Robinson, the performer, a great third baseman and Hall of Famer of the Baltimore Orioles—did you ever set your goals when you played in baseball to go into the Hall of Fame? And Brooks Robinson's reply to me was, Look, I just tried to go out there and play the best that I could every day, be the player I could be and reach the top of my potential.

And I agreed with him, that's what I attempted to do. If you would let the cards fall where they may, the Pro Football Hall of Fame was really not—it was the furthest thing from my mind. The Pro Football Hall of Fame represented the greats like Otto Graham, or Sammy Baugh, or Nagurski, Marion Motley, Jim Brown—I mean these are people that I read about, people that I emulated when I was a kid, but these were the true immortals, the icons. And I just never believed that those who would evaluate my play thought that I should belong in a place like that. I was enormously happy, proud, elated to have been selected and then to be selected in the first ballot.

I went in with Bobby Bell, who was a contemporary of

mine who played at the University of Minnesota in the Big Ten, truly one of the great, great linebackers of all time, and probably helped revolutionize that position because he had so many tremendous physical gifts—speed, quickness, a combination of that with strength, into an ability to see what offenses were doing and be in the right place at the right time. He was just extremely difficult for offensive backs who attempted to block him. He had that great athletic ability that he was flexible enough to rush the passer but get back into coverage, and he was one of the surest tacklers you would ever . . . and in addition to that really just a marvelous individual who was very gregarious and outgoing, but a great athlete and a great competitor.

Sonny Jurgensen, a guy I marveled for years watching on the sidelines. The things that he could do throwing the football, just phenomenal as a passer, pinpointing passing, precision, and you know, receivers always, in their dream of dreams, Gee, I'd like to play a season with Sonny Jurgensen. Yeah, I played with him in a couple of Pro Bowls. I got a chance to catch his passes from his hand, but the guy was a pure passer, and could do phenomenal things throwing the football. I just admired his work and, as I said, all pass receivers in their wildest dreams, say Well, geez, I'd like to play with this passer just one season.

But once I started playing as a regular for Gene Slaughter, I played my very first game, I remember and took pretty much of a good beating as a running back at that time. And I had my set of bumps and bruises, and I have to tell you, though, it kind of rocked my constitution, and then I wasn't quite sure that football was something that I wanted to continue. That was the first ball game that I played and so I struggled through the next week of practice, but the second week we were going to play in Canton. We were going to play a team that was a schoolboy powerhouse that was called Canton McKinley. And so as I prepared for that game I was still sore, and it took several days before I really started to feel good again.

But the night that we played Canton McKinley, Gene designed an offense that utilized me a lot. I scored three touchdowns, and all of a sudden the big hits didn't seem to matter. Well, the irony of all that was, as I scored three touchdowns across from the stadium, I was a stone's throw from the rotunda of the Pro Football Hall of Fame. I say that I was kind of at a crossroads, where I was vacillating about whether I wanted to continue to do that or not, and then it all happened for me in that stadium—twenty-five years later, less than 100 yards away on the rotunda steps, I was being accepted into the Pro Football Hall of Fame.

So that was a part of my induction speech, that twenty-five years earlier I was considering whether I wanted to do this or not because it was a rough sport, and yet that night playing a ball game in that particular stadium again it all opened up for me. It was revealed to me and all of a sudden the bumps and the bruises didn't matter that much, and subsequently I was standing on the steps of the Pro Football Hall of Fame.

Well, the emotional experience from that standpoint and seeing that all those things fell into place from the standpoint of the late Woody Hayes, my coach from Ohio State was there in the audience that day and supported me, my high school coach Gene Slaughter was there, my family and friends, and my hometown is a place called Warren, which is just fifty miles north of Canton. And I'd been over in Canton on numerous occasions to play scholastically, baseball and track and field also, so it brought back a lot of emotions particularly because again, football is a team sport, and one certainly realizes that the people are supportive of your efforts and you just don't get there alone.

I don't know if I really had a great day [in college]. Well, probably, again something similar at Ohio State. My last game of the season my sophomore year. I had a very big day against the University of Michigan, and that probably represented my greatest day because up to that point, I was an eighteen-year-old sophomore who had been highly touted, and I had what would have amounted to a so-so season by the standards of the pundits up to that point.

I played in the same backfield with Bob Ferguson, an All-American who certainly overshadowed what I was doing and what everyone else was doing. But so much was written about me as a high school player coming into Ohio State, I think the expectations were a lot greater. And it's not that I had a mediocre season, it was that the expectations were so great, and there were a lot of people who felt like I didn't live up to those expectations. But on that particular day, a lot of real good things happened, and happened well for me, and I had a big day rushing, and so the pundits in the newspapers seemed to justify the fact that I should have been in the Ohio State backfield all year based solely on that one day.

Well, I think I would probably choose to live the Hall of Fame ceremony. And I say that because as a part of my induction speech, it was the recognition of the fact that there were a lot of people there. Gene Slaughter was there and he's the guy who got me started. If he hadn't come over to the high school that day, I probably wouldn't have played high school football. I had a great baseball background. I was a better baseball player than football player—I played the outfield.

It's kind of ironic that in this period of time where they're talking about two-way players, I was told, because the baseball teams wanted to sign me since I was fifteen years old until I made a decision to go with the Cleveland Browns after being drafted by them. But I was told down the stretch that I had to play baseball or football. In those days both leagues, football and baseball, said, you're either going to do it for us or you're going to do it for the other guy. Take your pick. They didn't say, do both.

So Gene Slaughter impacted me so much, that what he said had almost special significance on that day I was fourteen years old. I mean, it seemed like I had never heard anything like that, so I was inquisitive enough to go out for high school football to see what it was all about based on what this man had told me. Woody Hayes was very instrumental in getting me to go to Ohio State and in my development not only as a football player, but as a student and young man, so he had a very significant and important impact on my life in college.

The only thing that I can say about the possibility of playing baseball and being a two-sport athlete is that from the time I was fifteen years old I was offered money, and of course I couldn't sign then, I was underage. But subsequent to that, some of the organizations tried to get me to leave school to go into professional baseball, but I refused to do it, obviously. So all of the events then, and the fact that I had a great game at Fawcett Stadium as a youngster, and then twenty-five years later as a result of that game that I probably decided to stay with football, I was there being inducted in the Pro Football Hall of Fame.

And then to be so honored in front of family, friends, and all those people who support me, and all those times things don't go particularly right but you always have the support of your family and those individuals who are close to you, that probably stood out more so because of the involvement of everybody than the things that were certainly meaningful, and that helped me along the way.

Greatest teammate? That one is kind of hard for me to answer because I can look over the period of years from high school, and if I were to choose one it would probably be a person who is kind of obscure to most people who follow sports and football in particular. It would be my high school teammate from Warren Harding, and he was an upperclassman, and I played baseball with him but I also played football with him, and his name is Jack Patillo. Jack embodied everything that I think you want in terms of a true leader who stood out there to be heard, to pull the team together, who didn't pull punches, who did everything one would expect of a true leader. I admired and respected him for his ability to stand out there.

I also admired and respected him as a player in terms of what he brought to the table. We have stayed and remained friends over the years, and in recent years he was elected to the local Warren High School sports hall of fame, which I am a member of too, and I sent him a congratulatory note because I couldn't attend the ceremony, but it was read at the ceremony and he, in turn, shared the feelings that he had, his mom had, his wife had and everyone had. He was the one player I respected more in terms of what his leadership brought to the field, brought to our teams.

Well, you know, I would have to say a guy I played against would have been Dick Butkus. You're talking about the way the game should be played. As if every play you're playing is absolutely the final play, that you're going to play and you're going to give 1,000 percent and give everything that you can into the game. Butkus epitomized that, not only in terms of his incentive, his motivation, his desire.

You know, football players, being that it is a tough game, have to take on the qualities of combativeness, ferociousness, and aggressiveness. He was a pure player in every sense of the word. The very purest, and if you could I guess put those components together and make a football player, he's probably the kind of player that you could—if you were Dr. Frankenstein and you could, I mean in terms of man-made. He was a great player, a great competitor and loved what he did. You could sense that he loved what he did, and gave you every ounce that he had to give on the football field.

Well, they would consider us to be opposites, but we were alike in many respects. People assume certain things, but it's a tough game and you have to play it tough, while neither man appeared to lessen that because of what I did as a wide receiver, I've been described as "graceful," "effortless"—I put a lot of effort in there, I worked extremely hard. I brought to every game a sense that I've got to play it hard and I've got to play it to the best of my ability. I've got to be as near perfection as I can possibly be, all of the elements that Butkus did. Our demeanors may have been different, but basically, internally if you look to see where we arrived and how we got there, you'd find a lot of similarities, I think.